More praise for *Ariel's Gift*

"Both narratively engaging and scholastically comprehensive." —Thomas Lynch, *Los Angeles Times*

"For anyone interested in the relationship between art and life, and drawn to the Hughes-Plath legend, *Ariel's Gift* will be required reading." —Elaine Showalter, *Princeton* magazine

"Wagner maintains a cool detachment. . . . This is a generous, respectful study, which, like its design, elegantly complements Hughes's *Birthday Letters*." —Lisa Allardice, *New Statesman*

"Wagner—knowledgeable, perceptive, and wise—guides us gracefully through Hughes' poems so that we see with a new clarity his responses to his life with Plath, and to her lamentable death." —*Kirkus Reviews*, starred review

"The fascination of the book is in the way it demonstrates the two poets' influence on each other." —Hugo Williams, *Daily Telegraph*

"The book is a commentary on *Birthday Letters*, gravely unfurling the biographical journey for which these most openly personal of poems are signposts, amplifying and interpreting." —Catherine Lockerbie, *The Scotsman*

W. W. NORTON & COMPANY · NEW YORK · LONDON

Erica Wagner

ARIEL'S GIFT

TED HUGHES, SYLVIA PLATH,
AND THE STORY OF *BIRTHDAY LETTERS*

First published in 2000 by Faber and Faber Limited
Copyright © 2000 by Erica Wagner
Poems by Ted Hughes © 1995, 1998 by the Estate of Ted Hughes
Poems by Sylvia Plath © 1960, 1965, 1971, 1981, 1989 by the Estate of Sylvia Plath

First American edition 2001
First published as a Norton paperback 2002

Originally published in England under the title
Ariel's Gift: A Commentary on Birthday Letters by Ted Hughes

Extract from "On His Work in the English Tongue" from *Electric Light* by Seamus
Heaney (published April 2001), reprinted by permission of Farrar, Straus & Giroux
Inc. Lines from Marianne Moore's poem "The Fish" are reprinted from her *Complete
Poems* (1981) by permission of Miss Moore's Literary Estate and Faber and Faber Ltd.

For information about permission to reproduce selections from this book,
write to Permissions, W. W. Norton & Company, Inc.,
500 Fifth Avenue, New York, NY 10110

The text of this book is composed in Berling with the display set in
Cloister Open Face
Composition by Molly Heron
Manufacturing by Quebecor Martinsburg
Book design by Blue Shoe Studio
Production manager: Leelo Märjamaa-Reintal

Library of Congress Cataloging-in-Publication Data

Wagner, Erica, 1967–
Ariel's gift : Ted Hughes, Sylvia Plath and the story of
Birthday Letters / Erica Wagner.
p. cm.
Originally published: London : Faber and Faber, 2000.
Includes bibliographical references and index.
ISBN 0-393-02009-6
1. Hughes, Ted, 1930– Birthday letters. 2. Plath, Sylvia—In literature. 3. Plath,
Sylvia—Marriage. 4. Marriage in literature. 5. Poets in literature. I. Title.
PR6058.U37 B5738 2001
821'.914—dc21   2001018310

ISBN 0-393-32301-3 pbk.

W. W. Norton & Company, Inc., 500 Fifth Avenue, New York, N.Y. 10110
www.wwnorton.com

W. W. Norton & Company Ltd., Castle House, 75/76 Wells Street,
London W1T 3QT

1 2 3 4 5 6 7 8 9 0

TED HUGHES

1930–1998

SYLVIA PLATH

1932–1963

Soul has its scruples. Things not to be said.
Things for keeping, that can keep the small hours' gaze
Open and steady. Things for the *aye* of God
And for poetry. Which is, as Milosz says,
"A dividend from ourselves," a tribute paid
By what we have been true to. A thing allowed.

—SEAMUS HEANEY
"On His Work in the English Tongue"

Dans le fond des forêts votre image me suit.

—RACINE
Phèdre

Contents

LIST OF ILLUSTRATIONS

INTRODUCTION:
THE ECSTASY OF INFLUENCE

WE HAVE GROWN accustomed to confession. It is not simply chat-show culture that has created a climate in which the most personal of revelations hardly seem shocking; the history of personal disclosure stretches back much farther than Oprah's first broadcast. In the fourth century St. Augustine gave us his *Confessions*; Jean-Jacques Rousseau delivered his in the eighteenth. Wordsworth's *Prelude*, the cantos of Byron's *Childe Harold*: poets and philosophers hoped to gain greater insight into themselves, and give their readers greater insight into their work, by laying bare their secrets.

It is hardly surprising. All of a writer's material—everything he (or she) sees, everything he hopes to transform in his art—passes through the filter of his consciousness. During and after the Romantic period, particularly, an attempt to understand the nature of that consciousness became part of the process of art. In the twentieth century, modern psychoanalytic theory having made its mark, that consciousness has often itself become the basis of art. Edmund Gosse's *Father and Son*, Thomas Hardy's *Poems of 1912–13* at the beginning of the century; the work of Robert Lowell, of Anne Sexton, of Allen Ginsberg in the 1950s and 1960s; nearer our own time, Tony Harrison's *School of Eloquence*, Douglas Dunn's *Elegies*—all offer a model for the art of confessional. Each a very different artist, but each, fueled by the desire to examine themselves before their readers, turning the artistic gaze inward. The revelation of the self was integral to both personality and art.

For most of his life, Ted Hughes did not reveal himself directly through his art. Although married for seven years to Sylvia Plath, one of the greatest of the twentieth century's confessional poets, Hughes's gaze turned outward. He looked to the natural world, to mythology and anthropology: he did not appear to look directly into his heart and show what he saw there to his readers. The suffering in his work— the tortured *Crow*, for instance—was never directly personal, but turned personal tragedy into metaphor and mythology.

He was an intensely private man in an era when privacy is not much allowed. He did not like to give interviews; he did like to go fishing on his own. He told very few people beyond his immediate family that he was dying of cancer. Furthermore, he maintained this privacy, this near-complete silence about his life, in the face of what might be regarded as years of grotesque, intrusive inquiry. He would not speak of his life with Sylvia Plath, of her suicide; he would not speak of the suicide of his lover, Assia Wevill—who also killed their daughter, Shura, when she killed herself— although he dedicated *Crow* to their memory. He refused to answer when the most devastating attacks were leveled against him. Although there were times when he was roused from his silence, it seemed only real extremity would drive him to express his feelings; and when he did, it was almost always to protect the two children he raised after Plath's death, Frieda and Nicholas.

And yet *Birthday Letters*, published in the last year of his life, is one of the most intimate and personal collections of poetry ever written. It seems all the more so because of what had gone before: Hughes was the last poet anyone would ever have expected to produce such a book. It burst into the world one winter without warning; it revealed the heart of a poet whom some had judged heartless; it brought to life the spirit of a great love that had existed between two great artists. It was a book no one ever expected to see. At the time of its appearance, in January 1998, the question "why now?" was often asked. When Ted Hughes died less than a year later, it seemed that, to put it most baldly, a real answer, a specific answer, to that question had been provided.

Yet that seems too simple. Eight of these eighty-eight poems appeared, after all, in Ted Hughes's *New Selected Poems* of 1994: "Chaucer," "You Hated Spain," "The Earthenware Head," "The Tender Place," "Black Coat," "Being Christ-like," "The God" and "The Dogs Are Eating Your Mother."* Stylistically, the book as a whole has much in common with the loose, dialogic style of *Moortown*, first published in 1979; and we might be able to look to that time for their beginnings. The last third of the book—less narrative and more preoccupied both with the aftermath of Sylvia Plath's death and with the spiritual fate of Plath and the poet himself—may date from the time of his illness.

What is not in question is that *Birthday Letters* is the artistic flowering of more than thirty years of pent-up emotion: this is the tidal force that gives the poems their power. When *Birthday Letters* was published, I wrote in *The Times* that Sylvia Plath—as, after her death by suicide at the age of thirty, shortly after her separation from her husband Hughes, so many critics and biographers attempted to fill the void she left—had been called the silent woman; but in truth, it was Ted Hughes who was the silent man. He had kept, as poet and biographer Andrew Motion put it, "a bristling badger-silence which seemed dignified to some, reprehensible to others, and fascinating to everyone." What became clear shortly after his death was that this was not simply a silence for public consumption; it truly existed in the poet's heart. After the poems' publication, he wrote of the almost miraculous release they had offered him, seemingly to his own astonishment. When *Birthday Letters* was made Whitbread Book of the Year three

---

*There are eleven more poems about his marriage to Sylvia Plath that do not appear in *Birthday Letters*; they were privately printed by The Gehenna Press as *Howls and Whispers*, in 1998, and illustrated with etchings by Leonard Baskin. However, as they are not available to the general reader, I have not discussed them in *Ariel's Gift*.

months after the poet's death, his daughter Frieda Hughes read aloud from a letter he had written to a friend:

> I think those letters do release the story that everything I have written since the early 1960s has been evading. It was a kind of desperation that I finally did publish them—I had always just thought them unpublishably raw and unguarded, simply too vulnerable. But then I just could not endure being blocked any longer. How strange that we have to make these public declarations of our secrets. But we do. If only I had done the equivalent 30 years ago, I might have had a more fruitful career—certainly a freer psychological life. Even now the sensation of inner liberation—a huge, sudden possibility of new inner experience. Quite strange.

That Hughes's work after Plath's death should be considered "evasive" is a startling thought. Certainly his poetry did not confront the matter of his private life in the manner of a memoir, but much of it was a powerful transformation of that life into the form of his art. Yet for Hughes at the end of his life, it appears, that transformation was not enough. The answer to the question "why now?", then, is not simply that the poet felt—as he wrote of Plath—the silent wing of his grave go over him, and was moved to speak because of that. That *Birthday Letters* should be the last book of Hughes's published in his lifetime certainly seems fitting; that the book brought a measure of peace to a man who had known much anguish is a fact, surely, to be welcomed, even by the poet's harshest critics.

It is true that some of the work he did after *Birthday Let-*

ters seems more directly autobiographical than what had gone before. In the months before his death, he was at work on a free translation of Euripides' *Alcestis* (published in October 1999): its tale of a king, Admetos, who is sentenced by the gods to die but allows his wife, Alcestis, to die in his stead, cannot but resonate with Hughes's own life. When Admetos' father, Pheres, accuses him:

> Look what you did: you let her die instead.
> You live now
> Only because you let Death take her.
> You killed her. Point-blank
> She met the death that you dodged . . .

Hughes confronts the accusation leveled against him, that he was responsible for Plath's death, in a way he never had before. But to view *Birthday Letters* in its proper context, to avoid seeing it simplistically as a kind of headstone over Hughes's long career, it is vital to acknowledge the reality of Hughes's silence to himself. It is vital to look, too, at what led him into that silence and how his breaking of it fits, quite organically, into his work as a whole.

Most important of all is to look where Hughes himself did in the writing of *Birthday Letters*: to the work of Sylvia Plath. *Birthday Letters* is no attempt to have "the last word" in an "argument"; it is not an answer to any accusations. All of Hughes's work is an expression of how permeable is the boundary between this world and the next, whatever that world may be. The poems conjure Plath to converse with her, and in so doing make the reader turn again to what she wrote and what she achieved. *Ariel's Gift* is an attempt to open up this dialogue between two people—both now dead—and make all of these aspects more accessible to the general reader. Through drawing on the details of their lives, as far as they can be ascertained, and of their work, and by making explicit the implicit connections Hughes created between *Birthday Letters* and Plath's writing, *Ariel's Gift* leads the reader through biography and poetry to a clearer understanding of Hughes's work.

BIRTHDAY LETTERS BEGAN with a marriage of true minds. Ted Hughes and Sylvia Plath were poets just embarking upon their careers—just embarking upon their lives—when they met in Cambridge at a party in February 1956. Yorkshire-born Hughes, the son of a carpenter, was twenty-five; he had graduated from Pembroke College in 1954, his degree delayed by two years' national service. Plath was twenty-three, and had left her native Massachusetts on a Fulbright Scholarship after graduating from Smith College in Northampton, Massachusetts, the year before. Both were passionate and ambitious; both were determined to change the way poetry in English was written. An audacious goal—but one they would each, in their very different ways, achieve.

Birthday Letters is Ted Hughes's account of their meeting, their falling in love, their marriage, the birth of their two children, Frieda and Nicholas. It is his account, too, of how the relationship failed in its seventh year, after which Plath, leaving their Devon home for a flat in London, committed suicide on a freezing February morning in 1963, laying her head in the gas oven of her kitchen while her children slept in a room she had sealed off from the fumes after placing milk and bread by their bedsides. At the time of her death, Hughes was already a very well known and much admired poet in Britain; Plath less so. Her first volume of poetry, *The Colossus*, had been moderately well received in 1961; her autobiographical novel, *The Bell Jar*—published under a pseudonym shortly before her death—hardly noticed at all.

Plath's fame, which finally eclipsed her husband's, came only after her death. *Ariel*, the book of forty poems that revealed her vivid, original and almost fearsome talent, was published in 1965, its editor Ted Hughes. Plath had died intestate, still married to Hughes, although they had separated; the role of literary executor thus fell to him. Readers of these ferocious, glittering poems wanted to know more about the woman who had written them: her work, as it continued to appear in the years that followed, seemed to satisfy some of that longing. *The Bell Jar* was published in the United States, under her own name, in 1971; two further volumes of poetry, *Crossing the Water* and *Winter Trees*, appeared that same year. Also published that year was part of a memoir by the poet and critic Al Alvarez, who had known Hughes and Plath in London and remained friendly with both after the couple had separated. Alvarez's powerful account, later incorporated into his book on suicide, *The Savage God*, revealed the despair of her final days and the manner of her death, little known at the time—and completely unknown to her children. Hughes was furious, and demanded that the *Observer*, which had run the memoir, refrain from publishing its second half; the Sunday newspaper acquiesced. Hughes wrote angrily to Alvarez that the account would be, for him and the couple's children, "permanent dynamite." For Hughes, at the time, the mere existence of the facts of Plath's death in the public mind was devastating.

Hughes's circumstances were not easy. On the one hand, he was faced with an artistic duty to the work of his late wife; on the other, with his wish to protect himself and his family from the intrusions and accusations of the press and the reading public. This difficulty was compounded by the nature of Plath's work: her unflinching gaze was forever directed at herself and those around her. She drew almost exclusively on her own experience. *The Bell Jar*, for instance, is a thinly disguised account of her breakdown and suicide attempt of 1953. In his introduction to her volume of stories, *Johnny Panic and the Bible of Dreams*, published in 1977, Hughes wrote of Plath's method:

> Nothing refreshed her more than sitting for hours in front of some intricate pile of things laboriously delineating each one. But that was also a helplessness. The blunt fact killed any power or inclination to rearrange it or see it differently. This limitation to actual circumstances, which is the prison of so much of her prose, became part of the solidity and truth of her later poems.

She recognized this difficulty herself, writing in her journal in 1959:

> I shall perish if I can write about no one but myself. Where is my old bawdy vigor and interest in the world around me? I

am not meant for this monastery living. Find always traces of passive dependence: on Ted, on people around me. A desire even while I write poems about it, to have someone decide my life, tell me what to do, praise me for doing it. I know this is absurd. Yet what can I do about it?

"I am I, which spells invulnerable," she wrote a few months before she first attempted suicide in 1953. But the self that provided a kind of armor for her work was battered by the force of her own pitiless regard.

Plath was a woman of her generation, determined to "have it all": though that phrase would have meant something different to her than it does today, several decades later. Plath wanted artistic fulfillment, yes, but she wanted to be able to combine that with being the perfect wife and mother. Marriage to Hughes—her intellectual equal and, as she saw it, in some ways superior—was an achievement in itself, and she seemed to feel no artistic rivalry. When *The Hawk in the Rain* was published in 1957, Plath expressed her delight that her husband should be published first, that she should follow in his footsteps. During the course of their marriage she was in his artistic shadow: whether or not she stood in that shade of her own free will—how much the pressure of time and circumstance set her there—could be endlessly and fruitlessly argued at several decades' remove. Certainly after her separation from Hughes (when the *Ariel* poems really began to flow) she felt freed of an oppression whose existence she had not recognized before, writing to her mother in November 1962: "Living apart from Ted is wonderful—I am no longer in his shadow, and it is heaven to be liked for myself alone, knowing what I want."

Her expression of her dissatisfaction with her marriage—revealed posthumously—combined with Ted Hughes's continuing editorial control over her material was an explosive mix. The pair parted unhappily; she killed herself shortly afterwards. Had he abandoned her and their children, leaving her to a lonely death? The gradual publication of her work coincided with the rise of the feminist movement on both sides of the Atlantic (Betty Friedan's *The Feminine Mystique* was first published in the year of Plath's death; Germaine Greer's *The Female Eunuch* appeared in 1970 and Marilyn French's *The Women's Room* in 1977); as Plath's poetic stature grew, so did her stature as a feminist icon, as the silenced voice of a generation. With this came the demonization, in some quarters, of Hughes, whose near-total silence on the subject only served as fuel to the fire.

Hughes was responsible for the publication of *Ariel*, the volume that made her name. When it appeared, in 1965, the poems were not in the order in which Plath had left the manuscript at the time of her death. Plath's *Ariel* began—as does the published volume—with "Morning Song," but it ended with "Wintering"; so the first word of the book was "love" and the last "spring." This gives the selection a positive, upward movement that the published collection does not have; the latter ends blackly, with the foreboding poems "Kindness," "Contusion," "Edge" and "Words." Hughes omitted, too, several poems critical of himself: "Mystic," "Purdah," "Brasilia" and "The Jailer" (". . . I dream of someone else

entirely. / And he, for this subversion, / Hurts me, he / With his armor of fakery, / His high cold masks of amnesia . . .").
This has been perceived as carelessness at best, censorship at worst.

In reviewing the *Collected Poems*—which finally appeared in 1981 and won the Pulitzer Prize—Katha Pollitt wrote of the destruction of the artistic pattern of Plath's manuscript:

> The *Ariel* we know ends on a note of absolute despair, and virtually invites the reader to luxuriate in the frisson of knowing that a week after writing "Edge" ("The woman is perfected. / Her dead / Body wears the smile of accomplishment"), Plath would herself be dead. The actual manuscript ended quite differently, on the note of triumph sounded by the magnificent cycle of bee poems, whose subject is the reclaiming of an autonomous womanly self. Its final word, as Plath noted, was "spring." Would it have made a difference to her reputation, I wonder, if Plath's pattern had been preserved, with the last poems added as a separate section?

Hughes's answer to those criticisms was given in an interview published in *The Paris Review* in 1995. Before her death, she had submitted many of the *Ariel* poems to literary magazines and had them sent straight back; no U.S. publisher, Hughes said, would touch the manuscript as she had left it.

> . . . I wanted the book that would display the whole range and variety. . . . Faber in England were happy to publish the book in any form. Finally, it was a compromise—I cut some things out and I put others in. As a result I have been mightily

accused of disordering her intentions and even suppressing part of her work. But those charges have evolved 20, 30 years after the event. They are based on simple ignorance of how it all happened. Within six years of that first publication all her late poems were published in collections—all that she'd put in her own *Ariel*, and those she'd kept out. It was her growing fame, of course, that made it possible to publish them. And years ago, for anybody who was curious, I published the contents and order of her own typescript—so if anybody wants to see what her *Ariel* was it's quite easy. On the other hand, how final was her order? She was forever shuffling the poems in her typescripts—looking for different connections, better sequences. She knew there were always new possibilities, all fluid.

Hughes made material available, as he saw it; almost never did he directly answer his critics. In November 1989, Hughes wrote to Anne Stevenson, whose biography of Plath, *Bitter Fame*, had just been published. Stevenson had the cooperation of the Plath estate—through Hughes's sister, then his literary agent, Olwyn Hughes—in the writing of the book, a cooperation she sometimes found overbearing, as her admission that parts of the book were "almost a work of dual authorship" reveals. Hughes, however, dissociated himself from the biography when it appeared, and told Stevenson of the reasons behind his reticence.

I have never attempted to give my account of Sylvia because I saw quite clearly from the first day that I am the only person in this business who cannot be believed by all who need to find me guilty. I know too that the alternative—

remaining silent—makes me a projection post for every worst suspicion. That my silence seems to confirm every accusation and fantasy. I preferred it, on the whole, to allowing myself to be dragged out into the bull-ring and teased and pricked and goaded into vomiting up every detail of my life with Sylvia for the higher entertainment of the hundred thousand Eng Lit Profs and graduates who—as you know—feel very little in this case beyond curiosity of quite a low order, the ordinary village kind, popular bloodsport kind, no matter how they robe their attentions in Lit Crit Theology and ethical sanctity. If they do feel anything more vigorous, it is generally something even lower: status anxiety, their professional angst on the promotion scramble.

Hughes's letter gives an indication to what extent the biographizing and analyzing of the work of Sylvia Plath had become, by that time, a kind of industry, a portion of its energy directed at persecuting Hughes—who became correspondingly defensive and paranoid. Robin Morgan, feminist poet (and later editor of *Ms.* magazine), wrote a poem calling for his dismemberment; she viewed him plainly as a murderer. The headstone of Plath's grave in Yorkshire was repeatedly defaced, the "Hughes" of her married name chipped away. As Germaine Greer has said—somewhat ruefully, after his death: "Feminists never had any intention of dealing with Ted Hughes. Ted Hughes existed to be punished—we had lost a heroine and we needed to blame someone, and there was Ted." By far the best discussion of the debates surrounding Plath's work and life and Hughes's handling of her estate can be found in Janet Malcolm's short but penetrating study, *The Silent Woman*. The uneasy balance

Hughes had to strike between his role as a father and husband and his role as literary executor is revealed in an essay entitled "Sylvia Plath and Her Journals," published in the United States in 1982.

The *Journals'* appearance followed that of her *Letters Home*: letters written, mostly to her mother, throughout the course of her life, which Aurelia Plath had sought permission from Hughes to publish after the publication in America of *The Bell Jar*. That novel, read autobiographically, was extremely wounding to Plath's mother; the bright, breezy tone of the high-achieving "Sivvy" found in *Letters Home* seemed a corrective to that. The much darker *Journals*, wherein Plath reveals all the doubts and fears she kept from her mother, offer a further correction; and so the pendulum of "truth" swung, back and forth.

But the *Journals* did not appear unedited. As Hughes wrote—making an awkward distinction between himself as impartial editor and partial husband:

Sylvia Plath's journals exist as an assortment of notebooks and bunches of loose sheets, and the selection just published here contains about a third of the whole bulk. Two other notebooks survived for a while after her death. They continued from where the surviving record breaks off in late 1959 and covered the last three years of her life. The second of these two books her husband destroyed, because he did not want her children to have to read it (in those days he regarded forgetfulness as an essential part of survival). The earlier one disappeared more recently (and may, presumably, still turn up).

The book that appeared in 1982 was marked by many elisions and omissions: many people mentioned in the *Journals*—particularly Aurelia Plath—were still around to be hurt, not least Hughes himself and the couple's children.

To many, the end result was deeply unsatisfactory. Peter Davison, who had been friendly with Plath from the end of her time at Smith, wrote in the *Washington Post*: "How can we content ourselves with a book so riddled with editorial expurgations, with omissions that stud the text like angry scars, with allusions to destroyed and 'disappeared' parts of the journals? . . . Does anyone imagine that Sylvia Plath herself, had she lived, would have permitted these journals to be set in type?" Yet while the *Journals* were published—and have been published, in full at last, in 2000—is it our business to "content ourselves" with anything? Hughes the husband, not the editor, must be recalled. As he said in 1995: "What I actually destroyed was one journal which covered maybe two or three months, the last months. And it was just sad. I just didn't want her children to see it, no. Particularly her last days." It seems worth remarking that Hughes need never have mentioned the destroyed journal's existence in the first place.

It is the confessional—and contradictory—nature of Plath's artistic output that continues to draw readers toward what it seems possible to imagine as the truth of her biography. Poems, stories, her novel—all hint at the existence of a true self which, if it could be revealed, might bring her back to life. But this is dangerous ground, and the footing beneath *Birthday Letters* is therefore equally treacherous. The work is biographical, yes; but the work is not the biography, the biography is not the work. As Judith Kroll has written in her study of Plath's work, *Chapters in a Mythology*:

> It is important to separate the aesthetic success of her poems from the biography, on which it does not depend. One can certainly read the poems just for biography or "confession," simply to "get the story" and "find out what happened to her"; but if one does this—as is fairly common among her readers—one has in a sense predetermined the scope of one's reading, prejudged what one is reading for ("the life of a suicidal, male-exploited genius"—the source and nature of whose genius is, however, oddly taken for granted; or not inquired into; or by some peculiar logic ascribed to her suffering). One therefore misses other meanings, not relevant to a focus on sensationalistic confessional aspects, by a priori screening them out.

There is nothing final about *Birthday Letters*. In the first place it is not a memoir, that most fallible of endeavors, but a work of art, and the nature of art is infinite. Poems—by Ted Hughes, by Sylvia Plath, by any poet—may be linked to events, but they are not those events; they are themselves. Nearly drowning out the clear voice of poetry are the many voices of those who knew these two poets, who have their perceptions, too, of what was "really" going on at this moment or that moment. I did not conduct many interviews during the writing of this book—none of the "so what did she say then?" variety. Recollections at a distance of several decades, corrupted, as such recollections must be, not only by the passage of time but also by opinion, conscious or unconscious, seemed of little use to me: they could not get me any nearer any kind of "truth," for that is, to my mind, simply never to be found.

One can say, to a certain extent, who, what, when, where; but why is trickier. "An early dramatic death gives one, in a literary sense, a real life, a throbbing biography," Elizabeth Hardwick said of Plath.

> People discovered they had known a vehement, disturbing genius in their schooldays; mere propinquity became a challenge, and the brief life has been the subject for memories of no special usefulness. Sylvia Plath does not come closer, shine more clearly. Poems have followed her poems, making their statements and to most of these her own harsh eloquence is the proper rebuke.

Hughes's poems, too, offer a rebuke to those who would, from the outside, try to solve the great mystery of his life.

Yet, if there are no solutions to be found in *Birthday Letters*, there are insights to be gained into how Hughes perceived the poetic task. For just as the arrival of *Birthday Letters* into the world was an astonishment, so was the arrival, in the postwar 1950s, of Hughes's voice. At the time the dominant voice in English poetry was that of "The Movement" (a term coined by J. D. Scott, literary editor of the *Spectator* magazine, in 1954), its exponents the anti-Romantic, witty and sardonic verses of Kingsley Amis, Philip Larkin, John Wain and Donald Davie, among others. But Hughes's work was rooted in the English rural landscape, steeped in an understanding of a continuous, mythic history that could encompass Blake's Albion as well as the destruction of the First World War. It also contained a larger understanding—through his readings of Robert Graves's seminal *The White Goddess*, first published in 1948, the works of Carl Jung, and books such as Paul Radin's *African Folktales* (1952)—of the great and universal stories that make us human and that we recreate in our own lives. He rejected the skepticism and rationality of The Movement, though his brand of Romanticism, while cousined to that of Wordsworth and Lawrence, was quite his own.

"His stride is the wilderness of freedom," he wrote in his portrait of a caged jaguar, which appeared in his first book, *The Hawk in the Rain*. Thirty years on, his placing of himself in the animal's eye, his naked language, does not shock. Then, what he did was new, though linked, of course, to the ancient. Another poem from that first collection, "The Man Seeking Experience Enquires His Way of a Drop of Water," has, even in its title, the feel of fairy tale, and endeavors to link its speaker to something universal and eternal, rejecting the self-centeredness of the mid-twentieth century. The speaker asks for the drop of water to tell him what made it what it is:

> So he spoke, aloud, grandly, then stood
> For an answer, knowing his own nature all
> Droplet-kin, sisters and brothers of lymph and blood,
> Listened for himself to speak for the drop's self.
> This droplet was clear simple water still.
> It no more responded than the hour-old child
>
> Does to finger-toy or coy baby-talk,
> But who lies long, long and frowningly

Unconscious under the shock of its own quick
After that first alone-in-creation cry
When into the mesh of sense, out of the dark,
Blundered the world-shouldering monstrous "I."

Hughes's perception of his poetic world was one of connection, not separation. As the poet could see with the eyes
of hawk or jaguar, could feel himself "droplet-kin," so the
work of the true poet was holistic. This philosophy is perhaps most clearly revealed in his *Shakespeare and the Goddess of Complete Being* (1992). This complex, difficult work
at times borders on the incomprehensible, and it was
received with hostility when it was published. Yet it reveals
Hughes's vision of the works of Shakespeare as an organic
whole—from the early poems to the plays from first to last
as an attempt to solve a "Tragic Equation." "The point here is
that though every play is made up, to some degree, of an
amalgam of his earlier styles, each one opens a core of
poetry, in the death—rebirth episode, that is absolutely
new"; this Hughes calls the "systole-diastole of Shakespeare's
poetic life." Hughes viewed his own writing as such a whole,
as he did the work of Plath, or any true artist. In this sense
the book can be taken as a commentary on Hughes's own
work, the solving of his own tragic equation.

Hughes's early life was shadowed by the great tragedy of
World War I, which had killed so many of his father's generation, emptying the valleys of his childhood of their young
men; his later life by the suicide of Plath, his first wife, and
then six years later the death, also by suicide, of his lover
Assia Wevill and their daughter Shura. The poet's attempts

to find meaning in painful and apparently random events of life took the form of a journey through myth, his own and others'. One of the most striking examples of this is 1970's *Crow*, an animal fable rooted in tradition, but whose humor and horror are all Hughes's own. *Gaudete*, published in 1977, leads a modern minister, Lumb, on a pagan journey through the underworld; even Hughes's laureate poems, collected in *Rain Charm for the Duchy* (1992), are powerfully connected to the cycle of British legend. His children's books, such as *The Iron Man*, published in 1968, had the strength of myth; his penultimate book, *Tales from Ovid*—Whitbread Book of the Year in 1997—transformed Ovid's legendary transformations into his own visionary verse.

Poetry, for Hughes, was animated by a shaping force whose energy was beyond the poet's control. In *Birthday Letters* he writes, in "Flounders," of a fishing trip taken with Plath as they traveled in America shortly after their marriage. It seems to be a tale of freedom, but it ends on a sense of imprisonment. Their actions are not their own but controlled by another force: "And we / Only did what poetry told us to do." As Robert Graves wrote in *The White Goddess*:

The poet is in love with *The White Goddess*, with Truth: his heart breaks with longing and love for her. She is the Flower-goddess Olwen or Blodeuwedd; but she is also Blodeuwedd the Owl, lamp-eyed, hooting dismally, with her foul nest in the hollow of a dead tree, or Circe the pitiless falcon, or Lamia with her flickering tongue, or the snarling chopped Sow-goddess, or the mare-headed Rhiannon who feeds on raw flesh. Odi atque amo: "to be in love with" is also to hate.

If Hughes was not a confessional poet in the conventional sense, however, the myth he built around himself and felt himself to be participating in was a kind of confession in itself. As he said in 1995,

> Goethe called his work one big confession, didn't he? Looking at his work in the broadest sense, you could say the same of Shakespeare: a total self-examination and self-accusation, a total confession—very naked, I think, when you look into it. Maybe it's the same with any writing that has real poetic life. Maybe all poetry, insofar as it moves us and connects with us, is a revealing of something that the writer doesn't actually want to say, but desperately needs to communicate, to be delivered of. Perhaps it's the need to keep it hidden that makes it poetic—makes it poetry. The writer daren't actually put it into words, so it leaks out obliquely, smuggled through analogies. We think we're writing something to amuse, but we're actually saying something we desperately need to share.

Look at the Reverend Lumb, in *Gaudete*, alive in a post-holocaust town in the North of England that has turned to a mass grave; he encounters a half-human, half-animal female who solicits his help, but Lumb only:

> . . . stands in confusion
> And looks round at the shadowed hollow faces
> Crowding to enclose him
> Eyepits and eyeglints
>
> He declares he can do nothing
> He protests there is nothing he can do

For this beautiful woman who seems to be alive and dead.
He is not a doctor. He can only pray.

Reviewing *Birthday Letters* when it appeared, Professor John Carey—discussing the abandonment of will to the Fate that haunts the work, the avoidance of responsibility—quite rightly fitted it into the larger cycle of Hughes's work:

> . . . In his vision human beings have always been dwarfed by what he has called "the elemental power-circuit of the universe"—a coercive force variously identified with the laws of science, or the giant figures of classical myth, or the brutal intensity of birds and animals. In this view of life (and who is to say it is false?), "responsibility" becomes a figment, valid only in the make-believe world of lawyers and moralists. We are moulded, directed and destroyed by cosmic forces beyond our control or understanding. Throughout *Birthday Letters*, this fatalism is relentlessly endorsed.

Believing as he did that Plath was a true poet, it is not surprising that Hughes viewed her work through a similar lens of myth and overarching structure. A myth—with its fury at and imagined reunion with her dead father—both seductive and dangerous. In his "Notes on the Chronological Order of Sylvia Plath's Poems," Hughes wrote:

> Most readers will perceive pretty readily the single centre of power and light which her poems all share, but I think it will be a service if I point out just how little of her poetry is "occasional," and how faithfully her separate poems build

up into one long poem. She faced a task in herself, and her poetry is the record of her progress in that task. The poems are chapters in a mythology where the plot, seen as a whole and in retrospect, is strong and clear—even if the origins of it and the dramatis personae, are at bottom enigmatic. The world of her poetry is one of emblematic visionary events, mathematical symmetries, metamorphoses. Her poetry escapes ordinary analysis in the way clairvoyance and mediumship do: her psychic gifts, at almost any time, were strong enough to make her frequently wish to be rid of them.

Hughes believed the exact nature of that task was abundantly clear. Two years before his death, he told the Israeli journalist Eilat Negev that

> All [Sylvia Plath's] creative work tells just one story: her Oedipal love for her father, her complex relationship with her mother, the attempt at suicide, the shock therapy. The novel and the poems all tell one story, and she never wrote about anything else. Whatever she wrote before, were metaphors on parts of this story. The power of these poems is because of her ability to cling to feelings of an eight-year-old, emotions that simmered for 20 years. And this naked little girl is at the bottom of all this.

Birthday Letters is powered by this perception of her life and her art. It is impossible to say whether Hughes was "right" or "wrong" to believe all her work falls into this predetermined structure: the point is that the book is built upon this notion, and the poems must be understood in this context. Here is the origin of the fatal helplessness that threads the book, haunted as it is by the presence of Fate, laced as it is with Hughes's repeated protestations of his ignorance of the situation ("I was the gnat in the ear of the wounded / Elephant of my own / Incomprehension," he writes in "Moonwalk"). For Hughes, Plath's artistic endeavor set her on a trajectory toward her death—the metaphor of the bullet is his, from "The Shot."

The voice of her late poems, in his view, is disembodied, the pure voice of poetry, uncontrollable, and the turning point for the arrival of this voice also gives a clue to the title of *Birthday Letters*. In November 1959, she wrote "The Stones," the last poem in her Roethke-influenced cycle "Poem for a Birthday."

> This is the city where men are mended.
> I lie on a great anvil.
> The flat blue sky-circle
>
> Flew off like the hat of a doll
> When I fell out of the light.

Of "The Stones," Hughes wrote that

> . . . In this . . . poem, the ruins are none other than her hospital city, the factory where men are remade, and where, among the fragments, a new self has been put together. Or rather an old shattered self, reduced by violence to its essential core, has been repaired and renovated and born again, and—most significant of all—speaks with a new voice.

It is this "new voice" that belonged to *Ariel*; Hughes then links the emergence of that voice directly to her death:

> It is doubtful whether we would be reading this journal at all if the "birth" recorded in that poem, "The Stones," had not happened in a very real sense, in November 1959. . . . It is unlike anything that had gone before in her work. The system of association, from image to image and within the images, is quite new, and—as we can now see—it is that of *Ariel*. And throughout the poem what we hear coming clear is the now-familiar voice of *Ariel*.

He calls this voice "the real thing." After she wrote "Pheasant," in April 1962, the transformation was, says Hughes, complete: "And at once the *Ariel* voice emerged in full. From that day on, it never really faltered again. During the next five months she produced ten more poems. The subject matter didn't alarm her. Why should it, when Ariel was doing the very thing it had been created and liberated to do?"*

It was a birthday, then, that was both a rebirth and a death; *Birthday Letters* crosses over the shadowy barrier between death and life by conjuring their subject, Sylvia Plath, so vividly that she seems to stand before the reader, vibrant with life—and radiating death. The poems, written with hindsight, seem to make her suicide inevitable. Hughes

---

*John Berryman's description of Theodore Roethke's work as "psychological, irreligious, personal . . . witty, savage and willing to astonish" could as easily be applied to Plath's; it is unsurprising that Roethke was an influence on her. Born in Michigan in 1908—his father was Prussian—he suffered the first of a series of breakdowns in 1936. He died suddenly of a heart attack in the year of Plath's death.

sees himself, in "The Table," unlocking the inner door that led her down to oblivion.

> I did not
> Know I had made and fitted a door
> Opening downwards into your Daddy's grave.

Al Alvarez, in his memoir *Where Did It All Go Right?*, refers to Plath's willingness—the willingness of the alpha student—to adopt Hughes's methods of ouija, horoscope, hypnotism; Hughes believed she had great "psychic gifts."

I don't think her "psychic gifts" were a power that came naturally to her; they were a symptom of her pathology. Hughes's loony methods for getting through to his creative underlife worked for him because, among other reasons, he was a man of unusual inner strength and assurance. Sylvia may have been saner and more sceptical than he was, but only intellectually; emotionally she was altogether more fragile. She had never got over her father's death, never finished mourning him and, because her mother wouldn't let the children go to the funeral for fear of upsetting them, she had never even buried the monster. For her, he was a scary absence, off somewhere out of sight, biding his time. With nightmares like those to contend with, Hughes's creative strategies would have worked on her like, say, the "recovered memory" games untrained rogue psychotherapists play on unwary patients—releasing the inner demons then stepping aside with no thought of the consequences. Because he truly believed in her talent he did it . . . in the name of poetry. He handed her the key she had been looking for to find her dead father and, always the good student, she went down into the cellarage, key in hand. But the ghouls she released were malign. They helped her write great poems, but they destroyed her marriage, they destroyed her.

BIRTHDAY LETTERS DEMONSTRATES the extent to which the poets influenced each other. Hughes's papers at Emory University in Atlanta, Georgia, and Plath's papers at the Lilly Library at Indiana University and at Smith College in Northampton, Massachusetts, show that the poets often worked on the reverse sides of each other's drafts; proof of their closeness, certainly, but also an indication of the cycle of influence that made their work. Hughes set Plath exercises—her poem "The Moon and the Yew Tree" was the result of such an exercise—and together they explored the effects of the occult on their work. Two years after her death Hughes spoke of the artistic link which, he believed, made them almost a single unit:

> . . . There was no rivalry between us as poets or in any other way. It sounds trite but you completely influence one another if you live together. You begin to write out of one brain. . . . It was all we were interested in, all we ever did. We were like two feet, each one using everything the other did. It was a working partnership and was all-absorbing. We just lived it. There was an unspoken unanimity in every criticism or judgment we made. It all fitted in very well.

Thirty years later, he would take their connection even further, believing that the sympathy that existed between them bordered on the supernatural. "Our minds soon became two parts of one operation," he said in 1995. "We dreamed a lot of shared or complementary dreams. Our telepathy was intrusive. . . ." To Eilat Negev, he spoke of the "supportive atmosphere" that exists when two writers share a space.

Whether this is an idealization of the situations that can arise when two artists—particularly artists as talented and ambitious as Hughes and Plath—share their lives is not the point. An understanding of Hughes's viewpoint increases the reader's appreciation of the necessary quality of these poems. Two feet, one mind: her death, then, a kind of severing of the self. When *Birthday Letters* won the Forward Prize for poetry in 1998, Hughes spoke of the book's intentions:

> My book *Birthday Letters* is a gathering of the occasions on which I tried to open a direct, private, inner contact with my first wife—not thinking to make a poem, thinking mainly to evoke her presence to myself, and to feel her there listening. Except for a handful, I never thought of publishing these pieces until this last year—when quite suddenly I realized I had to publish them, no matter what the consequences.

It is a kind of conversation—one-sided, but a conversation nonetheless. Plath may be gone, but her work remains; and so Hughes engages with her work, connecting with the imagery she used, the events she described. Poems like "Brasilia" and "The Rabbit Catcher" are not attempts to rewrite her poems of the same titles: they echo, they recall, they project into the future; they see darkly through the glass of her work. Plath's poetic voice is one of the most distinctive of the twentieth century; it is a mark of Hughes's artistic courage that he engages with it as he does.

Plath's ghost, of course, is not the only spirit that haunts this work. It is impossible to adapt a literary tradition—as Hughes did—without a thorough understanding and appreciation of that tradition; there is nothing new under the sun. Hughes's poems are one link in a chain of elegy and lament that stretches back to the very beginnings of poetry, and to which Hughes felt a fierce connection. It is possible to compare the sudden emergence of Plath's astonishing poetic voice with that of another American poet to whose work Hughes was very close, Emily Dickinson. Hughes edited a selection of Dickinson's poems in 1968; her rhythmic spring, her unflinching gaze at death are recalled by Plath's work although, without Christian faith, Plath's observance of the horses' heads turned toward eternity take on a darker character.

And there are close—some might say, eerie—parallels between *Birthday Letters* and Thomas Hardy's *Poems of 1912–13*, written after the death of his wife Emma Gifford. Hardy and Emma married in 1874; she died suddenly in 1912, after the couple had been estranged for a number of years: her strong Christian faith and his increasing unbelief were not a happy mix. But her death made him recall the happy days of their early courtship (memories he would later publish as *Some Recollections*), though he was distressed to discover, among her papers, an unflattering portrait of himself entitled "What I think of my Husband" (he destroyed the manuscript). Hardy's work foreshadows that of Hughes, as the poet addresses his late wife as "you":

Why did you give no hint that night
That quickly after the morrow's dawn,
And calmly, as if indifferent quite,
You would close your term here, up and be gone
   Where I could not follow
   With wing of swallow
To gain one glimpse of you ever anon!

So begins Hardy's first poem of his sequence, "The Going." Over the course of decades, language and style change; emotion—affection, regret—does not. Poems of Hughes's like "Freedom of Speech," which chart an imagined future, recall Hardy's "Family Portraits" or "The Pedigree."

More than subject and style, however, are belief and intent. Hardy's acceptance of "the Immanent Will that stirs and urges everything" also links him to Hughes; both saw a greater force not controlling, but overseeing human action. Choices are made within its framework.

The will of man is . . . neither wholly free nor wholly unfree. When swayed by the Universal Will (which he mostly must be as a subservient part of it) he is not individually free; but whenever it happens that all the rest of the Great Will is in equilibrium the minute portion called one person's will is free, just as a performer's fingers are free to go on playing the pianoforte of themselves when he talks or thinks of something else and the head does not rule them.

Birthday Letters reflects an imbalance, as Hughes saw it, in the Great Will; and it registers, too, what Harold Bloom called a sense of "belatedness": of writing within a larger poetic sequence of work which—from Shakespeare to Dante to Hardy to Plath—seems to anticipate his own.

Douglas Dunn's *Elegies*, written after the death of his wife Lesley in 1981 and published in 1985, offer a precedent in the late twentieth century; they show a kind of mirror image of *Birthday Letters*, their emotional focus on Dunn, left behind to mourn, rather than on his late wife. But go back even farther: it is worth noting that when Hughes read in public, his final selection was often an early Irish poem, "Donal Og."

> It is late last night the dog was speaking of you;
> the snipe was speaking of you in her deep marsh.
> It is you are the lonely bird through the woods;
> and that you may be without a mate until you find me.

The naked style of Hughes's lament is closer to that of "Donal Og" than it is to that of Hardy. "You promised me a thing that is not possible," the poet says to the departed love; the loss is almost greater than he can bear.

> You have taken the east from me; you have taken the west
>   from me;
> you have taken what is before me and what is behind me;
> you have taken the moon, you have taken the sun from me;
> and my fear is great that you have taken God from me!

After her death, the spirit of Plath survived in Hughes through his perception of the tradition of which they both were a part.

BIRTHDAY LETTERS APPEARED, so it seemed, out of nowhere. In the summer of 1997, Ted and Carol Hughes came to lunch at the Gloucestershire home of Matthew Evans and his wife, Caroline Michel. As Evans relates:

> At the end of the lunch Ted said, I have another manuscript for you, it's rather long. He went on—it's in the car; it's about Sylvia. I'll bring it to Faber in the next day or so. And I suppose I couldn't quite believe what I'd heard; they left, and he was down at the end of the drive before I realized what he'd said.

When he finally saw the manuscript a few days later, Evans was amazed and somewhat fearful: he knew its publication would have to be very carefully handled. Its existence was kept absolutely secret—a quite remarkable feat in the gossipy world of British publishing. The book was offered to *The Times* for serialization in November 1997; the paper paid £25,000 for the rights to the book. Poems don't fit easily into a newspaper, as Peter Stothard, the paper's editor, has remarked. But *Birthday Letters* was different: "It wasn't just the extraordinary quality of the poems, but they had this: these were real events that happened and this was a narration of them. This was first-rate art that had the qualities of a real news story. You can work in papers for decades and not come across something that has both of these qualities."

The Times published twelve of the poems between 17 January and 22 January 1998; I selected them and wrote the accompanying commentary that was the genesis of this book. There were certain poems Hughes did not wish taken out of context; on a photocopy of the book's table of contents, "Dreamers," "The Inscription" (taking the place of another poem, "The Laburnum," which appeared in the first proof I saw), "The Cast," "The Ventriloquist" and "Life after Death" are marked "NO" in Hughes's strong, sloping hand.

The first day of the serialization was twelve days before the book's actual date of publication, which Hughes had insisted be 29 January (and he requested that *The Times* print the date alongside publication details): the day the planet Neptune, the ruler of poetry, enters Aquarius, a constellation considered by astrologers to have much to do with collective awareness. Collective awareness there certainly was. Poets and critics who had never imagined they would see so much of Hughes's heart were astonished, and this book of difficult, complex poems became an instant bestseller on both sides of the Atlantic.

It was not just their subject matter that made the poems sensational. Their vivid directness of style, their epistolary immediacy, the manner in which they drew together all the poetic threads that had occupied Hughes throughout his life, gave them a tremendous power. As Al Alvarez wrote in *The New Yorker*: "[Hughes] takes the bare bones on which the biographies have been hung—Cambridge, Spain, America, Devon—and does what no biographer, however diligent and impartial, could ever do, he describes what it felt like to be there with her." Seamus Heaney, who was one of the few to have seen the book before its release, called it

a book of poems as solid as a sandbagged wall, as miraculous and yet as inevitable within the geology of imagination as a volcanic island. The immediate impression is one of wounded power healing and gathering and showing its back above the depths where it has been biding. To read it is to experience the psychic equivalent of "the bends." It takes you down to levels of pressure where the undertruths of sadness and endurance leave you gasping.

On the day the existence of *Birthday Letters* was revealed in *The Times*, Andrew Motion wrote of the symbolic, private language of the book's final poems, written to run parallel to the *Ariel* poems: "In the short term, these final poems will probably be less admired than the rest. In the fullness of time, they should be reckoned its finest achievement: poetry staggering under the weight of its emotional load, but keeping its dignity and purpose." A few weeks later, Michiko Kakutani, Pulitzer Prize–winning literary critic of the *New York Times*, wrote:

Written over the last few decades, the poems seem remarkably free of self-pity, score-settling and spin; rather, they draw a deeply affecting portrait of the couple's marriage while attesting to Mr Hughes's own impassioned love for Plath. Poems, however, are not biography, and these should not be read simply for the light they shed on the Hughes-Plath relationship. They should be read because they constitute the strongest, most emotionally tactile work of Mr Hughes's career. . . . Burned free of the detachment, condescension and contrivance that cramped much of his earlier work, they dazzle not only with verbal dexterity but also with clear-hearted emotion. They are clearly the work of a poet writing out of the deepest core of his being.

And yet there were doubts. James Fenton, reviewing the volume in the *New York Review of Books*, raised the question of self-justification. In "Fever," Hughes implies that he thought Plath's distress might be a form of crying wolf:

> To the hostile ear this will sound like a carefully placed piece of self-justification: Plath was self-dramatizing, so it was impossible to guess just how bad her state of mind was at any given time. My own feeling about this poem and the whole sequence is that the view given is perfectly plausible. As for the question of self-justification, it is, it must be, a legitimate aim of poetry. At the very least, the urge to justify ourselves may provide the first impulse for a poem. "saints will not mind from what angle they are viewed, / Having nothing to hide," Auden wrote. But the rest of us do mind. Indeed we should mind. How could we go through life with utter indifference to the angle from which we are viewed? What would such indifference imply?

Birthday Letters proved that Hughes had never been indifferent; he had perhaps, as Seamus Heaney has commented, been fearful that if he stepped into the arguments that swirled around his life with Plath, his "version" of events would become simply that, another version, with no special authority over the versions of those who had not lived it. The only way for him to enter this discussion was through the complex structure of his art. As Hughes said once of Douglas Dunn's accomplishment in the *Elegies*:

> It means the world becomes yours—whereas if you don't do it, it drifts away and takes a whole piece of yourself with it,

like an amputation. To attack it and attack it and get it under control—it's like taking possession of your own life, isn't it? Otherwise, it means whole areas of your life stand in front of you and stop you.

Still, it was possible to look at the poems simplistically, as a kind of excuse. The American poet Emily Warn wrote that

presenting Plath's suicide as a fait accompli makes me question Hughes's intent: did he seek through writing to truly understand the complexity of their relationship, or to create a fiction in which he and Plath are conjoined victims of a sealed fate? Because he so carefully constructs his case, I assume his purpose is to persuade others and free himself from any personal responsibility.

Robin Morgan reacted with characteristic rage; when she heard about the new book, "my teeth began to grind uncontrollably . . . I want to make it clear that Hughes didn't kill Sylvia, but that he drove her to suicide." And the critic James Wood remarked:

In the book's angriest poem, "Suttee," a work of astonishingly poor taste, Hughes plays on the idea of Plath as a mother who gave birth not to children, but to the evil baby of her own fragile survival from her suicide attempt. Like a good father, Hughes must look after not his children, but the death-baby that his wife has become. . . . "Suttee" should remind us, if we were in any doubt, that this is a book of anger and grief. Revenge and self-justification are inherent in this enterprise. I do not believe that Hughes, as an editor of

Plath's work, "silenced" her; quite the opposite. But *Birthday Letters* must amount to a kind of silencing because it is like listening to one half of a telephone call. . . . It is hard to ignore Hughes's bitterness. His poems are little epidemics of blame. This book is the progress of a hysteric, recorded by a husband who was not hysterical enough to comprehend his wife. . . .

What Hughes's purpose was in publishing *Birthday Letters* can never really be known. Hughes's account is of a release of psychic pressure; as to the question of why publish—as Michael Glover wrote in the *New Statesman*: "Now he has issued an open invitation to every amateur psychologist in the land to expatiate loudly and at whim upon his private life with Plath"—to Hughes, the poet's role, linked to an ancient bardic tradition, was a public one: the work exists in the open air. It is not a silencing, or one half of a telephone call, because what the poems do finally is return the reader to the well from which they sprang: the work of Sylvia Plath. To the poet Katha Pollitt, this was a weakness. Poems in *Birthday Letters* that take all or part of their titles from Plath's work ("Ouija," "The Rabbit Catcher," "Brasilia," "Black Coat," "Night-Ride on Ariel") are written "as if to answer, or contextualize, poems of hers. But Plath's poetry is one of intense compression and musicality, its imagery complex and ambiguous, whereas *Birthday Letters* is lax and digressive, the symbolism all on the surface, so these allusions, quotations and re-renderings serve mostly to remind us of what a great poet she was."

Plath's work is characterized by a rhythmic tension that binds all of her writing, however casual or conversational it might seem on the surface. She was a poet who schooled herself in form; her first collection, *The Colossus*, is often constricted by her adherence to it. It was *Ariel* that marked the leap free into something else: to work informed by a deep understanding of poetic texture but no longer constrained by it. It is this freedom that *Birthday Letters* seeks to echo; its laxness—and certainly, there are poetic longueurs over the spread of eighty-eight poems—is linked to its effort to make a "direct, private, inner contact" with Plath; these are part poem, part conversation. It is as well to recall Hughes's words of advice to young people who would try to turn their hands to poetry:

> . . . Imagine what you are writing about. See it and live it. Do not think it up laboriously, as if you were working out mental arithmetic. Just look at it, touch it, smell it, listen to it, turn yourself into it. When you do this, the words look after themselves, like magic. . . . The minute you flinch, and take your mind off this thing, and begin to look at the words and worry about them, then your worry goes into them and they set about killing each other.

Birthday Letters is nothing if not seen and lived. From the beginning of his poetic career, Hughes was trying to capture a quality that exists, as it were, beneath language; he himself referred to what he was trying to work with as "Some sort of language or set of sounds I can hear going on in the bottom of my mind, that's not quite English and not quite music. It's probably some sort of forgotten inherited language." Hughes's understanding of poetic form was just as great as

Plath's; he, too, broke away. By the time his third volume of poetry, *Wodwo*, was published in 1967, he had moved far away from the "well-made" poem in order to try to reach something deeper, more basic. The movement of poetry in the twentieth century has been an expansion of what the word itself might mean: the work of Gerard Manley Hopkins, when it first appeared, seemed just as startling and audacious as the work of Hughes. It is important to remember, too, that Hughes's language is grounded in his native dialect. As he said in an interview in 1971:

I grew up in West Yorkshire. They have a very distinctive dialect there. Whatever other speech you grow into, presumably your dialect stays alive in a sort of inner freedom . . . it's your childhood self there inside the dialect and that is possibly your real self or the core of it. . . . Without it, I doubt if I would ever have written verse. And in the case of the West Yorkshire dialect, of course, it connects you directly and in your most intimate self to Middle English poetry.

Hughes's work harks back more than most to the viscerality of *Beowulf* or *Gawain and the Green Knight*.

The work's vividness is sometimes shocking. A poem like "Suttee" cares nothing for the reader's squeamishness or sensibility: this is the truth as the poet perceives it, however distasteful that might seem. The impact of a poem like this is a reminder of the primal power of Hughes's work as a whole, of what an impact he had on the body of poetry in English. Hughes's work, with "its sensuous fetch, its redolence of blood and gland and grass and water, recalled English poetry in the Fifties from a too suburban aversion of the attention from the elemental, and the poems beat the bounds of a hidden England in streams and trees, on moors and in byres. Hughes appeared like Poor Tom on the heath, a civilised man tasting and testing the primitive facts," as Seamus Heaney wrote. What applies to streams and trees, moors and byres, also applies to the heart and the mind.

Ted Hughes is often compared to William Blake. Both were visionaries, though of very different sorts. Both saw the world, the poetic world, as a whole; both tried to cast off the shackles of tradition and create something entirely new; both understood the terrible beauty of the tiger. In "Milton," Blake wrote of the desire

To bathe in the waters of life, to wash off the not-human,
I come in self-annihilation & the grandeur of inspiration,
To cast off rational demonstration by faith in the Saviour;
To cast off the rotten rags of memory by inspiration;
To cast off Bacon, Locke & Newton from Albion's covering;
To take off his filthy garments, & clothe him with imagination;
To cast aside from poetry all that is not inspiration,
    That it no longer shall dare to mock with the aspersion of
        madness
Cast on the inspired, by the tame high finisher of paltry blots
Indefinite, or paltry rhymes, or paltry harmonies . . .
Who publishes doubt & calls it knowledge, whose science
    is despair . . .

The enduring power of *Birthday Letters* comes not from rhyme or reason, but from the grandeur of inspiration, from Hughes's ability, in the end, to wash off the not-human and engage with his humanity. In *Birthday Letters*, Ted Hughes honors the work and the person of Sylvia Plath. There is no greater gift of love than that honor.

Ariel's Gift

1 ◇ "A Crush of Diamonds"

THIS SECTION STARTS at the beginning of the sequence, "Fulbright Scholars," which depicts Ted Hughes's first sight—perhaps—of Sylvia Plath. She had arrived in Cambridge in the autumn of 1955, following her graduation from Smith College in Massachusetts. Ted Hughes had remained in Cambridge, on and off, after his graduation from Pembroke College the previous year. They met at a party in February 1956 and were instantly drawn to one another, as he reveals in "Trophies."

TWO YOUNG POETS at the beginning of their careers; both unknown, or nearly so. One a tall, dark-haired Yorkshire visionary, forceful and earthy; the other an American college girl, her shining surface the very image of wholesome, handsome America. Both were ambitious. Each would listen to what "poetry told them to do," and by the time *Birthday Letters* was published in January 1998, Ted Hughes and Sylvia Plath were, in their very different ways, among the best-known and best-loved poets of the century. Ted Hughes, in his poetic recounting of their seven years together, viewed their meeting and their marriage as destined: it is that destiny that governs the movement and shape of *Birthday Letters*.

That fate lay in an unimagined future when the sequence of poems begins. Sylvia Plath arrived in England from America in 1955, having graduated from Smith College. She had won a Fulbright Scholarship to study at Cambridge University. It was the acme of an already stellar academic career—at Smith she had been supported by a scholarship funded by the romantic novelist Olive Higgins Prouty, author of the popular radio serial *Stella Dallas*. "I feel that after I put down roots here, I shall be happier than ever before, since a golden promise hovers in the air along the Cam and in the quaint crooked streets. . . ." Sylvia Plath wrote to her mother shortly after her arrival, in October 1955. "Fulbright Scholars" gives the reader a first glimpse of the woman Ted Hughes would marry, as the poet gazes at a photograph of the Fulbright Scholars of that year, shortly to arrive in Cambridge. Plath was one of those scholars, but Hughes's doubt as to whether she was in the photograph, or whether he saw her there—

"Were you among them?"—shapes the drama of uncertainty that follows.

Hughes himself had already formally left the university, graduating the year before with a degree in social anthropology. His own background, one of rural, postwar austerity, was unsophisticated: his seeing the photograph coincides with his first experience of eating a fresh peach. "At twenty-five I was dumbfounded afresh / By my ignorance of the simplest things." Yet in his "ignorance" he is taking up the challenge of the poetic endeavor: his eating of the peach can be set against the nervous caution voiced by T. S. Eliot's Prufrock, who hesitates at this sensual commitment. Hughes's boldness, the boldness of an outsider, can be traced to his origins.

Hughes was born on 17 August 1930, the youngest of William and Edith Hughes's three children, in the Yorkshire Pennine village of Mytholmroyd. Hughes's father, a carpenter, had fought in World War I, one of only seventeen men of his entire regiment to return alive from Gallipoli—a diary in his breast pocket had stopped a bullet. The louring atmosphere of the landscape and the lingering devastation of the Great War made a powerful impression on the boy. Later he would write:

> Everything in West Yorkshire is slightly unpleasant. Nothing ever quite escapes into happiness. The people are not detached enough from the stone, as if they were only half-born from the earth, and the graves are too near the surface. A disaster seems to hang around in the air there for a long time. I can never escape the impression that the whole region is in mourning for the first world war. The moors don't escape this, but they give the sensation purely. And

finally, in spite of it, the mood of moorland is exultant, and this is what I remember of it.

From there the return home was a descent into the pit, and after each visit I must have returned less and less of myself to the valley. This was where the division of body and soul, for me, began.

When Hughes was eight and his mother came into a small inheritance, the family bought a newspaper and tobacco shop in Mexborough, in South Yorkshire, where he spent the rest of his youth—they returned to the Calder Valley in 1952. In 1948 he won an Open Exhibition to Cambridge from Mexborough Grammar School, but did two years of National Service in the RAF, at a radio station in the wilds of East Yorkshire.

He arrived at Pembroke College in 1951 to read English, but the tripos was, for Hughes, stifling. His friend, the poet W. S. Merwin, wrote of Hughes at this time: "At Cambridge he set out to study English Literature. Hated it. Groaned having to write those essays. Felt he was dying of it in some essential place. Sweated late at night over the paper on Dr Johnson et al—things he didn't want to read." Hughes himself, writing in 1993, recalled a dream he had then, of writing an English essay when a figure with the body of a man and the head of a fox walked into the room.

I saw that its body and limbs had just stepped out of a furnace. Every inch was roasted, smouldering, black-charred, split and bleeding. Its eyes, which were level with mine where I sat, dazzled with the intensity of the pain. It came up until it stood beside me. Then it spread its hand—a human hand as I now saw, but burned and bleeding like the rest of him—flat palm down on the blank space of my page. At the same time it said: "Stop this—you are destroying us."

The fox was always a totem for Hughes, from its signposting of the imagination in one of his early and most famous poems, "The Thought-Fox," to its crucial role in *Birthday Letters*, the fox cub in "Epiphany." He heeded this vision; and in his third year he switched to social anthropology, gaining knowledge in the myths and disciplines that would so fuel his writing. He graduated in the summer of 1954, and that summer his first poem appeared in *Granta*, a Cambridge literary magazine: "The Little Boys and the Seasons"—under the pseudonym of Daniel Hearing.

Although by the time Plath arrived Hughes had left the university, he was still tied to Cambridge by his literary connections. He worked at odd jobs in London—as a rose gardener; reading novels for development for the film company J. Arthur Rank—but returned to Cambridge to read in the library and to be with his friends, such as the Tennessean E. Lucas Myers, Daniel Huws, and a few others who made up the shifting crowd of "three of us, four, five, six—/ Playing at friendship," as he writes in "Caryatids (2)." Myers described Hughes's tall, striking figure:

He was an inch or so taller than Daniel and wore, as I recall, the brown leather greatcoat that had been issued to an uncle in World War I. His brown hair fell across the right side of his forehead and his voice modulated curiously at certain significant points in his speech. His eyes and his mouth were powerfully expressive.

Later, Plath would write to her mother of his "same black sweater and corduroy jacket with pockets full of poems, fresh trout and horoscopes."

Sylvia Plath's American upbringing was, of course, very different. She was born in Boston on 27 October 1932, to Otto Emil Plath and Aurelia Frances Schober Plath. Both parents were of German extraction, Otto having emigrated from Prussia at the age of sixteen, and Aurelia, twenty-one years his junior, a second-generation Austrian brought up just outside Boston. Otto Plath held a doctorate in entomology from Harvard—his specialty was the study of bees—although he lived by teaching German at Boston University, where he met Aurelia, at first his student. She would have a brief career as a high school teacher before her marriage, but once with Otto, gave it up to care for her home and her children: the couple were married on 4 January 1932. Sylvia's birth was followed by that of her brother Warren, just over two years later, in April 1935.

The household on Johnson Avenue in Winthrop, a Massachusetts seaside town, where Sylvia Plath spent her early years, was one where industry was highly valued. Her father's work, with Aurelia his devoted amanuensis, came before everything else—his *Bumblebees and Their Ways* was published in 1933, and that year he was invited to contribute an essay, "Insect Societies," to *A Handbook of Social Psychology* (1935). During the writing of this, Aurelia wrote:

The seventy-plus reference books were arranged on top of the long sideboard [in the dining room]; the dining table became his desk. No paper or book was to be moved! I drew a plan of the arrangement and managed to have friends in occasionally for dinner the one evening a week that my husband gave a course at Harvard night school, always replacing every item correctly before his return.

Aurelia's own studies were forced to one side. Her ambition she transferred to her clever daughter: early letters between the two, when Sylvia was as young as seven, show the cycle of achievement (by Sylvia) and praise (from her mother) that appeared to rule the poet's life. The need for achievement, for seeming perfection, was in conflict with a darker self, a conflict revealed most clearly if one reads her *Journals*,* streaked with black self-doubt, alongside *Letters Home*, the correspondence with her mother, which shows a jaunty, praiseworthy self. It is a duality that Hughes, in "Fulbright Scholars," reveals immediately when he imagines what he might have seen in the photograph, although at the time the darkness behind was invisible to him.

> Maybe I noticed you.
> Maybe I weighed you up, feeling unlikely.
> Noted your long hair, loose waves—
> Your Veronica Lake bang. Not what it hid.
> It would appear blond. And your grin.
> Your exaggerated American
> Grin for the cameras, the judges, the strangers, the
>   frighteners.

*The published *Journals* begin in 1950, just before she arrived at Smith.

For more insight into those "frighteners," and to the fear that was hidden behind her dyed-blond movie-star fringe, two poems in this first sequence are revealing: "The Tender Place" and "The Shot." The first begins as if it is a conventional love poem: "Your temples, where the hair crowded in, / Were the tender place." The next lines might at first seem a non sequitur:

> Once to check
> I dropped a file across the electrodes
> Of a twelve-volt battery—it exploded
> Like a grenade.

But this swift and shocking shift reveals more of Plath's history, and what she had suffered.

Sylvia Plath's domineering father had died in 1940, when Sylvia was eight, in part a victim of his own stubbornness. Otto Plath suffered from diabetes, but because of his distrust of doctors, this had gone undiagnosed and unchecked until stubbing his toe on a chest of drawers caused his foot and leg to become inflamed and discolored. At last a doctor was called, but it was too late: his leg was amputated in October, and less than a month later, on 2 November, he was dead. "I'll never speak to God again," Sylvia vowed upon hearing the news. By 1942, Aurelia, who now had to support her family, had found work teaching a course for medical secretaries at Boston University College of Practical Arts and Letters, and the family moved to Wellesley, Massachusetts, away from the ocean. Plath would come to seal away this early part of her childhood into a sea-glassy image of damaging and dangerous perfection. "I was only purely happy until I was nine years old," she wrote in her autobiographical novel, *The Bell Jar.*

After that—in spite of the Girl Scouts and the piano lessons and the water-color lessons and the dancing lessons and the sailing camp, all of which my mother scrimped to give me, and college, with crewing in the mist before breakfast and blackbottom pies and the little new firecrackers of ideas going off every day—I had never been really happy again.

She was always ambitious, always haunted by the specter of failure. "What is my life for and what am I going to do with it?" she wrote in her journal when she was eighteen. "I don't know and I'm afraid. I can never read all the books I want; I can never be all the people I want and live all the lives I want." She graduated from Bradford Senior High School in Wellesley in 1950, already a writer—she tried over and over again to get a story published in *Seventeen* magazine, sending in forty-five stories by the time she was eighteen years old. She finally succeeded with "And Summer Will Not Come Again," which appeared in August 1950, just before she entered Smith. The *Christian Science Monitor,* too, accepted a poem, "Bitter Strawberries," in the same month. And while she had high expectations for the literary career she wished to embark upon, she had, too, a desire to combine her work with a love of almost mythical completeness. In the summer of 1950 she wrote:

After a while I suppose I'll get used to the idea of marriage and children. If only it doesn't swallow up my desires to express myself in a smug, sensuous haze. Sure, marriage is self-expression, but if only my art, my writing, isn't just a mere sublimation of my sexual desires which will run dry once I get married. If only I can find him. . . . The man who will be intelligent, yet physically magnetic and personable. If I can offer that combination, why shouldn't I expect it in a man?

She left for Smith in September 1950 and appeared to flourish. While at Smith she came into the orbit of faculty member Mary Ellen Chase—Chase was influential in her decision, after she graduated, to go to Cambridge, but as early as September 1952 she wrote in her diary: "Today was good. Mr Crockett [her beloved high school English teacher] for two and one half hours in the afternoon, and after long talking in his green pine garden over sherry I got the flash of insight, the after-college objective. It is a frightening and wonderful thing: a year of graduate study in England. Cambridge or Oxford. . . ."

By her sophomore year she had been elected to an honors society for the arts, Alpha Phi Kappa Psi, was appointed to the editorial board of the *Smith Review* and served on Smith's Press Board, writing about the college for local newspapers. She was popular with her own sex and the young men who courted her: she wrote ecstatic letters to her mother of her social and intellectual success. "I love this place so," she wrote to her mother in 1952, "and there is so much to do creatively. . . . The world is splitting open at my feet like a ripe, juicy watermelon. If only I can work, work, work to justify all my opportunities."

In her journals of 1952, the summer in which she won $500 from *Mademoiselle* magazine for a story, "Sunday at the Mintons," she showed the division she felt between her creative self and her conformist, social self: how to balance between them?

It is like lifting a bell jar off a securely clockworklike functioning community, and seeing all the little busy people stop, gasp, blow up, and float in the inrush (or rather outrush) of the rarified scheduled atmosphere—poor little frightened people, flailing impotent arms in the aimless air. That's what it feels like: getting shed of a routine. Even though one has rebelled terribly against it, even then, one feels uncomfortable when jounced out of the repetitive rut. And so with me. What to do? Where to turn? What ties, what roots? As I hang suspended in the strange thin air of back-home?

Years later this image would give her the title of the novel that explored this period of her life, examining the stasis that made her feel that no matter what she did, "I would be sitting under the same glass bell jar, stewing in my own sour air."

In her junior year at college she was breathlessly busy: conquering a physics course, appointed next year's editor of the *Smith Review*, gaining the guest editorship at *Mademoiselle* that became the focal point of her novel, *The Bell Jar*— she spent the summer of 1953 in New York, working for the magazine. That her fashionable, girl-about-town facade was maintained at high cost is revealed through her harsh, deadpan portrayal of Esther Greenwood, her alter ego in the novel; Esther's attempts to get into the swing of the social, professional and sexual life of a young New Yorker are hampered by forces both internal (her own self-doubt) and external (a terrible case of food poisoning). Looking at the glamorous picture that appeared of "Esther" in the novel's fashion magazine, "everybody would think I must be having a real whirl," that she must have been "steering New York like her own private car."

> Only I wasn't steering anything, not even myself. I just bumped from my hotel to work and to parties and from parties to my hotel and back to work like a numb trolleybus. I guess I should have been excited the way most of the other girls were, but I couldn't get myself to react. I felt very still and very empty, the way the eye of a tornado must feel, moving dully along in the middle of the surrounding hullaballoo.

The novel gives the clearest account of the breakdown that followed when she went home for the summer after leaving New York. Her mother noted, flatly, "a great change in her: her usual joie de vivre was absent." She saw a psychiatrist who prescribed a course of electro-convulsive therapy (ECT): "somebody wired you up," as Hughes writes in "The Tender Place." "They crashed / The thunderbolt into your skull." Plath's own description of those events in *The Bell Jar* rattles the reader's teeth: "Then something bent down and took hold of me and shook me like the end of the world. Whee-ee-ee-ee, it shrilled, through an air crackling with blue light, and with each flash a great jolt drubbed me till I thought my bones would break and the sap fly out of me like a split plant." In the summer of 1960 she began her poem "The Hanging Man": "By the roots of my hair some god got hold of me. / I sizzled in his blue volts like a desert prophet."

Here, Hughes first acknowledges how that 1953 summer ended for Plath, with her suicide attempt on 24 August.

> The lights
> In the Senate House dipped
> As your voice dived inwards
> Right through the bolt-hole basement.

The bolt-hole basement was the crawl space underneath the Plaths' house, where Plath hid in order to swallow as many sleeping pills as she thought would kill her. ". . . I hit upon what I figured would be the easiest way out," she wrote later.

> I waited until my mother had gone to town, my brother was at work, and my grandparents were out in the back yard. Then I broke the lock of my mother's safe, took out the bottle of 50 sleeping pills, and descended to the dark sheltered ledge in our basement, after having left a note to mother that I had gone on a long walk and would not be back for a day or so. I swallowed quantities and blissfully succumbed to the whirling blackness that I honestly believed was eternal oblivion. . . .

(She swallowed too many pills, enough to make her sick. This saved her life.) She wrote in *The Bell Jar*: "Cobwebs touched my face with the softness of moths. Wrapping my black coat around me like my own sweet shadow, I unscrewed the bottle of pills and started taking them swiftly, between gulps of water, one by one."

For Hughes, "the tender place" at her temple is an embodiment of the suffering from which much of her art was made. Her poems were images of herself, created by turning what she saw when she looked inward toward the outside world, a desperately revelatory process. "She was incapable of free fantasy, in the ordinary sense," Hughes said of her. "If an image of hers had its source in a sleeping or waking 'dream,' it was inevitably the image of some meaning she had paid for or would have to pay for, in some way—that she had lived or would have to live. . . . Her internal crystal ball was helplessly truthful, in this sense." To Hughes, here, it is a kind of sacrifice: years later she still bears "the scorched-earth scars" of this time, and her work is the price she has paid.

> And your words,
> Faces reversed from the light,
> Holding in their entrails.

Here Hughes first acknowledges the overarching presence of her dead father. He makes her, it seems, Otto Plath's lost limb, a piece of himself amputated: "You your Daddy's leg." It is a theme he returns to at greater length in "The Shot," in which Plath appears as a bullet,

> gold-jacketed, solid silver,
> Nickel-tipped. Trajectory perfect
> As through ether.

While she is the bullet, however, her father is both "the god with the smoking gun" and "your real target."

After her suicide attempt, Plath was not found for nearly three days: the police were called, headlines in local papers clarioned her disappearance. She was finally discovered by her brother Warren and revived in Newton-Wellesley Hospital. Her cheek had been abraded by the concrete of the basement: she never lost the scar. Just before she met Hughes, she wrote of her suicide's mark:

> Being dead, I rose up again, and even resort to the mere sensation value of being suicidal, of getting so close, of coming out of the grave with the scars and the marring mark on my cheek which (is it my imagination?) grows more prominent: paling like a death-spot in the red, windblown skin, browning darkly in photographs, against my grave winter pallor.

She seems drawn to the scar, as Hughes's words indicate:

> Even the cheek-scar,
> Where you seemed to have side-swiped concrete,
> Served as a rifling groove
> To keep you true.

When her benefactor, Olive Higgins Prouty, came to hear of the incident, she offered to pay for psychiatric treatment at the renowned McLean Hospital in Belmont (Prouty had suffered a breakdown herself at one point). There Plath came under the care of a psychiatrist, Dr. Ruth Beuscher, whose friendship would support her for the rest of her life.

But, as Anne Stevenson writes: "Sylvia's psychotherapy also certainly opened up the dimensions of her Freudian psychodrama, revealing the figure of her lost, 'drowned' father, master of the bees, whose death she could never forgive nor allow herself to forget."

The trauma of this death and the torment it caused for Plath are reflected in "The Shot." Her father's death created a fatal lack. In March 1956, she wrote in her diary:

> I rail and rage against the taking of my father, whom I have never known; even his mind, his heart, his face, as a boy of 17 I love terribly. I would have loved him; and he is gone. . . . My villanelle was to my father, and the best one. I lust for the knowing of him; I looked at [Professor] Redpath at that wonderful coffee session at the Anchor, and practically ripped him up to beg him to be my father; to live with the rich, chastened, wise mind of an older man. I must beware, beware of marrying for that. Perhaps a young man with a brilliant father. I could wed both.

Later, Hughes fulfilled her desire for both father and husband. She wrote of him: "I identify him with my father at certain times, and these times take on great importance. . . . Ted, insofar as he is a male presence, is a substitute for my father: but in no other way. Images of his faithlessness with women echo my fear of my father's relation with my mother and Lady Death."

Hughes writes: "Your worship needed a god." She was filled with a restless energy that fed her constant striving toward success (good grades, publication, acclaim: "You rico-

cheted / The length of your Alpha career / With the fury /
Of a high-velocity bullet / That cannot shed one foot-pound
/ Of kinetic energy") and her near deification of the
boyfriends she chose. "Ordinary jocks became gods." She
wrote of one boy she met at Yale:

> Guess what [Myron Lotz] does in the summer! He pitches
> for the Detroit Tigers, and last summer earned $10,000! Isn't
> that amazing? Not only that, he comes from Austro-Hungar-
> ian immigrant parents who work in the steel mines and can
> hardly speak English. And he is going through Yale in three
> years, starting Yale Med School next fall. Did you ever hear
> of such a phenomenal character?

She would later view Hughes in the same vivid colors, make
him into a "phenomenal character" for her to adore.

Yet there was beneath this shining surface of perfection
a torment of "sob-sodden Kleenex"—Hughes's reference
here ironic, *Mademoiselle* magazine teenspeak, a ghostly
echo of Plath's young self. It was a torment that led her to
confuse her "gods," to blend Hughes, in the later years of
their marriage, with the image of her dead father. ". . . your
real target / Hid behind me," Hughes writes. His fusing of
the two "targets," himself and Otto Plath, calls to mind the
bitter closing stanza of her poem "Daddy," in which Plath
attempts a "resurrection" of her dead father after her suicide attempt:

> But they pulled me out of the sack,
> And they stuck me together with glue.
> And then I knew what to do.

I made a model of you,
A man in black with a Meinkampf look

And a love of the rack and the screw.
And I said I do, I do.

One of the texts influencing both Hughes and Plath in their early years together was Sir James Frazer's study of mythology, *The Golden Bough*, as Judith Kroll and other scholars have noted: "The marriage to and killing of her father by proxy are acts of what Frazer calls 'sympathetic magic,' in which 'things act on each other at a distance through a secret sympathy.'" It is a theme Hughes will return to in a later poem in the sequence, "Black Coat."

In "The Shot," Hughes adopts the position of confusion, of a lack of understanding that will dog him and this volume. The poem has a jerky, ballistic rhythm: as of squeezed-off rounds thudding into a target. In *Birthday Letters*, Hughes, as in so much of his poetry, lets go of formal poetic structures and creates his own. Uneven, unexpected, consonant-heavy rhymes and half-rhymes hammer reader and writer. The blows disorient him: unable to see what was happening at the time, he was "vague as mist, I did not even know / I had been hit." Hughes, whose long silence about his wife's death was seen by many over the years as an attempt to avoid blame, accepts it here:

In my position, the right witchdoctor
Might have caught you in flight with his bare hands,
Tossed you, cooling, one hand to the other,

Godless, happy, quieted.
                    I managed
A wisp of your hair, your ring, your watch, your nightgown.

These are the details that make her Sylvia, his wife; not Plath, the poet. Would she have been the poet she was if she were "godless, happy, quieted"? She was not so: that is the tension that drives *Birthday Letters*.

Sylvia Plath left McLean Hospital in February 1954 and returned to Smith. There, in April, she met Richard Sassoon, a junior at Yale who had heard about Plath through mutual friends and came to Smith to visit her. Distantly related to Siegfried Sassoon and with a European upbringing, his sophistication appealed to her; they began an ardent correspondence. The same month she learned she would be awarded a valuable scholarship by Smith; in May, *Harper's* published her poem "Doomsday."

In her senior year at Smith she continued seeing Sassoon, occasionally spending the weekend with him in hotels in New York. She was working on her senior thesis (significantly, for a young woman who seemed to have two such distinct sides to her personality, on the double in Dostoyevsky, "contrasting and comparing the literary treatment as it corresponds to the intention of psychological presentation," she wrote to her mother) and taking entrance exams for both Oxford and Cambridge in England, where she hoped to go for graduate study should her application for a Fulbright grant be successful: "My main bother this month is my Fulbright application," she wrote to her mother on 27 September 1954.

I've had numerous interviews with the head of the graduate office and all my former professors, all of which have at least resulted in most gratifying results: Elizabeth Drew, Newton Arvin, and Mary Ellen Chase have all agreed to write me letters of recommendation, and as they are all very big names in their field internationally, I should have an advantage there that might compensate for my mental hospital record. . . .

News of her success reached her in May 1955. With the backing of Mary Ellen Chase, she decided to begin her further studies at Cambridge in the autumn. She was at a peak of achievement, so it seemed: not only the Fulbright and Cambridge but a series of publications and prizes that epitomized the trajectory of what Hughes calls her "Alpha career" with good reason: that April she had been awarded the Alpha Phi Kappa Psi Award and the Alpha Award in Creative Writing at Smith (as well as the Christopher Prize—for stories emphasizing "the importance of personal responsibility and individual initiative in raising the standards of government, education, literature and labor relations," worth $100). And so in the middle of September, 1955, she set sail on the *Queen Elizabeth* for Europe.

She arrived in Cambridge in early October, a student affiliated to Newnham College and living, with others like herself, in Whitstead House on Barton Road. Of her lodgings she wrote to her mother:

The roof slants in an atticish way, and I have a gas fireplace which demands a shilling each time I want to warm up the room (wonderful for drying my washed hair by, which I did last night) and a gas ring on the hearth where I can warm up water for tea or coffee. . . . My books overflow everywhere and give me the feeling of color and being home. . . . I love the window-sofa—just big enough for two to sit on, or for one (me) to curl up in and read with a fine view of treetops. . . .

Another American at Newnham, Jane Baltzell—studying on a Marshall Scholarship—recalled an "almost professional sense of interior design" in Sylvia's room, with its scattering of costly art books, her full tea set of solid black pottery. She began to attend the lectures of F. R. Leavis; she met with Dorothea Krook, who became her supervisor and mentor, and who, when she first saw this tall, too smartly dressed girl (she had arrived in Cambridge carrying brand-new matching luggage) with her streaked blond hair, was struck by "the concentrated intensity of her scrutiny." At Christmastime Sylvia had her first visit to France: she went to Paris, and then to the south with Richard Sassoon.

She was back in Cambridge by early January 1956. Later that month she got a nasty shock, to which Hughes refers in "Caryatids (1)" and "Caryatids (2)." Two of her early poems, "Epitaph in Three Parts" and "Three Caryatids Without a Portico by Hugh Robus: A Study in Sculptural Dimensions" (only the former is available in the *Collected Poems*), had been published in a Cambridge student magazine, *Chequer*. Hughes's friend Daniel Huws, also a poet, published a piece mocking the two works.

"Caryatids (1)" offers the reader a cool appraisal of this unseen poem, through Hughes's eyes before he met her:

> It was the first poem of yours I had seen.
> It was the only poem you ever wrote
> That I disliked through the eyes of a stranger.

The grounds for his dislike are threaded through her juvenilia. Her very early work is precise, precocious; poems that experiment artfully with sound and sense. Hughes writes that the poem was "thin and brittle, the lines cold. / Like the theorem of a trap, a deadfall—set." As, in this poem, he shifts into the persona of his older self, he sees there are portents in these very early works of what is to come: the beginning of her use of stark, bright colors; her fascination with the sun-reflecting face of the moon. Yet Hughes, in the bright boldness of youth, had no eye for warning:

> In those days I coerced
> Oracular assurance
> In my favour out of every sign.

In "the white, blindfolded, rigid faces / Of those women" that appear in her early poem there is a foreshadowing of the deathly pallor that will haunt the work written near the very end of her life, such as "Paralytic" and "Edge."

Hughes and Plath had arrived at their meeting on very different trajectories: in "Caryatids (2)," Hughes looks back from a vantage point of scarred maturity to the insouciance and energy of youth, the carelessness of consequences, that gave rise to the darting criticism of Plath's caryatid poem.

> More to reach you
> Than to reproach you, more to spark

A contact through the see-saw bustling
Atmospherics of higher learning
And lower socializing, than to correct you
With our archaic principles, we concocted
An attack, a dismemberment, laughing.

Lucas Myers, in his memoir of Plath and Hughes, gives their disapproval the same throwaway, cynical tone. He says of her work at the time: "We disapproved of the poems in spite of their being well made, or rather partly because of it. Her ambition shined through them, or so we thought, and we thought it was not legitimate to write poetry, which should come down on the poet from somewhere, out of sheer will." He notes, however, that "only Ted hadn't commented." The language of "Caryatids (2)" hints at self-justification, but reproaches itself too: their principles are "archaic"; their socializing of a "lower" variety; but for all that the assault is no less savage—"An attack, a dismemberment," two words not softened by the "laughing" that follows. Stupidity, boredom, frivolousness and faithlessness: Hughes looks back with sorrow and reproach at his younger self. What he perceives as Plath's real self is hidden from him by her "blond veils"; he and his friends see only her "flaring gestures"—"I run flaring in my skin," she wrote in "Pursuit," inspired by Hughes—her "misfit self-display."

Hughes and his friends were dissatisfied with the quality of literary magazines produced around the university; they decided to start up their own. *St. Botolph's Review* (so named after St. Botolph's Rectory in Cambridge, where Lucas Myers had rooms) appeared—there was only one issue—in February of 1956, sold on the streets of the town the very morning that Plath had made her first visit to the university psychiatrist. Sassoon, it seems, was attempting to drop Plath: the damp chill of a Cambridge winter accentuated her misery. But on 25 February she wrote with more brightness to her mother that she would be going to a party at the Women's Union in Falcon Yard that evening for the new *Review*. The magazine, she said, "is really a brilliant counteraction to the dead, uneven, poorly written two literary magazines already going here, which run on prejudice and whim. . . . This new one is run by a combination of Americans and Britons, and the poetry is really brilliant, and the prose, taut, reportorial, and expert. . . ." She had been instantly taken with Hughes's poems (the magazine contained four of his verses: "Fallgrief's Girlfriends," "Law in the Country of Cats," "Soliloquy of a Misanthrope" and "Secretary"), and determined to meet "that big, dark, hunky boy," as she called him in her journal. She was looking for someone "to blast over Richard [Sassoon]; I deserve that, don't I, some sort of blazing love that I can live with. My God, I'd love to cook and make a house, and surge force into a man's dreams, and write, if he could talk and walk and work and passionately want to do his career. . . ."

Their meeting that night, as Hughes relates it in "St. Botolph's," is now literary legend, a legend fueled by her relation of the drama of the encounter. Hughes was attached at the time—his girlfriend, Shirley, the "loaded crossbow" of the poem—but no matter: the attraction was mutual and immediate. Hughes was a tall, handsome, striking figure; a contrast to the usual run of English boys, whom Plath had found, in the main, rather anemic. In the noisy room she quoted his poetry back at him, he mentioned his girlfriend, and then

> I was stamping and he was stamping on the floor, and then he kissed me bang smash on the mouth and ripped my hairband off, my lovely red hairband scarf which had weathered the sun and much love, and whose like I shall never again find, and my favourite silver earrings: hah, I shall keep, he barked. And when he kissed my neck I bit him long and hard on the cheek, and when we came out of the room, blood was running down his face. . . . Such violence, and I can see how women lie down for artists. The one man in the room who was big as his poems, huge, with hulk and dynamic words; his poems are strong and blasting like a high wind in steel girders

she confided to her diary.

The story would surface, too, barely disguised in her fictional account of it, "Stone Boy with Dolphin," written in 1957–58, when "Dody" meets "Leonard": "Teeth gouged. And held. Salt, warm salt, laving the tastebuds of her tongue. Teeth dug to meet. An ache started far off at their bone-root. Mark that, mark that. But he shook. Shook her bang against the solid-grained substance of the wall. . . ." As early as May 1953, Plath wondered in her journal:

> What to do? Think + create + love people + give of self like mad. Go outward in love and creation and maybe you will fall into knowing what you want simultaneously as what you want walks by your picket gate singing a never-again song with a nonchalant catch-me-quick hat aslant back on his

head and a book of "how life is a flea circus" under his einstein arm. . . .

It is hard to distinguish here whether "what you want" is a creative life—in the guise of a man—or the man himself; for Plath, Hughes was the perfect fusion of the two.

Here is Hughes's first glimpse, close up, of Plath's vitality and force. Here again is the oracular presence, the belief in fate, that guides Hughes in "Caryatids (1)." Here are Shakespeare, Chaucer, Dante: authors for whom the two would come to share a passion, authors of an earlier age when belief in magic and predestination were more common. The "disastrous expense" of the evening is a "planetary/Certainty," according to "Prospero's book"; this mention of what is perhaps Shakespeare's last play, *The Tempest*, is the first of many in *Birthday Letters*. As discussed in the introduction, Hughes viewed this play as a culmination of the mythology that Shakespeare had created in the body of his work: the union of Miranda and Ferdinand, Prospero's drowning of his book of magic, the final solution of the "Tragic Equation" presented in earlier plays. In *Birthday Letters*, Hughes will see his young self as a Ferdinand, sleepwalked into love by a force outside himself; his older self will carry echoes of Prospero, the magician finally ready to break his staff. Meeting, the two young lovers, like Miranda and Ferdinand, are helpless: "That day the solar system married us / Whether we knew it or not."

Other, more modern, images of fate are brought into play: "The hall / Like the tilting deck of the *Titanic*." Then he sees her. In retrospect he is so struck by her height ("your long, perfect, American legs") that he gives it a line of its own, and exaggerates it in memory: "Taller / Than ever you were again." Her wild force is brought out by his repetition, four times, of the word "joy"—but the brightness of her eyes is both "a crush of diamonds" and "a crush of tears." He recognizes, now, her aim: the way she directed herself at him like the bullet of "The Shot": "You meant to knock me out / With your vivacity." Just as he overcame her with his—on 3 March she wrote to her mother: "Met, by the way, a brilliant ex-Cambridge poet at the wild *St. Botolph's Review* party last week; will probably never see him again (he works for J. Arthur Rank in London), but wrote my best poem about him afterwards—the only man I've met yet here who'd be strong enough to be equal with—such is life."

At the end of "St. Botolph's," Hughes has the headscarf, torn from her hair, as blue. She wrote that it was red. Whom do we believe? That is not the issue. In writing—or even in revising—this poem, Hughes cannot have been unaware of Plath's recollection of her "lovely red hairband scarf," its color a match for the blood she left running down his cheek. One way of seeing this conflict is to view it as a reminder that memory is fallible; even (and especially) the memories of those who were direct participants in an event. Hughes acknowledges ellipses of memory again and again in this book, as he does in this poem: from these fractured memories are "stories" created. Hughes's story of the blue headscarf runs in parallel to the story of the red headscarf she tells in her journal. Neither, and both, are "true." As he writes at the end of "Visit": "It is only a story. / Your story. My story."

The story he tells in "Visit" took place a few weeks after their initial meeting. Hughes had returned to Cambridge from London and with Lucas Myers had discovered what they believed to be the location of her room—they made an excursion in darkness to wake her by flinging mud at her window; but they had the wrong window, and she was out that night, anyway.

> With my friend,
> After midnight, I stood in a garden
> Lobbing soil-clods up at a dark window . . .
>
> . . . Aiming to find you, and missing, and again missing.
> Flinging earth at a glass that could not protect you
> Because you were not there.

She has the tale, in her diary, too, entered on Sunday, 11 March; clearly influenced by a friend of hers informing her that Hughes was "the biggest seducer in Cambridge."

> He is on the prowl, all the fiends are come to torment me . . . last night they came, at two in the morning, Phillippa said. Throwing mud on her window, saying my name, the two mixed: mud and my name; my name is mud. She came to look for me, but I was sleeping. Dreaming of being home in Winthrop on a lovely new spring day, walking in pajamas down the streets of melting tar to the sea, the salt freshness, and squatting in the sea in a tangle of green weeds were clamdiggers with osier baskets, rising, one after the other, to look at me in my pyjamas, and I hid in spring shame in the trellised arbors of Day's home. . . . And all this while, those boys in the dark were treating me like what whore, coming like the soldiers to Blanche DuBois and rolling in the gardens, drunk, and mixing her name with mud. . . .

The poem reveals much about the lives of the two poets at that time. Hughes, aware enough of Plath to be, one senses, a little jealous of her friendship with Myers ("I heard of it [the friendship], alerted"), is working in London to save for his leap to being a full-time poet,

> Hoarding wage to fund a leap to freedom
> And the other side of the earth—a free-fall
> To strip my chrysalis off me in the slipstream.

He points to the rivalrous friendship that existed between Plath and Jane Baltzell, and the jealousy of his own girlfriend at the time—"she detested you."

When Plath heard about this escapade, she was ecstatic to hear that Hughes was back in Cambridge. ". . . let me have him for this British spring," she wrote in her journal. "Please, please . . . and give me the resilience & guts to make him respect me, be interested, and not to throw myself at him with loudness or hysterical yelling; calmly, gently, easy, baby, easy. . . . Oh, he is here; my black marauder; oh hungry hungry. I am so hungry for a big smashing creating burgeoning burdened love. . . ." Significantly, too, it is around this time that Richard Sassoon seems finally to have ended their relationship; she seems ready to move on.

She is not simply hungry for Hughes: she is hungry for a love that exists for her without her even knowing Hughes's nature. She has decided how things will be: Hughes is unaware. He writes in "Visit":

> Nor did I know I was being auditioned
> For the male lead in your drama,
> Miming through the first easy movements
> As if with eyes closed, feeling for the role.

He compares himself to a puppet, to the legs of a dead frog hooked up to electrodes: his picture of himself as helpless, as not in control, could not be farther from her image of him as her "black marauder." He is "unknown to you and not knowing you"—but it hardly seems to matter.

He comes across this hungry self in her journal years later, not then.

> Ten years after your death
> I meet on a page of your journal, as never before
> The shock of your joy
> When you heard that.

But more than joy there are the prayers and panic that were masked from him at the time. He points to the violent swings of her emotions: the alternative to joy was not mere unhappiness but

> the unthinkable
> Old despair and the new agony
> Melting into one familiar hell.

And yet the end of the poem offers a kind of redemption, melting her "actual words" into the words of their daughter, Frieda—although they are words of longing and absence. Frieda, born in 1960, is their future made flesh.

The future, in *Birthday Letters*, has its own existence, quite separate from Hughes and Plath. In the final lines of "Visit," he pictures himself clawing at the Cambridge soil as if he were trying to dig up something, and also calls forth a shadow of Plath's dead self, later buried in earth:

> Somewhere
> Inside that numbness of the earth
> Our future trying to happen.

This already-existing future allows *Birthday Letters* to share the "illusion of a Greek necessity" that Plath created for her own work.

Two poems in this first sequence give this future a vital, savage animal form. "Trophies" makes reference to the poem she wrote for Hughes immediately after she met him, entitled "Pursuit" (the one she referred to in the letter to her mother of 3 March), about a panther that takes on the shape of her "black marauder." "It is not bad," she noted of it in her journal entry for 27 February 1956. "It is dedicated to Ted Hughes." In her poem, the panther of passion stalks her, "hungry, hungry," as she was for Ted: "His kisses parch, each paw's a briar, / Doom consummates that appetite." But in "Trophies," Hughes puts Plath in the panther's grasp before they ever met, referring to the journey she had made through France with Richard Sassoon the Christmas before. The power of her outpourings of this time—

> Your effort to cry words
> Came apart in aired blood

Enriched by the adrenalins
Of despair, terror, sheer fury—

strikes him with an animal strength when he comes across it
years later:

After forty years
The whiff of that beast, off the dry pages,
Lifts the hair on the back of my hands.

Plath herself recognized this at the time of writing "Pursuit":
"It is, of course, a symbol of the terrible beauty of death, and
the paradox that the more intensely one lives, the more one
burns and consumes oneself; death, here, includes the concept of love, and is larger and richer than mere love, which is
part of it."

The panther, then, seeming to look through her "amber
jewels" of eyes, locks its jaws onto him. Again, Hughes is
helpless in the face of what is a "chemical process," and
again, as in "The Shot," he has no idea what hit him:

With a laugh I
Took its full weight. Little did I know
The shock attack of a big predator
According to survivors numbs the target
Into drunken euphoria.

—drunken as he was in "Visit." He is deluded into thinking
he is the victor, the one with the trophies (her hairband, her
earring, snatched at their first encounter as each relates). He
has, instead, been carried off himself.

A less likely wild beast is found in "the white calm stallion" of "Sam." The event of this poem took place before Hughes and Plath actually met: on 12 December, late the previous year, Plath went out riding with an old friend from Yale, Dick Wertz, and her horse, Sam, ran away with her. This led directly to the writing of one poem, "Whiteness I Remember" (1958):

> Whiteness being what I remember
> About Sam: whiteness and the great run
> He gave me . . .

and is also reflected in the power and pulse of "Ariel," four years later, the poet hauled through air and transformed by a force both beyond her control and part of herself.

For Hughes, then, this is an imagined recollection: "I can feel your bounced and dangling anguish, / Hugging what was left of your steerage." The runaway horse embodies his contention that she, that both of them, were prey to a higher, controlling agency of fate that demands a kind of worship: "It was grab his neck and adore him / Or free-fall." Her work, too, is perceived as the product of an almost separate self, having its own agency, saving itself at the expense of its writer's life:

> Maybe your poems
> Saved themselves, slung under that plunging neck,
> Hammocked in your body over the switchback road.

The gallop "was practice" for the later, deadly ride of "Ariel," in which Plath will write of how "The brown arc / Of the neck I cannot catch" dragged her toward oblivion.

Sam does not unseat her; Hughes, at the end of this poem, does, although there is confusion between actor and acted upon. You "fell off," he addresses her—or, in the next line, "Flung yourself off." Who, precisely, was the cause of the action can never be clarified. All that is clear and baldly stated is the end result:

> When I jumped a fence you strangled me
> One giddy moment, then fell off,
> Flung yourself off and under my feet to trip me
> And tripped me and lay dead. Over in a flash.

"Sam" blends her work, their lives, into a headlong rush to a swift and bitter end.

2 ◇ "BEAUTIFUL, BEAUTIFUL AMERICA!"

IN MARCH 1956, Hughes was staying in a London flat, 18 Rugby Street in Bloomsbury; Plath visited him there on her way to France, where she expected to meet Richard Sassoon, with whom she was still involved. But in Paris, Sassoon was nowhere to be found: and so Sylvia Plath turned her whole heart to Hughes. These next poems, from "18 Rugby Street" through to "The Owl"—the spring of 1956—shape the early days of their romance. Yet they also begin to explore Plath's interior torment: how, in Hughes's words, "the dark ate at you."

LATE IN THE MONTH of March 1956, Plath went down to London to meet Ted Hughes and Lucas Myers. At the time, Hughes was living in a flat in Rugby Street with no running water; the only bathroom was three floors down from his eyrie. No. 18 was

> a small early Georgian house, the odd one out at the end of a terrace of larger ones. On each floor was a living room with two windows facing south on to a lively street, a tiny kitchen beside it and, at the back, a small bedroom. The rooms still had their original panelling, covered in many coats of paint,

wrote Daniel Huws much later. Plath was on her way to France, for she had not yet given up on Richard Sassoon (on 13 March she wrote to her mother: "you know I am very much in love with Richard"); she resolved to visit him in Paris, where he was staying in the rue Duvivier.

When she arrived, however, Sassoon had gone, no one knew where. In "18 Rugby Street," his account of the first night he and Plath spent together, Hughes refers to her quest for Sassoon, writing of "the desperation of that search / Through those following days . . ." At the time she revealed her misery only to her journal, where she wrote, after arriving at Sassoon's empty flat:

> I had been ready to bear a day or two alone, but this news shook me to the roots. I sat down in [the concierge's] living room and wrote an incoherent letter while the tears fell scalding and wet on the paper. . . . I wrote and wrote, think-

ing that by some miracle he might walk in the door. But he had left no address, no messages, and my letters begging him to return in time were lying there blue and unread. I was really amazed at my situation; never before had a man gone off to leave me to cry after. . . .

To her mother she showed her other, brighter, face: "I have the loveliest garret in Paris, overlooking the rooftops and gables and [an] artists" skylight! . . . Perhaps the hardest and yet best thing for me is that Sassoon is not here . . . but I am getting most proud of my ability to maneuver alone. It is good for me, and I am beginning to enjoy it thoroughly. . . ." She noted this letter to her mother in her journal, "which gave her the gay side."

"18 Rugby Street" shuttles between the wonderfully vivid present of the poem—

> The catacomb basement heaped with exhaust mufflers,
> Assorted jagged shards of cars, shin-rippers
> On the way to the unlit and unlovely
> Lavatory beneath the street's pavement

—and the future. The poet looks ahead to the nights they will spend there after their wedding, sees how their son Nicholas's eyes will be like his mother's, though now, "For me yours were the novel originals." This time blending reinforces the sense of fate that is both implicit and explicit in *Birthday Letters*.

> Happy to be martyred for folly
> I invoked you, bribing Fate to produce you.

Were you conjuring me? I had no idea
How I was becoming necessary,
Or what emergency surgery Fate would make
Of my casual self-service.

He invokes her, she conjures him: a magic that obscures their
real selves and makes them actors in a drama. There is no
escape. Of 18 Rugby Street he has been told with fireside-
tale exaggeration:

It's possessed!
Whoever comes into it never gets properly out!
Whoever enters it enters a labyrinth—"

Later in that labyrinth, of course, he will find his Minotaur.

The other figures are just that: other—outside the lives of
Hughes and Plath: "That girl had nothing to do with the rest
of the house / But play her part in the drama." It is as if
Plath, whose whole life appeared to be played out as a
drama to herself, drew all those around her into the play as
well. And how could they help themselves? To Hughes, here,
she is a wonder, exotic: he flings description at her as if her
face is a whole world in itself—"aboriginal," "Apache," "Nose
from Attila's horde," "Navajo." Her face reflects what her
poetry does, "the sun's play and the moon's." Images draw
the reader to what lies outside the poem while always
remaining within it: the "great bird" of her excitement an
echo of the "Panic Bird" she wrote of as tormenting her in
her journal; the "bluish voltage" that was her flare of aura,
the electric charge of ECT. They could be seen as warnings;

but they are warnings that the poet, caught in the poem's present, is not ready to hear. Wordlessly, her scar speaks of her past anguish:

> And I heard
> Without ceasing for a moment to kiss you
> As if a sober star had whispered it
> Above the revolving, rumbling city: stay clear.

To him at this point this is not a star of Fate; this is simply a poltroon of a star," worthless, cowardly. He is lost in the wonder of her.

> You were a new world. My new world.
> So this is America, I marvelled.
> Beautiful, beautiful America!

Hughes remained on Plath's mind as she arrived in France in late March. "Arrived in Paris early Saturday evening exhausted from sleepless holocaust night with Ted in London," she wrote in her journal. ". . . I took myself in leash & washed my battered face, smeared with purple bruise from Ted and my neck raw and wounded too . . . now all Cambridge will be duly informed that I am Ted's mistress or something equally absurd. . . . Oh well, let them talk; I live in Whitstead and can ignore much." Her entry seems to indicate that they did not, in fact, have sex that night. Plath was forthright in her notes to herself about achieving "practical satisfaction" while maintaining "technical virginity"—she was, after all, a child of 1950s America.

After her disastrous visit to Europe, she was finally able to accept that Richard Sassoon was out of her life: "I took a plane from Rome through the mist-shrouded sky of Europe, to London—renounced Gordon [Lameyer, another boyfriend], Sassoon—my old life—and took up Ted." To her mother she wrote: "It is this man, this poet, this Ted Hughes. I have never known anything like it. For the first time I can use all my knowing and laughing and force and writing to the hilt all the time, everything, and you should see him, hear him!" She had found the god that Hughes said she was looking for in "The Shot": in her *Journals* she wrote, "I need Ted . . . as I need bread and wine." She called him, too, "my savior" and "the god creator risen." She locked on to him with ferocious passion and he fell under her spell: the strength of that is made evident in "Fidelity."

That spring Hughes gave up his London work and returned to Cambridge, staying with Lucas Myers in a house on Tenison Road. In "Fidelity," he describes his devotion to Plath as if he were the acolyte of a goddess. Among the "loose-lifers" and "day-sleepers" at Alexandra House—a British, or Civic, Restaurant run by the Women's Volunteer Service in Alexandra Street (just off Petty Cury) since the time of World War II—his existence takes on a priestly purity:

> A bare
> Mattress, on bare boards, in a bare room.
> All I had, my notebook and that mattress.

His writing, his notebook, is now allied with the mattress and his physical and spiritual passion for Plath. It is a rich, sensual time of fruitfulness and beginnings: he is aware of the "opening, bud-sticky chestnuts."

This love purified not only Hughes but, it seems, all others who came in contact with it. For Hughes did not sleep alone on his mattress: there was "a lovely girl, escaped freshly / From her husband," who, each night, lay naked in his arms. But no sexual element crept into their friendship:

> A holy law
> Had invented itself, somehow, for me.
> But she too served it, like a priestess,
> Tender, kind and stark naked beside me.

Of course, had she not been this virginal "priestess," perhaps Hughes would not have been able to resist her. Her "plump and pretty" friend "did all she could to get me inside her"; and, he addresses Plath:

> . . . you will never know what a battle
> I fought to keep the meaning of my words
> Solid with the world we were making.

These two girls, his desire for them, are the sacrifice he makes to their "unlikely future": that this romantic, dreamy poem ends with the violent image of a sinless child slaughtered to propitiate savage gods hints at the price that future will exact.

The disparity between the worlds the two poets came from cannot be overemphasized. In her eyes, he was the emblem of Natural Man—though with a wondrous poetic gift. He was "a large, hulking, healthy Adam . . . with a voice like the thunder of God—a singer, story-teller, lion and world-wanderer, a vagabond who will never stop." The clearest evidence of this is the different way they viewed their surroundings. Hughes's work, from his first book, *The Hawk in the Rain*, to *Tales from Ovid*, published in 1997, has always been closely connected to the natural world: his vivid images of animals and landscapes, whether familiar or exotic, stand out and endure. Plath's work is rarely so connected: much of it springs from her inner self and the private mythology she created around that self. Certainly, brought up as she had been in the United States, the English landscape that was bred in Hughes's bone was alien to her and, when first she tried to see it through his eyes, a wonder: a sense very clearly expressed by Hughes in "The Owl."

> I saw my world again through your eyes
> As I would see it again through your children's eyes.
> Through your eyes it was foreign.

Again he casts back to his younger self and forward from that point to the youth of their children: her delight is child-like,

> an incredulous joy
> Like a mother handed her new baby
> By the midwife.

"Anything wild, on legs" is strange to her, out of place even in its element, and he is like a kind of magician: "I made my world perform its utmost for you." The swooping, flightlike rhythm of the poem gives a sense of how the poet sees his soaring ability to conjure nature. But the performance, which he calls his "masterpiece," imitating the cry of a wounded rabbit and drawing a tawny owl to fly at his face, has sinister overtones: for the nocturnal owl, in many traditions, is the bird of death. The ancient Egyptians saw the owl as such; the owl's cry heralds King Duncan's death in *Macbeth*, the owl "the fatal bellman, / Which gives the stern'st good-night." Plath, in a grim depression in 1958, would write that she felt "as if a great muscular owl were sitting on my chest, its talons clenching and constricting my heart." Her poem of that year, "Owl," has "the pale, raptorial owl" as "fearfully soft"; "Rat's teeth gut the city / Shaken by owl cry."

So Hughes's performance, even if it was a masterpiece, could not protect Plath from the demons that haunted her. And there is, perhaps, another side to this: Seamus Heaney has identified Wordsworth's autobiographical boy—who, in *The Prelude*, blows "mimic hootings to the silent owls" and makes them answer back—as a metaphor for poetic creation; the first, imitative whistles the beginnings of the imaginative spark. So Hughes saw her early poetic work, written around this time: imitative preparation for the leap she would take into the full creative—but deathly—voice of the *Ariel* poems. The owl cry heralds wonder and final oblivion.

The "incredulous joy" revealed in "The Owl" is only one side of her personality; the other is the dark fear that Hughes, writing years later, acknowledges in both "The Machine" and "God Help the Wolf After Whom the Dogs Do Not Bark." As his body was placed between Plath and the destructive force of her father in "The Shot," so in "The Machine," too, there seems a possibility that Hughes's physical presence could keep her from fear and hurt:

> When you tried
> To will me up the stair, this terror
> Arrived instead.

It is a terror that she keeps at bay with acceptance and love procured, as Hughes writes in "God Help the Wolf," "with gifts of yourself." Her journal reveals her striving to be "perfect" in the instructions she occasionally gave herself: "Don't blab too much—listen more; sympathize and 'understand' people. . . . Don't criticize anybody to anyone else— misquoting is like a telephone game." Having fallen for Hughes, Plath will lecture herself sternly in how to keep him: "Re Ted," she wrote on 16 April 1956,

You have accepted his being; you were desperate for this and you know what you must pay: utter vigilance in Cambridge (rumor will be legion, but there must be no proof; never drink, keep calm) . . . whistling void in guts when he leaves with memory of his big iron violent virile body, incredible tenderness and rich voice . . . never complain or be bitter or ask for more than normal human consideration . . . let him go. Have the guts to make him happy: cook, play, read, but don't loose [sic] others—work for Krook, Varsity + home— keep other cups and flagons full—never accuse or nag—let him run, reap, rip—and glory in the temporary sun of his ruthless force.

She wanted so much; but her longing could never be revealed. In this poem, Hughes contends it was her striving for love in the "home of anger," her father's house, that kept her this way—her father's love was, after all, finally, terrifyingly unattainable. Hughes's ironic references in "God Help the Wolf" to sweetening his death, sugaring the bitterness of his death, recall that it was sweetness that killed Otto Plath: diabetes.

In both of these poems Hughes is firmly placed in the vantage point of the future, looking back on their uncomprehending, younger selves. In "The Machine," his own younger self bears the brunt of his reproach. He allows that even a dog would have scented the phantom fear, "might have stared at nothing / Hair on end," sensing the terror contained in her past. Here is his first reference to the fact that it was not simply her father's ghost that haunted her, but her living mother too: the mother for whom she wanted to be the perfect, brilliant, cheerful "Sivvy" who writes *Letters Home*— though in 1958 she would, in her journal, refer to her mother as "a source of great depression—a beacon of terrible warning." In her 1957 poem "The Disquieting Muses," she closes with a frigid description of her blank-faced guardians in their "gowns of stone," the setting sun "that never brightens or goes down."

> And this is the kingdom you bore me to,
> Mother, mother. But no frown of mine
> Will betray the company I keep.

Five years later, in "Medusa," she will betray the company she keeps, closing this bitter address to the "old barnacled umbilicus" with the stark rejection, "There is nothing between us."

Hughes writes:

> . . . the grotesque mask of your Mummy-Daddy
> Half-quarry, half-hospital, whole
> Juggernaut, stuffed with your unwritten poems,
> Ground invisibly without a ripple
> Towards me through the unstirred willows,
> Through the wall of The Anchor . . .

The Mummy-Daddy specter—out of which she made her art—heads toward him as inevitably (and as invisibly: the trees outside do not register the spirit pass) as the bullet of "The Shot": even in the most mundane place, a pub, even as he simply sinks his pint. It is inevitable that he, in ignorance, looks for a comfort he will not find: he finds his home in the "otherworld interior" of the grotesque mask that "Blackly yawned me" inside itself—but it will not be the home he expects.

In "God Help the Wolf," his reproach appears to turn outward. "There you met it—the mystery of hatred," he writes. The Colleges—all the institutions to which she was attached at one point or another (school, Smith, Cambridge) rolled into Hughes's collective representation—rejected her, in the view of the poem.

> It did seem
> You disturbed something just perfected
> That they were holding carefully, all of a piece,
> Till the glue dried.

The "something" they held was too fragile, too breakable, unable to withstand her vitality; the Colleges' glue calls to mind the image of Plath's poem "The Colossus," in which the poet vainly attempts to repair the broken statue of her father:

> I shall never get you put together entirely,
> Pieced, glued, and properly jointed . . .
>
> Scaling little ladders with gluepots and pails of Lysol
> I crawl like an ant in mourning
> Over the weedy acres of your brow
> To mend the immense skull-plates and clear
> The bald, white tumuli of your eyes.

An impossible mending: the glue won't hold, and for her breaking of the mold, the Colleges punish Plath. "They let you know that you were not John Donne," Hughes writes. (She wrote to her mother on 8 June 1957, following her exams, when she was "prevented . . . from absorbing anything, but only pessimistically rewriting the exams in my mind. A very nasty young don took this opportune moment for making a devastating and absolutely destructive attack on one of my poems by showing how 'hollow' it was compared to—guess who?—John Donne! Very typical of Cambridge criticism . . . and this coming at a time of nonwriting was especially trying.")

Plath was, almost always, enormously successful, academically, artistically and socially; yet she lived in a world of slights and damage that could easily tip her away from her fragile balance. When fellow student Jane Baltzell underlined in pencil some passages in Plath's books, Plath flew into a rage and wrote in her journal of 6 March: "I was furious, feeling my children had been raped, or beaten, by an alien"— and Jane she considered her friend. That hatred, surely, is a "mystery" in part because it was something of her own creation, a product of "your floundering / Drowning life and your effort to save yourself." The title and sensibility of "God Help the Wolf" echoes an early poem of Hughes's, "February," from *The Hawk in the Rain*, which conjures the ghost of the last wolf killed in Britain.

> The worst since has been so much mere Alsatian.
> Now it is the dream cries "Wolf!" where these feet
>
> Print the moonlit doorstep . . .

The wolf, for Hughes, is the savage force of creation, which Plath's orderly external world could not contain. "February" continues:

> These feet, deprived,
> Disdaining all that are caged, or storied, or pictured,
> Through and throughout the true world search
> For their vanished head, for the world
>
> Vanished with the head, the teeth, the quick eyes . . .

It was against the force of this wolf, Hughes contends, that she battled to save herself. It was an effort seemingly doomed from her girlhood. At the end of "The Machine," Hughes again echoes the stark colors of her own work, the black of death, the red of blood, as her terror takes him over and freezes him "forever" trying to escape its grasp. "The steps now stone," "the door now red," with Plath resurrected on that door's other side, create an image of Hughes himself trying, but never succeeding, to climb out of her grave.

3 ◆ "SPAIN WAS THE LAND OF YOUR DREAMS"

AS HUGHES WRITES in "A Pink Wool Knitted Dress," Ted Hughes and Sylvia Plath were married on Bloomsday, 1956. The next few poems in *Birthday Letters* take the couple through their honeymoon in Paris and through July, which they spent in Spain. Hughes blends the minutiae of their lives—the bullfight they attended in "You Hated Spain," her illness in "Fever," her concentrated intensity of skill in "Drawing"—with what he comes to see of her character.

SYLVIA PLATH AND Ted Hughes were married at St. George the Martyr in Bloomsbury—"St. George of the Chimney Sweeps" because of a plaque commemorating a nineteenth-century benefactor who provided £1,000 for "Christmas Dinners to Chimney Sweeps from all parts of London"—on 16 June 1956. The wedding was "a huge and miraculous secret," as she wrote to her brother Warren two days later: she was concerned that the college authorities at Newnham and the Fulbright Commission would cancel her scholarship if they found she had married ("the Victorian virgins wouldn't see how I could concentrate with being married to such a handsome virile man")—a fear that proved unfounded. "When Ted and I see you in Europe this summer," she wrote to her brother (then in Austria), "we'll tell you all the fantastic details of our struggle to get a license (from the Archbishop of Canterbury, no less), searching for the parish church where Ted belonged and had, by law, to be married, spotting a priest on the street, Ted pointing, 'That's him!' and following him home and finding he was the right one."

Her mother attended the wedding, but none of his family. She described to her brother the hectic lead-up to the wedding itself:

We rushed about London, buying dear Ted shoes and trousers, the gold wedding rings (I never wanted an engagement ring) with the last of our money, and mummy supplying a lovely pink knitted suit dress she brought (intuitively never having worn) and me in that and a pink hair ribbon and a pink rose from Ted, standing with the rain pouring outside in the dim little church, saying the most beautiful words in the world as our vows, with the curate as second witness [it is, in Hughes's account, the sexton] and the dear Reverend, an old, bright-eyed man (who lives right opposite Charles Dickens' house!) kissing my cheek, and the tears falling down from my eyes like rain—I was so happy with my dear, lovely Ted.

Her diary entry is breathless:

> Act of faith . . . We came together in that church of the chimney sweeps with nothing but love & hope & our own selves: Ted in his old black corduroy jacket & me in mother's gift of a pink knit dress. Pink rose & black tie. An empty church in watery yellow-gray light of rainy London. Outside, the crowd of thick-ankled tweed-coated mothers & pale, jabbering children waiting for the bus to take them on a church outing to the Zoo.

In her letter she tells, too, of chasing after the sexton: "A Pink Wool Knitted Dress" narrates the events of their wedding day but hints at what was to come: her future is "watch-towered," "searchlit" as if she is a prisoner within it, and her eyes are "like big jewels / Shaken in a dice-cup and held up to me"—jewels of chance and fate. She is physically transfigured by her emotion: "You shook, you sobbed with joy, you were ocean depth / Brimming with God" (Hughes's ironic but loving refraction of the "bag full of God" with "a head in the freakish Atlantic" that is Plath's "Daddy"). In an early echo of *The Tempest*, "You said you saw the heavens open / And show riches, ready to drop upon us."

She is physically transfigured by her love; she is similarly transfigured in an earlier poem about an event that took place a few months later, "Fate Playing," when, in October 1956, she nearly missed Hughes as he came down to London from Heptonstall. Not finding him, as she expected, at the bus station,

> I was really frantic, unable to understand why Ted wasn't on one of these [buses]; he'd bought reservations: so, in a fury of tears, I fell sobbing into a taxi and for 20 minutes begged him to hurry to King's Cross to see if by some miracle Ted might be there. I was sick, not knowing what to do but yell, but yell . . . through the streets of London. Well, to shorten the trauma, I walked into King's Cross into Ted's arms. He'd made the driver drop him off early so he could get to me sooner. . . . He looked like the most beautiful dear person in the world; everything began to shine, and the taxi driver sprouted wings, and all was fine.

In this poem, too, her physical self, as described by Hughes, is overwhelmed by her emotion; and gods, or the fates, are brought into the equation. On the platform

> I saw that surge and agitation, a figure
> Breasting the flow of released passengers,
> Then your molten face, your molten eyes
> And your exclamations, your flinging arms
> Your scattering tears
> As if I had come back from the dead
> Against every possibility, against
> Every negative but your own prayer
> To your own gods.

Here he is her "miracle," much as he will be at their wedding. At the end of this poem the earth weeps as she does, and will weep at their wedding—personified, for joy, after "the drought in August." But the extremity of her feeling, the overwhelming flood of her tears, seem out of proportion, the molten face and eyes hinting at a dangerous violence.

They left to honeymoon in Paris—with Aurelia Plath in tow—on 22 June. Plath's mother stayed with them a week. In "Your Paris," there is another view from the "post-war, utility son-in-law" encountered in "A Pink Wool Knitted Dress." The view of this honeymoon destination is very different, seen through the eyes of an American besotted by its foreign romance, from the just-post-wartime, post-Occupation Paris that a European sees. Plath sees

> . . . frame after frame,
> Street after street, of Impressionist paintings,
> Under the chestnut shades of Hemingway,
> Fitzgerald, Henry Miller, Gertrude Stein . . .

This was not Hughes's perception.

> While you
> Called me Aristide Bruant and wanted
> To draw les toits, and your ecstasies ricocheted
> Off the walls patched and scabbed with posters —
> I heard the contrabasso counterpoint
> In my dog-nosed pondering analysis
> Of café chairs where the SS mannequins
> Had performed their *tableaux vivants*
> So recently the coffee was still bitter

As acorns, and the waiters' eyes
Clogged with dregs of betrayal, reprisal, hatred.

He is somber, held back, the patron to her artist (Bruant was an early patron of Toulouse-Lautrec in Montmartre); and there is self-directed irony here, in his analysis of café chairs. There is also a darker reality and irony beneath that— particularly given that it will be she who appropriates, in her later work, Nazi imagery to such shocking and controversial effect.

"I was not much ravished by the view of the roofs." Hughes seems here to dismiss her tourist ardor with some bitterness. Mass death is for her, seemingly, only an "anecdotal aesthetic touch": her "lingo" is a "thesaurus of . . . cries"—innately shallow. But as the poem develops, something else is revealed: that this is simply her mechanism of protection. For her, Paris is really her memory of fruitlessly hunting Richard Sassoon:

> a desk in a *pension*
> Where your letters
> Waited for him unopened.

For Plath, the pain of past damage is never left behind. She is still lost in its labyrinth, and Paris

> Was a dream where you could not
> Wake or find the exit or
> The Minotaur to put a blessed end
> To the torment.

Compared to this, what, after all, is his dog-nosed pondering of "the odd, stray, historic bullet"? She calms herself with drawing and he is a "mere dog," a "guide dog," thinking he is protecting her but not understanding what she really needs protection from.

In July, they left Paris for Spain, and by the middle of the month had settled in Benidorm—which, in the mid-1950s, was not the tourist resort it is now. Plath, for the most part, wrote her usual contented letters to her mother: "Anyway, I have never felt so native to a country as I do to Spain . . . Spain is utter heaven," she wrote from Madrid on 7 July. "You Hated Spain," however, indicates that Hughes saw another side of his wife on their honeymoon: in Spain, he sensed her fear, her anger, and a kind of terrible recognition. Yet it was he, rather than Plath, who felt a native: "Spain / Where I felt at home." She becomes the "bobby-sox American," frightened by what seems a brutal, unvarnished country; but then, perhaps, her fear arises because it is a country she seems to know of old:

> Spain
> Was the land of your dreams: the dust-red cadaver
> You dared not wake with, the puckering amputations
> No literature course had glamorized.

Plath tried to make Spain bright and happy in her poem "Fiesta Melons," a slightly flat hymn to

> innumerable melons,
> Ovals and balls,

Bright green and thumpable
Laced over with stripes

Of turtle-dark green . . .

and in the notes she wrote in July: "The continuous poise
and splash of incoming waves mark a ragged line of surf
beyond which the morning sea blazes in the early sun,
already high and hot at ten-thirty; the ocean is cerulean
toward the horizon, vivid azure nearer shore, blue and
sheened as peacock feathers. . . ." More successful as a poem
than "Fiesta Melons" is "The Goring," reflecting a bullfight
they attended, where "Blood faultlessly broached redeemed
the sullied air, the earth's grossness." In "Departure," too, her
vision of the Spanish landscape is bleak and threatened:

Retrospect shall not soften such penury—
Sun's brass, the moon's steely patinas,
The leaden slag of the world—
But always expose

The scraggy rock spit shielding the town's blue bay
Against which the brunt of outer sea
Beats, is brutal endlessly.

Hughes's final image is hopeful and yet dreadful:

I see you, in moonlight,
Walking the empty wharf at Alicante
Like a soul waiting for the ferry,
A new soul, still not understanding,

Thinking it is still your honeymoon
In the happy world, with your whole life waiting,
Happy, and all your poems still to be found.

The light of the moon—"hard and apart and white," as she wrote in 1962's "Lesbos"—will become the bleak emblem of her bitterness, and he sees her here as if she is already dead, "a new soul" waiting to be ferried to the Underworld but fooled into believing that she still lives in the "happy world" of her honeymoon, not knowing that the poems "still to be found" will bring something other than happiness.

That deadly, bleached light floods the following poem, "Moonwalk." During that summer, Plath's moods fluctuated wildly. She wrote in her journal in July:

Alone, deepening. Feeling the perceptions deepen with the tang of geranium and the full moon and the mellowing of hurt; the deep ingrowing of hurt, too far from the bitching fussing surface tempests. The hurt going in, clean as a razor, and the dark blood welling. Just the sick knowing that the wrongness was growing in the full moon. . . . We go out leaving the light on in the house into the glare of the full moon. . . . We sit far apart, on stones and bristling dry grass. The light is cold, cruel and still. All could happen: the wilful drowning, the murder, the killing words. The stones are rough and clear, and outlined mercilessly in the moonlight. . . .

Here is the annihilating whiteness of "Moonrise," written in 1958—perhaps the "poem to be written so prettily" referred to here:

Death whitens in the egg and out of it.
I can see no color for this whiteness.
White: it is a complexion of the mind.

Five years later, she will begin the stark poem "The Moon and the Yew Tree": "This is the light of the mind, cold and planetary. / The trees of the mind are black. The light is blue."

This is a very different Sylvia Plath from the one who appears in "A Pink Wool Knitted Dress," although here again are the dice that connect the two. This Plath has a "mask / Bleak as cut iron." Coleridge's *Ancient Mariner* brings doom to his ship in the shape of a woman: "The Night-mare Life-in-Death was she, / Who thicks man's blood with cold"—and this is the presence that haunts Hughes, "throwing black-and-white dice," colors of the moon and its dark side. Hughes is uncomprehending. Is he "The doctor who humours, and watches / As the patient dies in his care"? He is fatally distanced from her:

> I could no more join you
> Than on the sacrificial slab
> That you were looking for. I could not
> Even imagine the priest.

Blame, in this poem, lies at the door of his ignorance and incomprehension (every stone is a "rosetta" he cannot decipher), but how could he understand if she did not either? For her, the moon was still "The raw lump / Of ore, not yet smelted and shaped / Into your managed talent"; and

> Your eyes
> Were in their element
> But uncomprehending and
> Terrified by it.

The poetic mask she makes from the images around her, both of her own creation and drawn from other sources (later, the following spring, when teaching at Smith, she will come to be greatly influenced by primitivist art, particularly that of de Chirico), is a fiesta mask worn not by Plath, it seems here, but by the "daemon" she becomes, and which is the demon that through her work still survives, "still gazes / Through it at me."

In Spain, too, she became ill with a bug, or food poisoning, as Hughes recounts in "Fever." It recalls an actual event—and Esther's poisoning in *Birthday Letters*—but also makes concrete her nameless anxiety and foreshadows her future. In her fever-dream, she climbed into a well:

> The cool of the dark shaft, the best place
> To find oblivion from your burning tangle
> And the foreign bug. You cried for certain
> You were going to die.

The shuttered Spanish house is already "a tomb." Hughes bustles about, making a vegetable soup—it had saved Voltaire from the plague, why not his wife from her bug? He admires himself in this role: "I fancied myself at that." But at the same time he is detached, questioning her desperation:

> Your cry jammed so hard
> Over into the red of catastrophe
> Left no space for worse.

The extremity of her reaction to her illness recalls the floods of her tears in "Fate Playing," and this time Hughes backs away:

> And I recoiled, just a little,
> Just for balance, just for symmetry,
> Into sceptical patience, a little.

As he saw himself and Plath then, he is rational, she is not, crying like a child for the "medicine cupboard" of her America. Yet these few lines, with their hesitant rhythm, their repetition of "a little," the remark "just for balance," make it seem as if the poet is slightly ashamed of his younger self.

Years later, his thought that she might be crying wolf leaves him observing his own coldness,

> . . . the blank thought
> Of the anaesthesia that helps creatures
> Under the polar ice, and the callous
> That eases overwhelmed doctors.

The phrase "I said nothing" tolls twice, as in the muffled ring of "the dead bell, the dead bell," which comes at the close of Plath's chilling poem "Death & Co.": "The stone man made soup. / The burning woman drank it." If she burns, he is only stone and unable to extinguish her suffering.

There was, however, contentment, too. Both Hughes and Plath were working hard at their writing (he on a book of Kiplingesque animal fables, later *How the Whale Became*; she on short stories for magazines), and in a letter to her mother, Plath described their days:

> We wake about seven in the morning, with a cool breeze blowing in the grape leaves outside our window. I get up, take the two litres of milk left daily on our doorstep in a can and heat it for my café-con-leche and Ted's brandy-milk . . . [to accompany] delectable wild bananas and sugar. Then we go early to market, first for fish . . . every day brings a different catch. There are mussels, crabs, shrimp, little baby octopuses, and sometimes a huge fish which they sell in steaks. . . . Then we price vegetables, buying our staples of eggs, potatoes, tomatoes and onions. . . . If only you could see how fantastically we economize. . . . I hope that never again in my life will I have to be so tight with money. We will one day have a great deal, I am sure of it.

This is the market he describes her sketching in the moving "Drawing." From Paris, Plath wrote to her mother of how, in Spain, she

> went about with Ted doing detailed pen-and-ink sketches while he sat at my side and read, wrote, or just meditated. He loves to go with me while I sketch and is very pleased with my drawings and sudden return to sketching. Wait till you see these few of Benidorm—the best I've ever done in my life, very heavy stylized shading and lines; very difficult subjects, too: the peasant market (the peasants crowded

around like curious children, and one little man who wanted me to get his stand in, too, hung a wreath of garlic over it artistically so I would draw that); a composition of three sardine boats on the bay with their elaborate lights, and a good one of the cliff-headland with the houses over the sea. . . .

Already, in "Your Paris," he has described the activity as her anesthetic, but the calmness it imparted to her seems to come at a cost: "Your poker infernal pen / Was like a branding iron," he writes; and the scene is not created but "imprisoned." But from the stillness of the scene, there is change in the offing: Benidorm, that had "a market place that still slept / In the Middle Ages" is about to disappear "under the screams of a million summer migrants / And the cliff of dazzling hotels." More than that—in three lines that take Plath gently from light to darkness—Hughes's wife will be lost to the death that made her a companion:

> As your hand
> Went under Heptonstall to be held
> By endless darkness.

Between that hand and his hand, there is still, however, a connection, as he writes not far from where she lies in her grave, conjuring the particular recollections that make memory so vivid—"Your shorts, your short-sleeved jumper— / One of the thirty I lugged around Europe—" Thirty years later the vivid life that insisted he carry thirty sweaters all around a continent is no more: "Now I drink from your stillness that neither / Of us can disturb or escape."

4 ◇ "THAT HOME WAS OUR FIRST CAMP"

HUGHES AND PLATH returned to England in the autumn of 1956, visiting Yorkshire—as Hughes relates in "Wuthering Heights"—before returning to Cambridge, where they found a home together. As can be seen in poems like "The Earthenware Head," "Horoscope," and "Ouija," the supernatural was alive for them both; husband and wife saw omens and portents all around them. But for the moment all seemed to point to good fortune.

THEIR HONEYMOON OVER, the Hugheses left Spain at the end of August, stopping off in Paris, where Hughes met Plath's brother Warren. Then she met with his family: returning to England at the beginning of September, they traveled up to the Beacon, Hughes's family home in Heptonstall. Plath seemed to like Hughes's parents, and was swept away by the romance of the place itself; writing to her mother on 2 September, she described "an incredible, wild, green landscape of bare hills, crisscrosssed by innumerable black stone walls like a spiders's web in which gray, woolly sheep graze, along with chickens and dappled brown-and-white cows. A wicked north wind is whipping a blowing rain against the little house, and coal fires are glowing." It is a description that cannot fail to recall "The Owl": the movie-set Yorkshire she describes is Hughes's world performing for Plath.

As Hughes relates in "Wuthering Heights," while in Yorkshire they walked across the moor to Withins, a ruined farmhouse on the moors above Haworth, supposedly the site of Emily Brontë's *Wuthering Heights*, in the company of Hughes's Uncle Walter. "We had a picnic in a field of purple heather," her letter continues,

and the sun, by a miracle, was out among luminous white clouds in a blue sky. There is no way to Wuthering Heights except by foot for several miles over the moors. How can I tell you how wonderful it is. Imagine yourself on top of the world, with all the purplish hills curving away, and gray sheep grazing with horns curling and black demonic faces and yellow eyes . . . black walls of stone, clear streams from

which we drank; and, at last, a windy side of a hill. I began a
sketch of the sagging roof and stone walls. . . .

Hughes's poem delineates the differences, but also under-
lines some similarities, between Plath and Emily Brontë.
Brontë, who, like Plath, had begun writing at a precociously
early age, was also dead by the age of thirty, and her sister,
Charlotte, writing about the former's Gothic masterpiece
after her death, felt obliged to note the "horror of great darkness" that loured over the work; a darkness found, too, in
Plath's late writing.

The poem sees the countryside less romantically than
Plath's gushing letter to her mother:

> The leakage
> Of earnings off a few sickly bullocks
> And a scatter of crazed sheep.

But when Plath saw this "sodden, raw-stone cramp of
refuge,"

> You breathed it all in
> With jealous, emulous sniffings. Weren't you
> Twice as ambitious as Emily?

Perching in a tree for a picture, she is "doing as Emily never
did," is "full of life and hope and future" where Emily was "a
dying prisoner." And yet, in Hughes's poem, something in
this place understands what lies in store for her, that there is

real connection between the two writers in the flame of their talents:

> And the stone,
> Reaching to touch your hand, found you real
> And warm, and lucent, like that earlier one.

The ghost who "maybe" sees her, gains an understanding of her—where her husband, at that time, did not. In Plath's poem "Wuthering Heights" (written later, in September 1961), she writes of how

> the wind
> Pours by like destiny, bending
> Everything in one direction.
> I can feel it trying
> To funnel my heat away.
> If I pay the roots of the heather
> Too close attention, they will invite me
> To whiten my bones among them.

But term was about to begin, and the couple returned to Cambridge. They searched for a place to live, and found a flat on the ground floor of a house near Grantchester Meadows, 55 Eltisley Avenue, as Hughes relates in the brooding, ominous "55 Eltisley." This is the second of three poems in *Birthday Letters* that take their titles from homes the Hugheses made for themselves; eight others* are linked to specific

---

*"St. Botolph's," "Wuthering Heights," "Child's Park," "The Badlands," "Fishing Bridge," "Grand Canyon," "Karlsbad Caverns," and "Stubbing Wharfe."

places by their titles. Place and recollection are inextricably linked: this imagery of location makes *Birthday Letters* a kind of memory palace, a series of visual images that bring a lost time vividly into the present.

"55 Eltisley" is a poem very different in tone from the bright letter Plath wrote to her mother, happily describing their new abode:

> We share a bathroom with a Canadian couple upstairs and have the whole first floor: living room, bedroom, large sort of dining room, antique but sturdy gas stove and pantry . . . [the landlady] assured us we could paint the walls (now a ghastly yellow) as long as we didn't choose purple or orange. . . . The rent is 4 pounds a week, plus expenses for gas, light, phone and coal. We'll keep the place extravagantly warm! . . . It even has two apple trees in the ragged little back yard and a bay tree. It's got pots and pans, old kitchen silver and a few old sheets for the double bed. I'll make it like an ad out of House and Garden with Ted's help. . . .

Both poets, at this time, were meeting with success: Plath's poem "Pursuit" had been accepted by the *Atlantic Monthly*, and a few more were taken by *Poetry* (Chicago). Hughes was recording some poems by Yeats for the BBC, and got a job teaching in a local boys school. In January 1957, he had his first poem accepted by a British magazine, *Nimbus*.

Initially, Plath had feared that the college authorities would react badly to the news of her marriage and that she might even lose her scholarship. When, however, she at last notified the Fulbright Commission, she was met with congratulations, not wrath. One of her particular supporters was her supervisor, Dorothea Krook, referred to in "55 Eltisley"; "Wendy" is Wendy Christie (later Campbell), a South African friend of Krook's who sat in on some of Plath's supervisions. Plath moved in with Hughes, who had "claimed our first home / Alone," in mid-November 1956. Plath wrote to her mother of her happiness—although she does, even at this stage, identify Hughes with her father.

> We have such lovely hours together. . . . We read, discuss poems we discover, talk, analyze—we continually fascinate each other. It is heaven to have someone like Ted who is so kind and honest and brilliant—always stimulating me to study, think, draw and write. He is better than any teacher, even fills somehow that huge, sad hole I felt in having no father. . . .

Wendy Christie recalled the extraordinary pairing that made up this marriage:

> About this time I remember them both very clearly at a party I gave (standing by the fireplace, talking to some people, both of them smiling and smiling, almost incandescent with happiness). The Dean of Ted's college arrived and was standing in the doorway casting a delicately nauseated eye over the assembly when it came to rest on Ted. "You do know some extraordinary people," he murmured. I thought Ted so genuinely extraordinary that I laughed aloud and so did he, but the good dean spoke with feeling since Ted had apparently posed a certain problem for the college for a part of his time there. He lived with such vehemence, and such a perfect absence of self-consciousness, and such a total indif-

ference to the modes of the Establishment that it was not always easy to preserve both Ted and the appearances which were thought to be necessary. At this party a friend of mine said as he was leaving, indicating Ted and Sylvia, "something going on between those two," and I said, "Well, yes, they've just been married." And indeed something was undoubtedly going on. They seemed to have found solid ground in each other. Ted's gusto took more constructive forms and Sylvia had found a man on the same scale as herself. Her vividness demanded largeness, intensity, an extreme, and Ted was not only physically large, he was unafraid: he didn't care, in a tidy bourgeois sense, he didn't care a damn for anyone or anything.

Yet "55 Eltisley" hints that already there were darker undercurrents in the marriage. Dorothea Krook would later remark on glimpsing at this time in Plath "the passionate rage which has since come to be recognised as a dominating emotion of her poetry." The atmosphere Hughes conjures in this poem does not seem an auspicious one for beginning a life together. Moving in, he looked for omens and found one: a bloodstain on a pillow left, it appears, by the now-dead husband of the widow who had vacated the house.

> She had left the last blood of her husband
> Staining a pillow. Their whole story
> Hung—a miasma—round that stain.
> Senility's sour odour. It had condensed
> Like a grease on the cutlery.

He becomes obsessed with puzzling out the source of the blood and tries

   . . . not to inhale the ghost
That clung on in the breath of the bed.
His death and her bereavement
Were the sole guests at our house-warming.

The poem hints at her possessiveness of him. While her journals at the time show her in love and confident in that love, Hughes is to her "my man." Hughes refers again to Coleridge's *Rime of the Ancient Mariner*, the Albatross a possibility of redemption lost: "You yourself were a whole Antarctic sea / Between me and your girl-friends." Hughes creates images of a kind of happiness, heavily blinkered: he is "happy to stare at a candle," he lives in "rainbow darkness." Already it seems that Hughes could see Plath becoming enclosed in the gassy, poisonous atmosphere of the "Bell Jar" that would give her only completed novel its title, transfixed by the distant image of a familial happiness frozen and in the past.

Both were busy that autumn and winter. Plath, who was diligent about keeping both her own and her husband's poems in circulation for possible publication, typed out forty of his poems and sent them out, under the title *The Hawk in the Rain*, to Harper Brothers, in New York, for a New York Poetry Center competition to be judged by Marianne Moore, Stephen Spender and W. H. Auden. Hughes got a job teaching at a secondary modern school; Plath was writing and continuing to study.

One of the poems she composed early in that year was "The Lady and the Earthenware Head" (among others were "Hardcastle Crags," "The Thin People," "On the Difficulty of

Conjuring up a Dryad"), a reflection of which is found in Hughes's "The Earthenware Head." Plath's poem arose from a clay sculpture of her head made by a roommate at Smith; somehow superstitious, she could not throw it away:

Fired in sanguine clay, the model head
Fit nowhere: brickdust-complected, eye under a dense lid,
On the long bookshelf it stood
Stolidly propping up thick volumes of prose: spite-set
Ape of her look. Best rid
Hearthstone at once of the outrageous head;
Still, she felt loath to junk it.

It was a poem of which she was, initially, very proud; later she changed her mind, calling it "too fancy, glassy, patchy and rigid—it embarrasses me now—with its ten elaborate epithets for head in five verses." It is a change of heart Hughes reflects in his poem:

You ransacked thesaurus in your poem about it,
Veiling its mirror, rhyming yourself into safety
From its orphaned fate.

In the end it was Hughes's idea that they take it out to Grantchester Meadows and set it in the branches of a willow tree. "Ted suggested we walk out into the meadows and climb up into a tree and ensconce it there so it could look over the cow pastures and river," she wrote to her mother on 8 February 1957.

I returned there for the first time today, and there it was, high up on a branch-platform in a gnarled willow, gazing out over the lovely green meadows with the peace that passes understanding. I like to think of leaving "my head" here, as it were. Ted was right: every time I think of it now, I feel leaves and ivy twining around it, like a monument at rest in the midst of nature. . . .

Hughes writes, in "The Earthenware Head":

> Above head height, the socket of a healed bole-wound,
> A twiggy crotch, nearly an owl's porch,
> Made a mythic shrine for your double.

The imagery of the head separated off from Plath recalls the dual nature of her personality, and casts her as a female Orpheus, her head still singing though severed from her body. Plath was fearful of its falling into the river, it seems: as Anne Stevenson points out, the drowned head is an image that recurs in her later poems, in "All the Dead Dears" and "Words"; it then seems significant that in Hughes's "The Earthenware Head," he writes with certainty of the head's drowning: "Surely the river got it. Surely / The river is its chapel. And keeps it." For she did "drown," her suicide putting her face to face with "the Father / Mudded at the bottom of the Cam." She called the head "evil"—he repeats it twice—as if it represented the evil in herself, now "washed from it," after its submergence, after her death.

That was, however, a distant darkness. Spring brought good news for both of them. In February, they heard that Hughes had indeed won the New York Poetry Center competition with *The Hawk in the Rain*; the next month Plath received confirmation of a teaching post at Smith, to begin in the coming autumn, which Mary Ellen Chase had been trying to arrange for her. Olive Higgins Prouty, on hearing the news, wrote that so many thrilling things happening to them "frightens me a little," and urged her protégée, ". . . Sometime write me a little poem that isn't intense. A lamp turned too high might shatter its chimney. Please just glow sometimes. . . ." But it was a warning that fell on deaf ears. It must have seemed as if the successful future of which they had dreamed was opening up before them; as if the portents of good fortune that they had looked for in ouija and horoscope—as Hughes relates in the two poems so called—were being made good.

Plath herself wrote a poem called "Ouija" in 1957: "It is a chilly god, a god of shades, / Rises to the glass from his black fathoms," the work begins. In her *Collected Poems*, edited by Hughes, he includes as a note to this a longer, previously unpublished work, "Dialogue Over a Ouija Board." He remarks:

> SP occasionally amused herself, with one or two others, by holding her finger on an upturned glass, in a ring of letters laid out on a smooth table, and questioning the "spirits." The following "Dialogue Over a Ouija Board" (which she never showed, though it must have been written some time in 1957–58), used the actual "spirit" text of one of the ouija sessions. The spirit named here [Pan] was the one regularly applied to. His news could be accurate. (The first time he was guided through Littlewood's football coupon, he predicted all thirteen of the draws made on the following

Saturday—but anticipated them, throughout, by just one match. The first dividend at that time, in 1956, was £75,000. The spirit's later attempts were progressively less accurate and very soon no better than anyone else's.) Usually his communications were gloomy and macabre, though not without wit.

Plath gave her own account in a letter to her mother:

> I do wish we could win the pools. Pan (our Ouija imp) has been getting better and better about it and tells us more and more accurately. Last week we got 20 points out of a possible 24 (which would be a fortune of 75,000 pounds, given out every week). We keep telling Pan we want it so we can have leisure to write and have lots of children, both. . . .

This is the spirit who, thirty years later, inhabits Hughes's own "Ouija." It is worth looking more closely at his first appearance in Plath's "Dialogue."

Here the two characters calling the spirit are Sibyl and Leroy—both names charged with symbolism: the woman prophesying the future; the man the king. Once they have got beyond asking for the pools results (because the spirit is "more philosopher, it seems, / Than financier"), Leroy wishes to question further; Sybil is more cautious.

> Do you
> Honestly want to find if you'll have a fling
> At fame or not? As for love, I figure when we're
> Out of it will be time and plenty for us
> To court remorse.

She prefers to ask about the afterlife, to which Leroy replies:

> That's because
> You don't quite believe in it. You're deaf to real
> Dangers, but don't mind hearing about the ones
> In hell, since hell's a fairytale.

But she enquires after her father, to be told he is "in plumage." (Later, Hughes will write of this ouija work: "Her father's name was Otto, and 'spirits' would regularly arrive with instructions for her from one Prince Otto, who was said to be a great power in the underworld. When she pressed for a more personal communication, she would be told that Prince Otto could not speak to her directly, because he was under orders from the Colossus. And when she pressed for an audience with the Colossus, they would say he was inaccessible. It is easy to see how her effort to come to terms with the meaning this Colossus held for her, in her poetry, became more and more central as the years passed." Plath wrote to her mother in 1958 that "Pan claims his family god, 'kolossus,' tells him much of this information. . . .")

The couple, however, begin to argue over Pan, Leroy accusing Sibyl of having scorn for Pan but too much credulity when his words suit her purposes; they end by smashing the glass that calls him. When Sibyl asks Leroy if he feels wiser for what Pan has said he replies:

> I felt drawn
> Deeper within the dark, and as I pitched further
> Into myself and into my conviction

> A rigor seized me: I saw cracks appear,
> Dilating to craters in this livingroom,
> And you, shackled ashen across the rift, a specter
> Of one I loved.

This specter, "shackled ashen across the rift," is the Plath who seems to appear at the end of Hughes's "Ouija," when he asks their pools-predicting spirit about fame. In his version, the rebuke made by Plath is not Sybil's almost casual, flippant dismissal of the question.

> Your tears flashed, your face was contorted,
> Your voice cracked, it was thunder and flash together:
> "And give yourself to the glare? Is that what you want?
> Why should you want to be famous?
> Don't you see—fame will ruin everything."

In this construction of events, however, he is seized by no dark rigor: it is as if she is the sibyl, prophesying what is to come.

In hindsight, Hughes wonders if she had heard a whisper from the "still small voice" warning of the price that she— that they both—would pay. In a sense it is the same inner voice, or inner image, that appears in a poem slightly later in the sequence, "Horoscope." Here too, her interest in the conventional supernatural is eclipsed by her own more powerful, self-created mythology.

> You wanted to study
> Your stars—the guards
> Of your prison yard, their zodiac.

But here the planets, like the spirit of "Ouija," seem ineffectual; they "muttered their Babylonish power-sprach"; her scarred face is of equal, if not greater, significance. Her destiny lies within frighteningly easy reach, within the work she created out of her own suffering:

> You only had to look
> Into the nearest face of a metaphor
> Picked out of your wardrobe or off your plate
> Or out of the sun or the moon or the yew tree
> To see your father, your mother, or me
> Bringing you your whole Fate.

Plath was studying for the exams she took in the summer: Part II of the English tripos. Three papers were compulsory: essay, criticism and composition, and tragedy. She would sit her optional papers on the English Moralists, the history of English literary criticism and Chaucer. In the early mornings, she and Hughes sometimes walked across Grantchester Meadows, not far from where they lived.

> It is a country on a nursery plate.
> Spotted cows revolve their jaws and crop
> Red clover or gnaw beetroot
> Bellied on a nimbus of sun-glazed buttercup . . .

she wrote two years later, in "Watercolor of Grantchester Meadows." Hughes's "Chaucer" recalls one morning when, on a walk, she stopped and stood on a stile and began to declaim all she could remember of the *Canterbury Tales* to an audience of cows. "We began mooing at a pasture of cows," she wrote to her mother on 8 April, resolving to put the scene in her novel,

> and they all looked up, and, as if hypnotized, began to follow us in a crowd of about twenty across the pasture to a wooden stile, staring, fascinated. I stood on the stile and, in a resonant voice, recited all I knew of Chaucer's *Canterbury Tales* for about twenty minutes. I never had such an intelligent, fascinated audience. You should have seen their expressions as they came flocking up around me. I'm sure they loved it!

Two points stand out in Hughes's vivid, affectionate poem. The first is that the Wife of Bath was "your favourite character in all literature." There is irony here, in the unconventional Wife with her five late husbands, her tale of women's desire for sovereignty—for while Plath was, in her art, no conventional woman, she bound herself to conventional notions of femininity, choosing to project the image of the happy co-ed that is seen particularly clearly in *Letters Home*. It is an image Hughes was most aware of, writing to his sister Olwyn in 1957:

> Her immediate "face" . . . when she meets someone is too open and too nice—but that's the American stereotype she clutches at when she is in fact panic-stricken. Or perhaps— and I think this is more like it—her poise and brain just vanish in a kind of vacuous receptivity—only this American stereotyped manner keeps her going at all.

Yet she fought against it, too, particularly near the end of her life, when she rose with the dawn to write before her children awoke, and when she wrote bitter poems like "The Applicant," fueled by a furious mockery of marriage, a spiteful rejection of all she once held so dear.

What also springs clearly from this poem—and this is a recurring theme throughout the book—is the slippery, elusive quality of memory, particularly happy memory. Of her voice in the wide air, he writes: "It must have sounded lost"—almost as if he hadn't been there.

> How did you stop? I can't remember
> You stopping. I imagine they reeled away—
> Rolling eyes, as if driven from their fodder.
> I imagine I shooed them away.

Certain images hold, frozen like photographs:

> But
> Your sostenuto rendering of Chaucer
> Was already perpetual

Other images vanish in time, ungraspable, lost for ever.

Plath took her exams in late May; she got a 2.1. She had by now put together a book of poems for submission to the Yale Series of Younger Poets, to be judged by W. H. Auden. By late May she knew *Two Lovers and a Beachcomber* had been chosen as a finalist for the prize. She was able to tell her mother this news, too, on 10 May:

> FABER & FABER, the British publishing house, has just written to accept Ted's poetry book for publication in England. Not only that, but Mr. T. S. Eliot (who is on their staff)

read the book, and the publisher writes: "Mr. Eliot has asked me to tell you how much he personally enjoyed the poems and to pass on to you his congratulations on them."

They spent their first anniversary in Yorkshire, with Hughes's family; then in late June they set sail on the *Queen Elizabeth* to America, where Plath would begin teaching at Smith in the autumn. Before that, however, they had seven weeks in a cottage in Eastham, Cape Cod—a wedding gift from Aurelia Plath.

5 ◦ "What Happens in the Heart Simply Happens"

THE HUGHESES SPENT the summer of 1957 in Cape Cod; Ted Hughes revels in America in "The Chipmunk." They had a summer of sunning and writing and fishing, as he tells in "Flounders." In the autumn, they moved to Northampton, Massachusetts, so that Plath could start teaching at Smith— an experience that frightened her, as "The Blue Flannel Suit" relates. So they resolved to live from their earnings as writers, and in September 1958 moved to Boston, where they found an apartment, 9 Willow Street. In mid-December, Plath began analytic treatment with Dr. Ruth Beuscher again; analysis that would give her access to the demons of her past.

HERE, THEN, WAS Hughes's first actual encounter with "beautiful, beautiful America!"—and it is fitting that this first encounter should be expressed in an animal poem, settling on a creature he never would have met in his native land, "The Chipmunk." *Tamias striatus*, with its five black stripes, neat brown body and inky eyes, is only found in the eastern United States: "A first scout of the continent's wild game, / Midget aboriginal American." In "18 Rugby Street," lovingly examining Plath, Hughes describes the "aboriginal thickness" of her mouth; she is here explicitly connected to this sprightly American creature, and not just because "In a flash-still, retorting to my something, / You made a chipmunk face." Its eyes "popping with inky joy" recall the "squeeze of joy" in her jewel eyes in "St. Botolph's."

It is as if this connection brings them together: until the moment the chipmunk "globed me in a new vision,"she had remained alien to him, "American, airport-hopping superproduct." And yet a shadow lurks at the end of this poem.

> And suddenly,
> Just in that flash—as I laughed
> And got my snapshot for life,
> And shouted: "That's my first ever real chipmunk!"—
> A ghost, dim, a woodland spirit, swore me
> To take his orphan.

A supernatural creature exacts a hidden promise from the unknowing Hughes, darkening this bright time. "Flounders," too, seems a bright poem, but is clouded even in its opening, which is an anxious question: "Was that a happy day?" It recalls a day in their summer of writing, sunbathing and swimming: having gone fishing, they were nearly swept out to sea in their rowboat in rough weather; a passing motorboat rescued them and as they came inshore they were able to land a good catch, success rescued from the teeth of near disaster.

Yes, it seems, it was a happy day—the kind of happiness that comes from the abnegation of responsibility: "our map / Somebody's optimistic assurance." The story of "Flounders" is the story of what doesn't happen in their lives, in their marriage: when "the wind / Smartened against us, and the tide turned, roughening," there is no "big, good America" to find them, no "power-boat and a pilot of no problems," no sudden, miraculous bounty from the sea. Now, years later, it appears to the poet as a vision of a different life, " a toy miniature / Of the life that might have bonded us / Into a single animal, a single soul—" but it is not to be. It is a brief escape, "a visit from the goddess, the beauty / Who was poetry's sister." But it is poetry, not this goddess, who will guide them to a darker fate for which, in the poet's eyes, neither is responsible: "And we / Only did what poetry told us to do."

Their bright summer also had its shadows, as her journals reveal. Plath was struggling with short stories that she hoped to see published in American magazines such as the *Saturday Evening Post* and *Mademoiselle*. They were not turning out as she wished and she wasn't having much success in working on her novel of Cambridge life. "Yesterday was the first day of work: a bad day. Spent time on a very desperately elaborate psychological idea and wrote maybe one good image . . . to a raft of brittle, stilted artificial stuff. No touch-

ing on my deep self. This bad beginning depressed me inordi-
nately." She feared she was pregnant—she very much wanted
children, but not until, as she saw it, she had made her
name: "No children until I have done it," she wrote emphati-
cally. In August, *Two Lovers and a Beachcomber* came back,
rejected by Yale. Her husband did have some success that
summer: "The Thought-Fox" was accepted by *The New
Yorker*, though it had been rejected a year earlier.

When the summer was nearly over, the Hugheses moved
to Northampton, to a house on Elm Street. Plath had looked
forward to teaching at Smith, but now, as "The Blue Flannel
Suit" relates, she was beset by terror.

> You waited,
> Knowing yourself helpless in the tweezers
> Of the life that judged you, and I saw
> The flayed nerve, the unhealable face-wound
> Which was all you had for courage.

She wrote in her journal at the time:

Last night I felt the sensation I have been reading about to
no avail in James: the sick, soul-annihilating flux of fear in
my blood switching its current to defiant fight. I could not
sleep, although tired, and lay feeling my nerves shaved to
pain & the groaning inner void: oh, you can't teach, can't do
anything. Can't write, can't think. And I lay under the nega-
tive flood of denial, thinking that voice was all my own, a
part of me, and it must somehow conquer me and leave me
with my worst visions: having had the chance to battle it &
win day by day, and having failed.

She did not feel up to the task before her; she resented it, too. "Woke up after 9 hours sleep still exhausted + rebellious, not wanting to drag my drugged body to a lecture platform . . . ," she wrote on 21 February 1958.

Ted says: "In twenty-five minutes you'll be talking to a class." I dawdled over coffee in the thick brown pottery mug, waiting for the coffee-revelation, which didn't come, bang, into clothes, torn webbed stockings, out into the dull-mat-finished gray morning, raw as an oyster + jamming into gear to the parking lot, the gold hand on the clocktower on college hall standing at 9. Ran up ice path gritted with sand, bang, bell rang, into class in a daze, with faces looking up, expecting me to say something, + me not there, blank, bored, hearing my voice blither on ironic structure of the *Oedipus* which I realize I don't understand myself. . . . How glad I was when the bell rang. . . .

Even to her mother, she wrote:

I keep feeling I could make up some good stuff out of my head to teach them about symbolism or style, but have so little time as yet, and so am always deathly nervous. I must make up little brief 5-minute lectures on topics, for I am a hopeless extempore speaker. If I only knew my "subject" or was an expert, but I am struggling enough to review mere grammar and term paper forms. . . .

She had a heavy load—teaching work ranging from *Antigone* to Yeats, via *The Duchess of Malfi, The Master*

Builder, Oedipus Rex and *The Waste Land.* She had a varied, demanding audience—

> Girls with bear-skin caps from public schools in the wilds of Minnesota (who confessed, with humble desire for improvement, to never reading a whole book) sat next to elegant blonde young ladies from the best New York City preparatory schools deep, at the moment, in Sartre, or *Finnegans Wake.* With a few exceptions, most of my students were glisteningly eager to work. . . .

—which must have made her burden seem even heavier. Hughes indicates that this black fear was, at least, half-concealed from Hughes at the time. "I had supposed / It was all OK." He is blinded by "the gleam of your finish," her public face; but "now I know, as I did not" what apprehension she felt, what judgment she imagined, what inevitable failure she saw looming: "What a furnace / Of eyes waited to prove your metal." She is dressed in her blue flannel suit (when she got the job, she had written to her mother from England about preparing her "look" for teaching, "I am thinking of having a suit or two tailor-made here") like a soldier for battle. It is a "mad, execution uniform," its very ugliness expressing her misery and fear; how ill-fitting is the garment of conventionality she wishes to wear. Her head is "pathetically tiny," her scar lumpish: she is a mask like her feared double in "The Earthenware Head."

The end of the poem makes a strange, sad blending of past and future when, for an instant (contradicting his earlier disclaimer of ignorance), "I saw that what gripped you . . . Were terrors that had killed you once already." But did he understand, then? For the next line appears confused: "Now, I see, I saw, sitting, the lonely / Girl who was going to die." He shifts back to his past unknowingness—"But then I sat, stilled, / Unable to fathom what stilled you"—before returning to a terrible, eternal present, and her eternal stillness:

> as I am stilled
> Permanently now, permanently
> Bending so briefly at your open coffin.

The image of Hughes never unbending away from her open coffin (although he bends over it only "so briefly") is haunting.

By November, Plath was discontented enough with teaching—which swallowed a huge amount of her time and energy, making it nearly impossible for her to write—that the Hugheses decided to leave Northampton at the end of the academic year, and try freelancing in Boston. They were encouraged in this by a new friendship with the poet W. S. Merwin—who had given a glowing review to *The Hawk in the Rain* in the *New York Times Book Review* in October—and his wife Dido. But in the meantime, Hughes got a semester of teaching at the University of Massachusetts at Amherst, where he taught freshman English ("which in American usually means: how to write a clear sentence," Plath wrote to Dorothea Krook), a sophomore general literature course that took him from *Samson Agonistes* to Molière to Thoreau, and an advanced course in writing. Plath was finally inspired to a great burst of writing by a commission from *ARTnews*, which led her to explore the work of Klee, Rousseau and de Chirico; she was, she wrote to her mother, "overflowing with ideas and inspirations."

But her journals of this time reveal her unhappiness, a blackness reflected in "Child's Park," which looks back at the summer of 1958. Plath, in her entry for 11 June 1958, tells how she and Hughes used to walk in a nearby park and pick a single rose for their living room. One day they encountered a group of girls taking flowers from the park's rhododendron bushes. Plath was moved to fury, which she tamed for her formal poem, "Fable of the Rhododendron Stealers," but let fly in her journal:

> These girls were ripping up whole bushes—that crudeness and wholesale selfishness disgusted and angered me. I have a violence in me that is hot as death-blood. I can kill myself or—I know it now—even kill another. I could kill a woman, or wound a man. I think I could. I gritted to control my hands, but had a flash of bloody stars in my head as I stared that sassy girl down, and a blood-longing to [rush] at her and tear her to bloody beating bits.

It is this "homicidal / Hooded stare" of Plath's that Hughes conjures in "Child's Park":

> What did they mean to you, the azalea flowers?
> Those girls were so happy, rending the branches,
> Embracing their daring bouquets, their sumptuous
> trousseaux,
> The wet, hot-petalled blossoms.

Note that in this poetic recreation of the event, the flowers are not rhododendrons but azaleas, the flowers she would use to lead her to the ghost of her dead father—who was

buried alongside the "Azalea Path" in the Winthrop Cemetery—in "Electra on the Azalea Path."

Her rage is incomprehensible to Hughes at the time: it is
"your plutonium secret." "You breathed water," he writes,
removing her from the realm of ordinary, air-breathing mor-
tals—and pulling the reader toward the same image from a
poem she wrote around this time, "Full Fathom Five." Its title
was drawn from Ariel's song in *The Tempest* and it unleashes
the image of the drowned father/god entangling his daugh-
ter/worshipper:

> Your shelled bed I remember.
> Father, this thick air is murderous.
> I would breathe water.

(It is an image she explores as early as 1952, in her eerie
tale "Sunday at the Mintons"; and in 1945, when she was
not yet twelve, Aurelia Plath had taken her two children to
see a local theater production of *The Tempest*, the first play
Plath had seen. Aurelia Plath wrote of her daughter's fascination with the play, the "celestial occasion" of their going
to see it.) "Full Fathom Five" was, too, an early choice for a
book title:

> It relates more richly to my life and imagery than anything
> else I've dreamed up: has the background of *The Tempest*, the
> association of the sea, which is a central metaphor for my
> childhood, my poems and the artist's subconscious, of the
> father image—relating to my own father, the buried male
> muse and god-creator risen to be my mate in Ted. . . .

Her vision, in "Child's Park," seen through his eyes, skews the natural world, a woodpecker suddenly seeming like a ptero-dactyl:

> The devilry
> Of the uncoiling head, the spooky wings,
> And the livid cry
> Flung the garden open.

But it is a deadly garden, "the pit of the hairy flower," "the mouth of the azalea" seductively sexual and malevolent. The ghost of her father becomes entwined, as she admitted in her *Journals*, with the image of her husband: her fear of Hughes's faithlessness recalling her father's abandonment of her in his death. Her father's death she had viewed as a betrayal; at Cambridge she had written to herself, ". . . I cry so to be held by a man; some man, who is a father." In "Child's Park," hers is a poisoning fury and fear against which the Hughes of this poem is helpless: "I stepped back." Nothing can ever be the same:

> That glare
> Flinging your old selves off like underthings
> Left your whole Eden radioactive.

In June, when the term was over, the Hugheses had a week in New York, where they visited the poet Marianne Moore at her home in Brooklyn, as Hughes relates in "The Literary Life." According to Plath in a letter to her mother, Moore "was lovely at her home in Brooklyn and admires Ted very much and served us strawberries, sesame-seed biscuits and milk and talked a blue streak." A little while later Plath wrote to Moore, asking if she would give her a reference for a grant application, and she sent the poet a group of her poems. But Moore didn't like Plath's work and sent her, as she wrote in her journal,

> a queerly ambiguous spiteful letter in answer to my poems and request that she be a reference for my [Eugene] Saxton [grant]. So spiteful it is hard to believe it: comments of absolutely no clear meaning or help, resonant only with great unpleasantness: "don't be so grisly" . . . "you are too unrelenting" . . . and certain pointed remarks about "typing being a bugbear," so she sends back the poems we sent. I cannot believe she got so tart and acidy simply because I sent her carbon copies. . . .

Moore's *Collected Poems* had been published in 1951. She was an acknowledged giant of American poetry: T. S. Eliot called her one of the few producers of durable poetry of her time. A biology major at Bryn Mawr College in the early years of the century (she was born in 1887 and died in 1972), she wrote with a detailed, close observation that Plath would surely have admired; in her famous poem "The Fish," Moore writes that they

wade

through black jade.
Of the crow-blue mussel-shells, one keeps
adjusting the ash-heaps;
opening and shutting itself like
an
injured fan.

Her rejection of Plath turns this precision, in Hughes's poem, to closed-mindedness. She lives up a "narrow stair," in a "bower-bird bric-à-brac nest, in Brooklyn." Her talk—like Hughes's stabbing alliteration of "b's"—is a "needle," her face a "tiny American treen bobbin / On a spindle"; and the young poets are at first in awe: "Why shouldn't we cherish her?" Her dismissiveness is shattering to Plath, and to Hughes, who, furthermore, has to attempt to repair the damage: "I carried you back up," while Moore is unaffected, "tight, brisk, / Neat and hard as an ant." "A decade later," after Plath's death, she meets Hughes in England; this time, of course, her tone is different.

Hughes's bitterness is undisguised. She praises "Ocean 1212," "your little near-posthumous memoir"—note the quotation marks around the title, reminding the reader that Miss Moore, despite her praise, cannot recall that the piece is actually called "Ocean 1212-W," after Plath's grandmother's phone number during her childhood. "(It was all she wanted to say)": this parenthetical note hints at an urgent, but hidden guilt beneath the "great hat-brim's floppy petal." She is, in Hughes's eyes, "tinier than ever," her lips like "a child's purse," her cheek "a bat's wing": darting, spiritlike, and slightly sinister. Hughes is "heavy as a graveyard." She searches for "the grave / Where she could lay down her little wreath," but she cannot find it. There can be no happy conclusion to this bitter little tale.

Yet that summer, two of Plath's poems, "Mussel Hunter at Rock Harbor" and "Nocturne" (later "Hardcastle Crags"), were accepted for publication by *The New Yorker*. This was a great victory: publication by that magazine had long been her goal, and she had pursued it as assiduously as, earlier in her life, she had sought acceptance by *Seventeen*.

The literary life beckoned. In September they moved to Boston, then full of luminaries: Robert Lowell, his wife Elizabeth Hardwick, Archibald MacLeish, Robert Frost, Adrienne Rich, George Starbuck, Anne Sexton. Plath found a job in October, typing records for the psychiatric clinic of Massachusetts General Hospital, work that gave her material for the short story "Johnny Panic and the Bible of Dreams." But in a poem titled for the two-room apartment they found on Beacon Hill—9 Willow Street—Hughes grapples with the wild unhappiness that was threatening to overwhelm their lives. The apartment, near to the summit of Beacon Hill, was pleasant, as Plath wrote to Dorothea Krook:

> We have a little two room apartment: I write in the living-room-diningroom-kitchen (pullman, all in one wall, hostile to any elaborate housewifery, which is good) while Ted's study is in the bedroom, a desk of two fine sturdy planks in a window niche. . . . We take long walks to the wharfs to watch the gulls, ships, and crab-merchants; read aloud, read silently. . . .

At first there seems to be a good omen in Boston, when they find their building numbered for the Muses, and Hughes, indeed, was having some success: the *Atlantic Monthly* took his poem "Dick Straight-up"; "The Thought-Fox" won the Guinness Prize back in England; the *Atlantic*, however, turned down Plath's work, and she began to feel panic as she worked at her typewriter:

You hammered your new Hermes,
Your Panic Bird chipping at the old egg,
While I rolled in my sack, with my lumber,
Along the bottom of the Charles.

(Her "Panic Bird" flew through her Boston journal: "But although it makes me feel good as hell to express my hostility for my mother, frees me from the Panic Bird on my heart and my typewriter (why?), I can't go through life calling Dr. Beuscher up from Paris, London, the wilds of Maine long-distance . . ." reappearing, "conquered," some months later.) Now Hughes places himself at the bottom of the river, in the water with her drowned father-god—where they will both be by the third stanza of the poem. With brown paper over his windows and earplugs in his ears, he huddles away from her and from himself,

each of us festering
A unique soul-sepsis for the other,
Each of us was the stake
Impaling the other.

Here again is the helpless blindness to their situation, the "spectre-blinded searching," the happiness fled like a bird "before we could identify it." It is blindness then made flesh in a bat found sick in daylight on Boston Common, which Hughes tries to rescue. It is unwilling to be helped: "It reared up on its elbows and snarled at me, / A raving hyena." There is nothing for it but sacrifice:

I had to give it my finger.
Let the bite lock. Then, cradling it,
Gently lifted it . . .

It seems to him an insignificant wound until he recalls that American bats have rabies: a reminder of how foreign he is, how dangerous his situation is, how strange. This is the real omen, the real portent, stated baldly by Hughes at the end of the poem:

It confirmed
The myth we had sleepwalked into: death.
This was the bat-light we were living in: death.

The cold brilliance of death, which Plath captured so memorably in her *Ariel* poems, glares over all: there is, in this version of events, no escape.

The deadly connection, in Plath's perception, between Hughes and Otto Plath, which is hinted at in "9 Willow Street"—and which, in *Birthday Letters*, seems to be absorbed by Hughes himself—is further explored in a poem slightly later in the sequence, "Black Coat." The poem hinges on an ellipsis of recollection, searches for more memory. "I remember going out there," it begins.

The tide far out, the North Shore ice-wind
Cutting me back
To the quick of the blood—that outer-edge nostalgia,
The good feeling. My sole memory
Of my black overcoat.

He writes as if in answer to Plath's poem "Man in Black," which puts "you" in a bleak landscape of grey sea, a "dun / Barb-wired headland" and "snuff-colored sand cliffs." Plath's poem (which is made of seven three-line stanzas and is a single, unfurling sentence) closes:

> . . . And you, across those white
>
> Stones, strode out in your dead
> Black coat, black shoes, and your
> Black hair till there you stood,
>
> Fixed vortex on the far
> Tip, riveting stones, air,
> All of it, together.

That this "you" is Hughes seems confirmed by his own poem; and yet both works substantiate the idea that it is her father, too. The dead black of the coat in Plath's poem points to this; as does the image of Otto Plath as a "fixed vortex" in her life, always threatening to suck her in, as the grey sea sucks. Hughes's poem hopes for a new start, seeing himself as separate from her but connected with her Atlantic Ocean:

> Me and the sea one big tabula rasa,
> As if my returning footprints
> Out of that scrim of gleam, that horizon-wide wipe,
> Might be a whole new start.

The new start is not to be: for once again he is caught out, as in "The Shot":

>   . . . I had no idea I had stepped
>   Into the telescopic sights
>   Of the paparazzo sniper
>   Nested in your brown iris.

That sniper sees him and the ghost of her father as one:

>   The body of the ghost and me the blurred see-through
>   Came into single focus,
>   Sharp-edged, stark as a target . . .

Her dead father crawls from the sea—which Hughes has imagined will offer him freedom—and in Plath's remorseless gaze, "he slid into me." It was during their time in Boston—in March 1959—that Plath visited her father's grave in Winthrop for the first time. "In the third yard, on a flat grassy area looking across a sallow barren stretch to rows of wooden tenements, I found the flat stone, 'Otto E. Plath: 1885–1940,' right beside the path, where it would be walked over. Felt cheated," she wrote in her journal. "My temptation to dig him up. To prove he existed and really was dead. How far gone would he be?" In the poem written after this visit, "Electra on the Azalea Path," she closes simply: "It was my love that did us both to death."

The deadly myth she created for herself is also explored in Hughes's loose, imagistic poem "The Bird," which draws from different parts of their life—walking on Boston Common, seeing a burning building, drinks in a Cambridge college, her death—collaging them together in a kind of dream.

Under its glass dome, behind its eyes,
Your Panic Bird was not stuffed. It was looking
For you did not know what.

She is the "glass dome" (Plath herself wrote of being in a "glass caul" in her *Journals*) holding in the Panic Bird—an echo of her bell jar—as fragile and miraculous as the crystal glass that, at a party just after their marriage, shattered like ice, seemingly without explanation.

My eyes
Had locked on a chunky tumbler
Solid with coins (donations to pay for the booze),
Isolated on a polished table.
I was staring at it when it vanished
Like a spinning grenade, with a bang.
The coins collapsed in a slither. But the table
Was suddenly white with a shatter of tiny crystals.

She keeps hidden from him, as he sees it, the fears that drive her. "You told me / Everything but the fairy tale." And once again he depicts himself as a sleepwalker, caught in someone else's nightmare: "step for step / I walked in the sleep / You tried to wake from." Around this time she would write in her *Journals* of the "great, stark, bloody play acting itself out over and over again behind the sunny façade of our daily rituals, birth, marriage, death." If Hughes, through his knowledge of anthropology and his interest in myth, had access to that deep-seated drama, he did not—according to this poem— apply that knowledge to his own life.

The image of the Panic Bird is transposed onto the eagle of America and the eagle of her father's Germany.

> What glowed into focus was blood suddenly
> Weltering dumb and alive
> Up through the tattooed blazon of an eagle.
> Your homeland's double totem. Germany's eagle
> Bleeding up through your American eagle
> In a cloud of Dettol.

To Hughes, here, it is the central figure of her myth incised on her skin, and in this poem it stands for her suicide, the death that was always within her: "It wanted / To be born, pecking at the glass." She fosters its existence, in this poem seeming to turn everything she saw into fuel for her inner fire. As they gaze at a burned-out building,

> You howled
> With your sound turned off and your screen dark
> For tragedy to go on—to hell with the curtain.
> You willed it to get going all over again . . .

Hughes is unaware of what burns behind the blackness. The day it breaks free and the glass dome vanishes is the day of her death in the cold February of 1963, when snow "all but barricaded London," and is linked with the icy shatter of the glass full of coins, magically broken: "A cake of frozen snow / Could have crashed in from space."

Panic was much in her mind at this time. Her involvement with psychiatric records at the Massachusetts General Hospital fueled the short story, "Johnny Panic and the Bible of Dreams" (only published after her death, in the *Atlantic Monthly* in 1968). Its narrator has a job much like Plath's, but her secret self accumulates information for Johnny Panic, her god of fear. It is a disturbing, powerful story, its dreamlike—nightmarish—imagery pinned down by the reality of Plath's own experience at the hands of psychiatrists: "They extend me full-length on my back on the cot," the narrator says when she is finally caught by the Clinic Director and readied for shock treatments.

> The crown of wire is placed on my head, the wafer of forgetfulness on my tongue. The masked priests move to their posts and take hold. . . . From their cramped niches along the wall, the votaries raise their voices in protest. They begin the devotional chant:

> > The only thing to love is Fear itself.
> > Love of fear is the beginning of wisdom.
> > The only thing to love is Fear itself.
> > May Fear and Fear and Fear be everywhere.

The frozen night of her death, the coldness of that earlier winter in Boston when each was a stake to impale the other, is recalled again at the beginning of "Astringency," as the poet remembers the polluted city river: "I always think of the Charles River / Frozen." It seems a river of despair, poisoning a million worms—until a goldfish caught by a fisherman seems to give a ray of hope: "Brainstorm of the odds!" But once again Hughes's memory fails him, and he cannot recall if he saw this alone or with her:

> Were you with me
> When I saw an amazing thing,
> Right there at the edge of the Charles?

But his memory for another kind of astringency is clear, when they stand together at the edge of the river,

> . . . watching
> The sliding ring of ripple
> That each small, tired wave threw over the rock
> "Like a lariat," you said.
>
> The sole metaphor that ever escaped you
> In easy speech, in my company . . .

The real astringency is her self-censor, the force he is unable to identify and so notes with question marks. The metaphors are like shoals of fish, netted:

> Who caught all
> That teeming population, every one,
> To hang their tortured eyes and tongues up
> In your poems? To what end?

In Hughes's eyes, her dark, tortured imagery festers inside her.

Despite the threatening overtones of "Johnny Panic," that winter Plath returned to psychiatric care—in December 1958, she began to visit Dr. Beuscher again, the doctor she had seen in McLean Hospital. She would see Beuscher weekly for all her remaining time in Boston; her journal from this time analyzes her fears, her doubts, her panics. Of her mother's telling her of her father's death, she wrote: "I hate her for that." It was with Ruth Beuscher that she most deeply explored the "fairy tale" that Hughes, by his own account, didn't even know existed, or had to understand. With Beuscher she focused her distress on the loss of her father in her childhood; she explored the resentment she felt toward the mother for whom she had to perform, the mother she blamed for killing her father. With Beuscher, too, she came to see Otto Plath and Hughes as, in some ways, two halves of a whole—appearing to fear that her mother might destroy Hughes as she had destroyed Otto Plath. She "felt a fear also that she might appropriate Ted as hers and kill him, or kill him through me? In spirit or maleness is as bad as physically."

Yet she had accomplished much in Boston: she had written six stories, a children's book (*The Bed Book*, not published until 1976), and had two poems, "Watercolor of Grantchester Meadows" and "Man in Black," accepted by *The New Yorker*. And in April 1959 there was good news— Hughes was awarded a $5,000 Guggenheim grant on the tenth of the month; the same spring they were invited to Yaddo, the artists' colony in Saratoga Springs, New York, for the following autumn. By the end of May she wrote in her journal: "I feel that this month I have conquered my Panic Bird. I am a calm, happy and serene writer. . . . I have done, this year, what I said I would: overcome my fear of facing a blank page day after day, acknowledging myself, in my deepest emotions, a writer, come what may."

1 A picture of Otto: Otto Plath in 1930.

2 The literary life: Marianne Moore talking to Sylvia Plath, April 1955.

Sylvia Plath tours the stores and forecasts
MAY WEEK FASHIONS

WITH May Week just around the corner like some fair Country of C o c k a i g n e — but barely visible through the present smog of Tripos exams—we set out to discover what the well-dressed Newnhamite or Girtonian might wear for punting, cocktails and balls.

From large department stores to small specialty shops, Cambridge offers a fine, colourful selection of spring fashions which should enable our Cambridge undergraduates to rival the most chic and charming of imported London models.

We chose a different Cambridge shop to outfit us for each occasion and picked featured and favourite styles for photographs. While aware that our assignment was for a newspaper article rather than for private purchase, department managers kindly donated advice, information, and much time, treating us,

Strapless white cocktail dress.

Indeed, like a Saturday Cinderella.

bathing suits

To begin with bathing suits, perfect for beach holidays and very safe punting. At Robert Sayle's on St. Andrew's Street.

thing from picnic to sunglasses (12/6); a flamboyant red-and-white striped towelling stole with big pockets and black-tasseled fringe (24/9); and finally, to complete the whole ensemble, a white terrycloth beachcoat with attractive full circular yoke (73/6). H a p p y swimming, everyone!

cocktail dress

Our cocktail and dance dress featured at Joshua Taylor's (see picture) is a strapless white cotton by Jean Allen, patterned with pink rosebuds and green leaves; the marvellous pouf skirt billows most bouffant over its triple crinoline petticoats (£10 12s. 6d.). Draped from the front to a pert bow in back, this gala outfit sports its own cover-up bolero and so becomes suitable for afternoon garden parties or champagne soirées overlooking G r e a t Court, Trinity.

Runners-up: A poppy-red button-down jumper dress in French c o t t o n put out by Continentals (at £4 7s. 6d.), with square open neck and cool, clean-cut flared skirt; also, a green-and-white striped cotton dress by Estrava, fresh as a mint julep, with off-the-shoulder boat neck, cuffed pockets at hip

3 Sylvia Plath in *Varsity*, the Cambridge University newspaper, May 1956.

4 Ted Hughes and Sylvia Plath in Yorkshire, 1956.

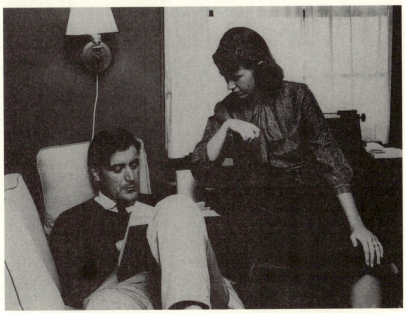

5 Ted Hughes and Sylvia Plath in their Boston apartment, 9 Willow Street, 1958.

MEMORANDUM

To _____ From _____

6 & 7 Hughes and Plath worked closely together, often writing on the backs of each other's drafts. Here, handwritten on Smith College paper, is a draft of Hughes's story 'Harvesting', with a typescript page of Plath's 'Runaway' on the reverse.

Sam turned right to enter the white stable doors, with the white
horse's head painted on them in a black circle. A sturdy, docile head,
like Sam's. ~~And~~ Sam ~~had~~ greyed, palpably, as he clopped onto the
paving and stood, waiting for Mavis to dismount, *his patience. The dogged*
patience of the long-sufferer, the meek, who have not yet inherited the earth.
The square red-faced girl came out of a stall with a deadpan *, are growing*
dubious about
the value of
meekness)
face. "Did you have a nice ride miss?"

"Lovely," Mavis said, swinging herself down to the pavement.
She extricated her foot from the stirrup, which had slipped up on
her ankle and caught it. "Perfectly lovely."

"Sam's a good horse," the girl said sturdily, patting his
flank with a certain awkwardness. "Safe as they come. You ask
for him next time."

"I will," Mavis said. *You may be sure of that."*

8 The Badlands: Ted Hughes overlooking the North Dakota prairies, July 1959.
9 Sylvia Plath on Yellowstone Lake, Yellowstone National Park, Wyoming, July 1959.

10 Sylvia Plath and Frieda outside the front door of Court Green, Devon,
December 1961.
11 Sylvia Plath with Frieda and Nicholas on the lawn at Court Green, August 1962.

12 The Cambridge home of Hughes and Plath: 55 Eltisley Avenue.
13 No. 18 Rugby Street, Bloomsbury, London

14 The Church of St George the Martyr, Bloomsbury, where Hughes and Plath were married in June 1956.
15 The last London home of Hughes and Plath: 3 Chalcot Square, near Primrose Hill.

16 Daffodils: Sylvia Plath with Frieda and Nicholas Hughes outside Court Green, 1962.

6 ◊ "Right Across America We Went Looking for You"

IN THE SUMMER of 1959, the Hugheses set out on a trip across America, seeing the sights of the wide West: "The Badlands," "Karlsbad Caverns," "Grand Canyon"—the last poem pulsing with life as Plath discovered she was pregnant. But the bleached, harsh light of the wild landscape is less than benevolent. By the autumn of that year, when they began their residency at the artists' colony at Yaddo, a dark and fiery spirit shadowed Plath, as Hughes visualizes in "Portraits."

THE PLAN WAS now to spend the summer traveling across America—in a car borrowed from Aurelia Plath—before returning to New York for their stint at Yaddo. They traveled north to Ontario, west to Wisconsin and the Dakota Badlands, then to Montana; to Yellowstone, Lake Tahoe and San Francisco; then south to Los Angeles, east across the Mojave Desert, and, taking in the Grand Canyon, to New Orleans before heading to Tennessee, Washington D.C., Philadelphia, and then back to Boston.

In "The Badlands," Hughes envisions their journey as a dark quest. "Right across America / We went looking for you." "You" is Plath's poetic self, the savage creator of the *Ariel* poems with their stark colors echoing the bleached, bright, wide landscapes of the American West.

> Lightning
> Had ripped your clothes off
> And signed your cheekbone.

He connects her, through the lightning, to the destructive events of the twentieth century, which she took so much to heart: the bombing of Hiroshima and Nagasaki; the electrocution of Julius and Ethel Rosenberg for spying for the Soviet Union in June 1953, the same summer that Plath tried to kill herself (her horror at their judicial murder provides the opening motif of *The Bell Jar*). Here is her scarred, suicidal self, which Plath becomes helplessly—Hughes's words echoing her poem "The Hanging Man":

> You only knew it had come and had gripped you
> By the roots of the hair

And held you down on the bed
And stretched across your retina
The global map of nerves in blue flames,
Then left you signed and empty.

Her emptiness needs filling; but what will fill it is to be feared. "One thing to find a guide, / Another to follow him."

Hughes paints a landscape that is not beautiful, but terrible, "staked out in the sun and left to die . . . Loose teeth, bone / Coming through crust, bristles," where the sun has gone "sullenly mad." "The colors assert themselves with a sort of vengeance," Plath would write of the North American landscape in "Two Campers in Cloud Country." "Each day concludes in a huge splurge of vermilions / And night arrives in one gigantic step." Here, Hughes writes, is "empty, horrible, archaic—America," very different from the "beautiful, beautiful America" that is his first image of the country as seen in his wife. Once again a solitary animal appears, spiritlike, an omen. It is a mouse, whose very survival is a mystery:

Where was his food?
And what was he doing here
In this solar furnace
Of oxides and firedust?

The manic energy of the tiny rodent could be the sign of a breakdown, could be "some uncontainable surplus of joy," the polarized extremes an embodiment of his wife's dual personality.

Plath reacts as she did to the earthenware head. " 'This is evil,' / You said. 'This is real evil.' " Hughes remains ignorant, uncomprehending. " 'I kept saying, 'What is it?' " Any happiness is elusive. "Fishing Bridge" only allows for a glimpse of the possibility of contentment, beginning: "Nearly happy." Rock Lake, Ontario (about which "Two Campers in Cloud Country" was written), was one of their first destinations, where they fished for three days before heading into Wisconsin by the edge of Lake Superior—"that threshold of the great lake." Here, as in "Flounders," they easily catch their fill, though this time Hughes hints that there is no miraculous bounty. Instead they simply have an unfair advantage, and their success is jaded:

> No problem
> Catching our limit dozen
> Of those weary migrants, pushing and pushed
> Towards their spawning gravels.

The poem pauses on a threshold, opens a crack in the door of their future, then shuts it.

> What I remember
> Is the sun's dazzle—and your delight
> Wandering off along the lake's fringe
> Towards the shag-headed wilderness
> In your bikini. There you nearly
> Stepped into America. You turned back,
> And we turned away.

For an instant, they might reclaim the America of possibility and hope that he first encountered—but the pair are instructed that there is something else they should seek.

The voice urged on
Into an unlit maze of crying and loss.
What voice? "Find your souls," said the voice.
"Find your true selves. This way. Search, search."

Turning away from the surface of the shining lake, they will find only the death at the heart of the labyrinth the voice has built for them, the two of them once again sleepwalking to their fate.

That voice from inside the labyrinth was, by Hughes's lights, both Plath's doom and her salvation, as the very end of the poem "The 59th Bear" reflects. This strongly narrative poem is based around their time in Yellowstone, the huge national park that stretches from Wyoming into Montana and Idaho. It tells the story of their adventures there among the bears, who are more savage, as it turns out, than their Disneyesque appearance would have tourists like Hughes and Plath believe—although significantly, again, it is Plath who becomes fearful first, Plath who comprehends the darkness and the danger. Hughes sees only an American nature arrayed for their convenience: "Eagles were laid on too," he writes, as if a great controlling hand, operating for their benefit, was putting on a show. The bears at first are "camera stars," performing at sunken trash bins; they are like "jolly inflatables." How each misunderstands the other's culture can be seen by comparing this poem with "The Owl" and "Wuthering Heights."

But in the night a bear ransacks their car, ripping out a window and devouring all their food.

> I got out my hatchet,
> Pitifully unimaginative.
> I was remembering those amiable bears.
> That's how it happens. Your terrors
> Were more intelligent, with their vision—

Plath's "vision" is proved right when the following day they hear how a man at a neighboring campsite, attempting to shoo away a marauding bear, has been killed with one swipe of a paw. Plath had written to her mother after their adventure, telling her the colorful tale:

> There in the blue weird light of the moon, not 10 feet away, a huge, dark bear-shape hunched, guzzling at a tin. . . . We lay there for what seemed like years, wondering if the bear would eat us, since it found our crackers so interesting. Just as we were relaxing and felt the dawn starting to lighten, we heard a heavy shuffling tread. The bear, back from its rounds, had returned to the car. Ted stood up to look out the back window—it was all I could do to keep him from going out before to check on the damage—and reported that the bear was at the back of the car, halfway in the left rear window. It had discovered our oranges. From then until sunup, we lay listening to the bear squeeze the oranges open and slurp up the juice. It was interrupted only by a car which drove by and scared the bear to run toward the front door of our tent. It tripped on the guy ropes anchoring our porch and for a moment the whole tent shook so we thought it had decided to come in. Then there was a long silence. Then more orange-squeezing. We got up, rather shaken. The car window had been shattered to the root, and wiry brown bear hairs stuck all along the edge of it.

Two months later, while at Yaddo, Plath transferred the whole experience into a story, also entitled "The 59th Bear," published in the *London Magazine* in 1961—although in her journal she called it "a stiff artificial piece." In her story, the wife, Sadie, counts bears with her husband, Norton, until a bear attacks their car. Unlike Plath, however, Sadie does not attempt to keep her husband from going out to the bear: "'Do something.' Sadie huddled down into the nest of blankets. 'Shoo him away.' Her voice challenged him, yet his limbs were heavy." Norton does try to shoo the bear away—hence the bear-shooing man in the actual event as Hughes's "doppelgänger," in his poem: Sadie wills him to die. It was a portrait of a marriage from which parallels could not fail to be drawn; a hurtful story, surely, to her real, nonfiction husband—whose hurt at the time comes clear in his poem:

> I did not see
> What flicker in yours, what need later
> Transformed our dud scenario into a fiction—
> Or what self-salvation
> Squeezed the possible blood out of it
> Through your typewriter ribbon.

Here, if not completely explicated but at least indicated, is the burden of the last line of his earlier poem, "The Bear," which made its first appearance in *Wodwo* in 1967. This earlier bear is a mysterious totem,

> digging
> In his sleep

Through the wall of the Universe
With a man's femur.

"He is the ferryman / To dead land," the poem closes. "His price is everything."

The younger Hughes, author of "The Bear," did not see the "self-salvation" that Plath sought in creating her painful tale; but this is the key to the work. ". . . The death hurtling to and fro / Inside your head, had to alight somewhere," he writes now. Its resting place then was on his own shoulders, himself transmuted into her fiction: but it was a resting place that was merely temporary.

Yet there was life, too, in Plath. Just before they left for the trip she had had a scare, when she had been told by a doctor that she was temporarily infertile. Since she was a woman who believed that part of her destiny was to bear children, this had thrown her into despair. In a later poem, "A Childless Woman," she wrote in the persona of barrenness: "This body / This ivory / Ungodly as a child's shriek." While in Boston she had written in her journal: "I would bear children until my change of life if that were possible. I want a house of our children, little animals, flowers, vegetables, fruits. I want to be an Earth Mother in the deepest sense." On this trip across America, Plath became pregnant, and "Grand Canyon" gives the first inkling of this, her plenitude suffusing all his language and imagery:

Not a brimming glass of orange juice—
But you were suddenly more than careful
Not to spill a drop.

The Canyon itself is triumphantly "America's big red mamma!", a woman satiated,

> Now letting the sun, with changing colours,
> Caress her, as she lay open.
> We drifted our gaze through—like a feather
> Lost in the afterglow of her sensations.

They have not abandoned their quest, however, for "oracular assurance": the Canyon seems an oracle, "America's Delphi." "Grand Canyon" reminds the reader of Hughes's interest in shamanism. Poets and shamans share access to an inner world; Hughes has called the shamanic flight "one of the main regeneration dramas of the human psyche: the fundamental poetic event." The shaman is called, often in a dream, and must undergo a spiritual death and rebirth. Hughes called *Wodwo*, haunted by its totems of "The Green Wolf" and "The Bear," "a descent into destruction of some sort."

"Grand Canyon," while echoing with the new life that springs within Plath, also offers such a descent. "We had sweated the labour, the pilgrimage. / Now we wanted the blessing." But the blessing offered is mixed, mysterious. The PAUM! of the Navajo drum, the noise of which is devouring, resonates against Plath's womb, their baby "in her quaking echo-chamber." When the drums have finished, there is this sign: their precious bag of water has been stolen, and Hughes is again a sleepwalker, uncomprehending. Yet here, too, is a glimpse of a brighter future, an echo of the drum, thirty years later: "Close, itself, ours as the voice of your daughter—

/ PAUM!" It was a future glimpsed in the shamanistic journey of the couple who appear in his earlier poem, "Bride and groom lie hidden for three days"; where spiritual disintegration is healed in rebirth:

> So, gasping with joy, with cries of wonderment
> Like two gods of mud
> Sprawling in the dirt, but with infinite care
>
> They bring each other to perfection.

Omens accumulate as their journey continues. At the National Park of Carlsbad Caverns, in New Mexico, there is a colony of several million bats, which, each summer evening, spirals out from the caves like a living cloud to catch the insects upon which they feed. Here, in "Karlsbad Caverns," is this whole crew of bats—recalling and amplifying the single, lost or damaged bat that appeared in "9 Willow Street":

> Presumably the whole lot were happy—
>
> So happy they didn't know they were happy,
> They were so busy with it, so full of it,
> Clinging upside down in their stone heavens.

Hughes envies their exclusive, enclosed world, the safety of the group, an existence that can be calculated "to the minute." Solitary, the "9 Willow Street" bat was savage: here, collectively, there is only contentment—or at least, a presumption of that state. "The bats' meaning / Oiled the unfailing logic of the earth," their existence part of a deep connection that seems "a rebuke to our flutter of half-participation."

Yet during their visit, this unfailing logic does fail. A storm brews up, and the bats "dived out of the height / Straight back into the cave—the whole cloud." The bats, though seemingly governed by even stricter rules of Fate than those that bind humans, "knew how, and when, to detach themselves / From the love that moves the sun and the other stars." To that terrible love, Hughes and the pregnant Plath are still chained.

On 10 September 1959 they were back East—at Yaddo, formerly a magnificent private estate and now an artists' colony in Saratoga Springs, New York. She had a studio in the West House, a room she described as "low-ceilinged, painted white, with a cot, a rug, a huge, heavy darkwood table that I use as a typing and writing table with piles of room for papers and books." The grounds, she wrote to her mother, were beautiful: "I particularly love the scenic beauty of the estate: the rose gardens, goldfish pools, marble statuary everywhere, woodland walks, little lakes."

The Hugheses stayed until November, and Plath completed the poems for her first book, *The Colossus*, during their stay. They included "Blue Moles," about two dead moles she and Hughes found in the grounds, and "The Manor Garden," which blends a shadowy depiction of the landscape with intimations of her pregnancy. While her journals of this time show her initially depressed over her lack of progress with her prose work, by the end of October she had reached a kind of poetic breakthrough with the composition of the seven-sectioned "Poem for a Birthday" (heavily influenced by the work of Theodore Roethke), which blends, in her own myth, the search for her lost parent with the transformation of herself into the "other," a self released by climbing onto a bed of fire. This doubling, or halving, of herself was crucial to her work and her personality. As Anne Stevenson writes in *Bitter Fame*:

> Sylvia seemed egotistical, however, not because her ego was strong, but because it was perilously weak. Between her rigid, genteel-mother construct, on the one hand, and the suppressed Medean furies of a "real self," on the other, her ego was ground between upper and nether millstones, allowing her only two options for action. Either she could remain a pathetic victim, a homunculus with barely a chance of survival, or she could fight back with all the bitterness of deeply aggrieved injury—which in her writing is mostly what she did.

It is this aggrieved self that Hughes confronts in the disturbing "Portraits." Hughes writes of a portrait done of Plath while at Yaddo, by a friend—a portrait now vanished. The painter gets

> carried away
> When he started feeding his colours
> Into your image.

He is provoked, it seems, by a spirit.

> Suddenly—"What's that? Who's that?"
> Out of the gloomy neglected chamber behind you

Somebody had emerged, hunched, gloating at you,
Just behind your shoulder—a cowled
Humanoid of raggy shadows. Who?
Howard was surprised. He smiled at it.
"If I see it there, I paint it. I like it
When things like that happen. He just came."

The image he makes of Plath, beside the shadowy figure, shows her "new-fired idol brilliance." Looking at
Hughes's view of Plath's work, it is worth noting that he
saw this time at Yaddo as the point of her artistic transformation, or rebirth, particularly as seen in her poem "The
Stones," a section of "Poem for a Birthday," written in
November 1959. Its imagery, of the shattered self repaired
and born again, "speaks with a new voice," Hughes has
written. "It is unlike anything that had gone before in her
work. The system of association, from image to image and
within the images, is quite new and—as we can now see—
is that of *Ariel*."

The Hughes of "Portraits" has a rare moment of insight: "I
saw it with horrible premonition," he says of what he saw in
the painting. He doesn't know what the creature is, but he
knows it is a demon, that Plath is "a bait, an offering" to it.
But it is a seductive image too, with Plath

> Molten, luminous, looking at us
> From that window of Howard's vision of you.
> Yourself lifted out of yourself
> In a flaming of oils, your lips exact

—as seductive as the snake that arrives in this Eden.

> We watched
> A small snake swim out, questing
> Over the greenhouse dust.

It is "a bronze prong / Glistening life" that nearly hypnotizes Hughes. But Howard—who in this poems seems to have the qualities of a sibyl—sees it plain. " 'You like it,' he said, / 'Because it's evil. It's evil, so it thrills you.' " Again, as in "The Earthenware Head" and "The Badlands," the forceful repetition of "evil" returns to that word its ancient religious power, the power of a curse.

Plath is mysteriously silent, keeps her own counsel. Hughes leaves the reader with the image of her bowed over this new work she is undertaking, "as over a baby"—she carries their child within her—"Conjuring into its shrine, onto your page, / This thing's dead immortal doppelgänger."

7 ◇ "I LET THAT FOX CUB GO"

HUGHES AND PLATH spent Christmas of 1959 with his family in Yorkshire while they tried to decide where they would make their home, as "Stubbing Wharfe" relates. In the end they settled on London, and found a flat in Primrose Hill where, as Hughes recounts in "Remission," Frieda Rebecca Hughes was born on 1 April 1960. Their flat was small, they had a new baby, it was a difficult time; and "Epiphany" shows that Hughes seems to have come to a critical point in his relationship with Plath. By the summer of 1961, which they spent with the Merwins in France, Plath

was pregnant again—although "A Dream" and "The Minotaur" scent death, rather than new life, in the air.

WHEN THE HUGHESES left Yaddo and returned to England, they headed north, to Ted Hughes's family home in
Yorkshire, for Christmas. The holiday would be a respite
before they had to decide where to settle down, a matter
more urgent now that Plath was pregnant. "Stubbing
Wharfe" indicates they considered—or at least Hughes suggested—that they might find a home in his native county;
this poem foreshadows how true that would eventually
become for her.

Hughes describes an unromantic England, not Plath's
imagined England—similar here to his descriptions in
"Wuthering Heights" or even "55 Eltisley." Outside the
"gummy dark bar" is

> The shut-in
> Sodden dreariness of the whole valley,
> The hopeless old stone trap of it.

Already it seems a graveyard place: "This gloomy memorial
of a valley, / The fallen-in grave of its history . . ." Plath
appears in despair, the fate or chance that flung her ("like a
thrown dice") across the ocean the agent of her misery. "The
sparkle of America"—echoes again of her glittering dream-
Atlantic—is gone from her.

Yet, as he sips his Guinness, its "bitter liquorice" like an
elixir, Hughes is charged with an idea.

At that black moment
Prophecy, like a local owl,
Down from the deep-cut valley opposite
Made a circuit through its territory—
Your future and mine.

The owl of prophecy is by now familiar to the reader. Suddenly "my certainty of the place was visionary."

"These side-valleys," I whispered,
"Are full of the most fantastic houses,
Elizabethan, marvellous, little kingdoms,
Going for next to nothing."

It is a vision that Plath doesn't see: "You had no idea what I was talking about." She is caught up both in the imagery of her past, her vanished, beautiful America with its "sun-shot Atlantic lift," and her future, as "a silent / Wing of your grave went over you." Her future home waits for her in a way she nearly sees: "you saw only blackness, / Black nothing, the face of nothingness . . ." The sudden appearance of a band of local bowls players is both a relief and a Dantesque vision. Their wild mirth calls to the poet's mind an image of "souls tossing in a hell." All at once he sees, "helpless laughter, agony, tears," the three ideas inseparable, confused as their hilarity is filtered through the screen of Plath's dark gaze. "I had to smile. You had to smile. The future / Seemed to ease open a fraction." It only appeared to do so: in Hughes's drama of fate, such appearances are deceptive.

They did not look for a home in Yorkshire, despite Hughes's vision. They arrived in London in January 1960, at first staying with Daniel Huws and his German-born wife, Helga, back at 18 Rugby Street. They house-hunted frantically; and finally, with Plath due to give birth in six weeks' time, found an unfurnished flat at No. 3 Chalcot Square, in Primrose Hill. In part with the help of the Merwins, who had returned from Boston just ahead of them, they began to establish themselves in London. Bill Merwin introduced Hughes to Douglas Cleverdon, a radio producer for the BBC's Third Programme (he produced Dylan Thomas's *Under Milk Wood*); Hughes recorded some of his stories for transmission, and a verse play, *The House of Aries*, was accepted for production in the autumn. Hughes's next book, *Lupercal*, was published in March and went into a second printing in June; a children's book, *Meet My Folks!*, came out early the following year.

And Plath found a publisher for the work now called *The Colossus*: on 10 February 1960, she signed a contract with Heinemann for publication in the autumn. Delighted, she wrote to her mother, "They do very few, very few poets at Heinemann and will do a nice book. . . . It is dedicated to that paragon who has encouraged me through all my glooms about it, Ted." On 24 March, the paragon received a telegram informing him that *The Hawk in the Rain* had won the Somerset Maugham Award—£500, to be spent traveling.

As "Remission" relates, Frieda Rebecca Hughes was born in the early morning of 1 April 1960. It was an easy, swift delivery at home, and Plath was helped by the Indian midwife Hughes describes, Sister Mahdi. "Remission" is a strange title for a poem about a birth; it is a term now used most often of a cancer's retreat, and means forgiveness, or pardon of a sin, or respite. Frieda's arrival is just such a respite, a momentary escape from "the death who had already donned your features." For Plath, despite her success and the forthcoming birth of the baby, did not appear to be happy; friends of the Hugheses who saw them in London at the time describe her possessiveness of Hughes, her seemingly inexplicable rages and aggression. Yet motherhood was something she had longed for: "That was the you / You loved and wanted to live with," Hughes writes, alluding to the way Plath compartmentalized herself into daughter, wife, poet, mother. "I think being mountainous-pregnant was my favorite feeling, & I wish I could prolong it," she wrote to her American friend Lynne Lawner some months after the baby was born.

She has a birth-drawn self and a death-drawn self: "Remission" relates the two. Significantly, this is the midpoint of *Birthday Letters*, the forty-fourth poem out of the eighty-eight, and as such it is balanced between life and death. The former, birth-drawn self ". . . was the you you shared with the wild earth. / It was . . . the Paradise / Your suicide had tried to drag you from." But the scales tilt, and Death is closer on her heels in the following poem, "Isis," which takes its name from the Egyptian goddess who was both magician and protector of the dead. The Hugheses had a print of Isis on the wall of their Chalcot Square flat, taken from a French astrology book published by Editions Le Seuil (the original is in the Bibliothèque Nationale in Paris). Is Plath, in this poem, perhaps under the protection of that dark goddess?

It seems, in Hughes's vision, that Isis guarded Plath as they drove through the States. He imagines she had resolved the "macabre debate" in her head between Life and Death:

"He [Death] could keep your Daddy and you could have a child." The poem is a battleground for the opposed forces of Life and Death, Life at first taking precedence, but Death still along for the ride. "Was Death, too, part of our luggage?" Hughes asks. "Unemployed for a while, fellow traveller?" His questioning tone reveals again his ignorance at the time, the mystery his life was to him. Death and Life are inextricably entwined: Isis is "Magnae Deorum Matris,"* the great mother of the gods. She has the barren moon between her hipbones, as if it is death to which she will give birth; but she is, too, crowned with ears of corn, symbol of life and fruitfulness.

Plath is not, however, to be allowed to escape. The poem takes away from her possession of the birth of her child. "Our Black Isis had stepped off the wall," Hughes writes. She inhabits the body of his wife: "The great goddess in person / Had put on your body, waxing full." Plath gives birth, gives Life, but her body is only "borrowed / By immortality and its promise," and Death, sulking in her papers, back in her bedroom, will return.

In Chalcot Square, Hughes wrote in a tiny, cramped vestibule in the hallway at a card table borrowed from the Merwins; later that summer he would have the use of Bill Merwin's study. They did not have a great deal of space. Al Alvarez has written:

> The Hugheses' flat was one floor up a bedraggled staircase, past a pram in the hall and a bicycle. It was so small that

---

*Hughes uses the genitive case for the Latin, which allows the line to scan. He may have been drawing on the phrasing of medieval Latin, which is often uneven in this respect.

everything appeared to be sideways on. You inserted yourself into a hallway so narrow and jammed that you could scarcely take off your coat. The kitchen seemed to fit one person at a time, who could span it with arms outstretched. In the living room you sat side by side, longways on, between a wall of books and a wall of pictures. The bedroom off it, with its flowered wallpaper, seemed to have room for nothing except a double bed. But the colors were cheerful, the bits and pieces pretty, and the whole place had a sense of liveliness about it, of things being done. . . .

The cramped spaces made visitors grate on Plath's nerves; although she was euphoric at Frieda's birth, her daughter must have caused strain, too. Plath's *Letters Home*, at this point—her journals from this date do not survive—are blithely positive (she describes dinner at the home of T. S. Eliot: "He was marvelous. Put us immediately at ease . . . I felt to be sitting next to a descended god; he has such a nimbus of greatness about him. . . ."); others have described a less relaxed Plath. In her memoir of Plath, published in Anne Stevenson's *Bitter Fame*, Dido Merwin wrote of this time and described

> the inescapable blast of active hostility that she [Plath] directed at each individual who happened to be involved. This nonstop dispensation of condemnatory Schadenfreude made for a climate of sickened bewilderment that was (and still is) unforgettable and, I suspect, not believable for anyone who never came into contact with the anger of which Sylvia wrote: "I have a violence in me that is hot as death-blood."

This active hostility is reflected in the next poem, "Epiphany." Once again through the medium of an animal appearing out of context, out of nowhere, like the owl of "The Owl" or the bat of "9 Willow Street" or the snake of "Portraits," "Epiphany" explores the mysterious turning point in a relationship, the moment when one or both partners realizes, for a reason that may seem unrelated to the event that has provoked the realization, that something has changed, something is over. The reader can recall the fox-headed spirit that moved Hughes at Cambridge; or know that Hughes, writing to Plath's biographer Anne Stevenson, compared the guarding of Plath's legacy to a boy who holds a fox cub to protect it from hounds, but must allow himself to be bitten (an image that also suits "9 Willow Street").

In this poem, the epiphanic event is the peculiar offer of a fox cub to Hughes, for sale for a pound, as he walks the London streets not far from their home: "A fox-cub / On the hump of Chalk Farm Bridge!" he writes with astonishment. A man walks toward him with something hidden under his coat:

> I glanced at him for the first time as I passed him
> Because I noticed (I couldn't believe it)
> What I'd been ignoring.

The fox's wildness seems to stand for a kind of containment in Hughes: the fear he has been holding back, or his own poet-self, constrained by marriage and baby ("A new father—slightly light-headed / With the lack of sleep and the novelty"). He knows what the fox will grow into; can envision its "mannerless energy," its "old smell," a "long-mouthed, flashing temperament" and "a vast hunger for everything beyond us." Could such wildness be brought into their "crate of space"? Hughes, standing in the street, looking at the fox, "my thoughts . . . like big, ignorant hounds / Circling and sniffing round him," thinks not.

The poem, at this point, hints that the crate of space is too tight round Hughes's shoulders, too; but the end retreats from such condemnation. Instead, the epiphany offered is the understanding that it was his refusal to try to bring that wildness, that fox, into their lives that cost him so dear:

If I had grasped that whatever comes with a fox
Is what tests a marriage and proves it a marriage—
I would not have failed the test. Would you have failed it?
But I failed. Our marriage had failed.

Hughes's work, however, brought him only success. They had, now, a good income from the BBC: his stories "The Rain Horse" and "Harvesting" were broadcast at the end of the year; he had translated parts of the *Odyssey*, too, for broadcasting. Plath was also recording, contributing to *The Poet's Voice* series, broadcast in November. In March 1961, *Lupercal* won the prestigious Hawthornden Prize, and early in April, Peter Hall commissioned him to write a play for the Royal Shakespeare Company. But Christmas, at the Hugheses' in Yorkshire, was strained—it was the last time Hughes's sister Olwyn saw Plath, and their parting was not a happy one. In February of 1961 Plath suffered a miscarriage and then later that month had her appendix out. Her hospital stay, however, provoked new, fine poems, "Tulips" and "In Plaster"; in March, she began work on her novel, *The Bell Jar*. In May, she wrote to her mother of "GOOD NEWS GOOD NEWS GOOD NEWS"—Knopf would bring out *The Colossus* in New York.

By June, Plath was pregnant again, and Aurelia Plath came over from America; in part to look after Frieda while the Hugheses had a two-week holiday in France, staying for some of the time with the Merwins at their house in the Lôt. Driving down in their Morris Traveller, they passed through the Pas-de-Calais and stopped in Rheims, the setting of "The Gypsy." It is a poem that begins on a note of cautious hope, Hughes a spider weaving a path to their future—"maybe." Plath seems bright: "You were writing postcards, concentrated. / In your mac. Midmorning, the air fresh." There is another, animal-like interruption, the "dark stub gypsy woman" like "a weasel testing every crevice." She holds up a pendant, which Plath does not even see before refusing it—though it may be of St. Nicholas, the name they will give to their second child. And so the gypsy woman curses Plath: "Vous / Crèverez bientôt"—You will soon be dead—and vanishes.

Plath seems not to hear. "But you / Went on writing postcards." Instead, the weight of the curse falls on Hughes alone, the weight of a

> much older religion
> In me alone, to be carried
> Everywhere with me . . .

It is Hughes who fears her curse—seeing her face as a quipu, the ancient Peruvian device for recording information via knots in thread, suggesting that she is the possessor of some ancient wisdom. He tries to counter the weight of that old religion with charms spoken in ancient, formal Welsh verse:

> For days I rhymed
> Talismans of power, in cynghanedd,
> To neutralize her venom.

Plath is peculiarly oblivious. He hints at how bound up she was in her own world: how "deafened, maybe, / By closer explosions," her own internal distress muffling human contact. It is worth noting, in this context, the erratic behavior she could display, which seemed so strange to those around her. Their subsequent stay with the Merwins was unhappy. Plath seemed distressed whenever Hughes suggested he might leave her alone; when she was unavoidably left by herself, she consumed an entire dinner meant to feed a group of people, according to Dido Merwin's dramatic account. "It was Ted who was finally forced to admit that . . . there was nothing for it but to cut their stay short and take Sylvia away," Merwin writes in her account of Plath. "It was then that I asked him why he never put his foot down, and he told me that it would only make things worse; that 'she couldn't be helped that way.' . . . Apart from when she was sleeping, eating, sunbathing or playing cards . . . their stay at Lacan had been one long scene—a kind of macabre marathon for all concerned."

What Hughes writes seems evidence of her new distance from the world, a drawing-in to her inner demons. Here is the "still virulence," the "gathered pallors," of the disturbing "Berck-Plage," which she wrote after they had stopped by that beach on the way down to the Merwins (although Hughes has noted that at the time of their visit, she showed no sign of distress):

> On the balconies of the hotel, things are glittering.
> Things, things—
>
> Tubular steel wheelchairs, aluminum crutches.
> Such salt-sweetness. Why should I walk
>
> Beyond the breakwater, spotty with barnacles?

Her poem is haunted and haunting. Hughes begins, in "The Gypsy," to build an image of his wife as she would become, the nearly possessed creature who, as he saw it, was author of the *Ariel* poems, removed from the world, pulling toward death, already "in a soldier crypt." The same pulling away from the warm world is seen in "A Dream," which also draws on the French trip, the appearance of Chartres Cathedral echoing the spire of Rheims in the previous poem:

> The spectacular up-spearing
> Of its tonnage pierced us
> With the shadow-gloom and weight of the sacred.

Here the shadow-gloom comes from—her dream? his dream? It isn't clear. "Your worst dream / Came true," the poem begins, but the events appear "In your dream or mine?" It does not matter: the effect is the same.

Strange letter box.
You took out the envelope. It was
A letter from your Daddy. "I'm home.
Can I stay with you?"

The question has only one answer: "For me, a request was a command." The little Breton jug filled with money, "with everything we had," recalls the coin-filled glass of "The Bird," so full and so easily, mysteriously smashed. Here, however, it is Plath who smashes the jug, "Into shards, crude stars, / And gave them to your mother." The jug recalls, too, the smashed glass from her ouija "Dialogue," the oracle refused and broken, its fearful truth. The escape into life that a poem such as "Remission" seemed to offer now looks as if it was too good to be true. The poet's attempt to dismiss the dream ("Not dreams, I had said, but fixed stars / Govern a life") is both knowingly wrong-headed (in the context of the poem) and an appropriation of the inexorable end of her poem "Words," written just a few days before she took her life: "From the bottom of the pool, fixed stars / Govern a life." The fixed stars of Fate, inescapable, invade even dreams.

Now the center of the labyrinth that the reader entered in "18 Rugby Street" has been reached, and "The Minotaur" is discovered at its heart. Released in this poem is the violence that appears in dream form in the previous poem: Plath smashes Hughes's mother's "heirloom sideboard— / Mapped with the scars of my whole life." It is a violence that seems out of all proportion to the event that provoked it; she is "demented by my being / Twenty minutes late for baby-minding." But Hughes's reaction to her violence, sarcastic,

critical, is truer than he knew at the time, and his words now
have a terrible resonance:

> "Marvellous!" I shouted, "Go on,
> Smash it into kindling.
> That's the stuff you're keeping out of your poems!"

Even later, calmer, considered, he held to this contention,
reflecting the controlled chill of much of her pre-*Ariel* work.
"The poetry of the *Ariel* poems was no surprise to me," he
wrote in an essay, "Publishing Sylvia Plath." "It was at last the
flight of whatever we had been trying to get flying for a
number of years. But it dawned on me only in the last
months which way it wanted to fly." He has, to his horror,
given her the answer, given her her death, taken her to

> The bloody end of the skein
> That unravelled your marriage,
> Left your children echoing
> Like tunnels in a labyrinth . . .

Hughes retreats from the awfulness of it, a pulling back
hinted at earlier in the sequence at the end of "Grand
Canyon," when the unborn Frieda was "your daughter." Here
again it is your marriage (not their marriage); your children
(not their children); the second person scrambles backwards,
away from the awful vision at the center of the labyrinth:

> the horned, bellowing
> Grave of your risen father—
> And your own corpse in it.

8 ⬦ "THEN THE SCRIPT OVERTOOK US"

IN AUGUST 1961, the Hugheses began their search for a home in the country, finally settling on Court Green, a rambling, ancient house in Devon. But their move away from London was a mistake, as Hughes sees it in "Error"; his heart knows it is wrong before his mind does, as is made evident in "The Lodger." There were happy events in Devon. On 17 January 1962, Plath gave birth to their son, Nicholas Farrar Hughes; that spring, daffodils filled their garden with bright blooms. But as the summer of 1962 drew on, the undercurrents of Plath's struggle were strong and swift: "Dream Life" paints her as haunted nightly by her father's ghost; "Suttee" portrays a birth opposed to the arrival of little Nicholas: the deadly birth of her *Ariel* poems, with Hughes their midwife.

THE HUGHESES HAD decided to leave London. To that end, when they returned from France, Aurelia Plath continued to look after Frieda while the pair drove through Devon and Cornwall, looking for a house they could afford and that would offer them the peace they both felt they needed to get on with their real work, their writing.

The house they finally found, Court Green in North Tawton, Devon, was a former manorhouse and rectory, with a thatched roof: Hughes returned to it after Plath's death and remained there to the end of his life. It was large, with a stable at the back and a small ruined cottage in the grounds; there were apple trees and a great wych elm growing at the edge of a moated prehistoric mound. The windows of what would be their bedroom looked out over a lawn to the nearby church and churchyard. Plath described the house in a letter to Helga Huws, written in October 1961:

> It is . . . very very ancient . . . with castle-thick walls in the original back part and almost 10 rooms, yet very compact and not at all rambling, feeling almost small (except when I look at the floorspace . . .). We have a U-shape of out-buildings around a cobbled courtyard—a big thatched barn, stables(!), and a thatched cottage which someday we would like to make into a guest house for mothers-in-law and such people. But those are all 10-year plans. The house is white, with a black trim and this primeval peaked thatch. We have just over two acres of land, mostly stinging nettle, but Ted is dig-

ging up the big vegetable garden and we'll hope to live on them—he's already put in strawberries, and we have about 70 apple trees, eaters and cookers—though sadly the crop this year is very poor everywhere and we are almost through ours. And blackberries everywhere in season. I have a tiny front lawn carved out of the wilderness—a laburnum tree, lilacs, and a few rose bushes. We adjoin the town church, Anglican, with its own 8 famous bell-ringers.

Before they moved, however, they had to dispose of the Chalcot Square flat. They eventually accepted an offer from a young Canadian poet and his wife, David and Assia Wevill. And in late August, just before they moved, Plath at last completed *The Bell Jar*; she heard, too, from Knopf in New York that *The Colossus* would be published in the spring of 1962. Her black mood seemed to have lifted—but the poetry that began to come from her as they settled in Devon reveals a dark current still running strong. It was at this time, in September, that she wrote of the invitation to death and burial found in "Wuthering Heights."

This strange, seductive shadow hangs over the poems in *Birthday Letters* that chart the couple's move away from London, to the setting Hughes—both of them—hoped would be idyllic. In "The Pan" and "Error," there is no breath of hope: straight away things have gone wrong. "The Pan," like "Epiphany," hinges on a single, seemingly random object that refracts, in the poet's mind, the slanted light of his life.

> When he stopped at last in the long main street
> Of the small town, after that hundred
> And ninety miles, the five-o'clock, September,

Brassy, low, wet Westcountry sun
Above the street's far end, and when
He had extricated his stiffness
From the car crammed with books, carrier bags
Of crockery, cutlery and baby things,
And crossed the tilting street in that strange town
To buy a pan to heat milk and babyfood
The moment they arrived
Hours ahead of their furniture
Into their stripped new house, in their strange new life,
He did not notice that the ironmonger's
Where he bought the pan had been closed
And empty for two years.

"The Pan"'s threatening atmosphere is not sensed by the "he" of the poem, in the poem's present: he is a ghost already, looking back on his own life—this is one of only two poems in the book written in the third person, where the poet looks at himself all the way through. The place they arrive, their new home, is a "strange town," the life they are going to is a "strange new life." There is no comfort offered here, only distraction, a crowded car, their new house "stripped"—and as he (somehow, by a ghostly process) buys a pan from a shop long closed, he is observed by a projection of himself, whose haunting silence contradicts the image of the "happy car" that, at the end of this doom-laden poem, is almost pathetic.

The poem is constructed of two rushing, breathless sentences: it has the headlong drive of their flight down to Devon, its pace and rhythm that of pursuit. It only calls itself to a kind of halt in its last two lines, when he does not recognize the man on the pavement staring at him, does not rec-

ognize that it "was himself—knowing their whole future /
And helpless to warn them."

This double of himself is somewhat reminiscent of the
doubling that occurs in Hughes's mythological sequence of
1977, *Gaudete*, in which the clergyman Lumb is swept away
to the spirit world and replaced by a Dionysian double who
wreaks havoc among his parishioners. Lumb's splitting is a
materialization of the divided self, of the actor and the
observer, the spiritual and the physical. Hughes wrote of
Gaudete:

> . . . what I held in focus as I wrote was a sense of the spirit
> energy staggering through the crassness of the living cells . . .
> and emerging in its way as stupefied and benighted, and
> going about its mission almost somnambulist, almost uncon-
> scious. . . . The battery image of the poem was of transcen-
> dental energy jammed—unconscious and deformed in the
> collision—into dead-end objects, dead-end claustrophobic
> egos. . . .

This is the atmosphere of "The Pan": the stalled town, the
pan, those dead-end objects that jam the energy trapped in
the car between Plath and Hughes. Something is clearly
wrong. "Error," the next poem is titled: what could be more
plain? Not bad luck or mischance but mistake, his mistake. "I
brought you to Devon." It is his will, and yet, it is not: he is
still unknowing, sleepwalking again, "I sleepwalked you /
Into my land of totems." There is no chance in this poem; he
and his wife—she is "gallant and desperate and hopeful"—
are too different, too separate. She has to leave behind all she

is to follow him, "stripping off / Your American royalty," her "flashing trajectory" of adolescent dreams. The house rots around them like a coffin, and he cannot fathom her thoughts as she sits at the table Hughes made for her from a plank of elm in September, "staring at the blank sheet of white paper."

"This was Lyonnesse," he writes, and the line brings into the reader's mind the work of both Plath and Thomas Hardy. "Lyonnesse," a poem that Plath wrote in October 1962, makes symbolic reference to her sense of suffocation in Devon, returning as it does to her underwater imagery: "It was not a shock—/ The clear, green, quite breathable atmosphere". Referring to "the Lyonians," she writes of how

> the big God
> Had lazily closed one eye and let them slip
> Over the English cliff and under so much history!

"Lyonnesse" is a term denoting the north and northwest coast of Cornwall; Tennyson and Swinburne used it in their Arthurian romances. Hardy recalled his first meeting with his wife, Emma Gifford, at St. Juliot in Cornwall in his lyric "When I set out for Lyonnesse." Plath, in her poem, identifies Hughes with the English landscape and history to which he was so bound; it drowns her, and her poem ends with a chilling line: "The white gape of his mind was the real Tabula Rasa."

Hughes, in "Error," admits to the white gape. Now, years later, he can see how everything is threatening, alien, seen through her eyes. The village women—"stump-warts, you called them"—"jabbered hedge-bank judgements, a dark-age dialect." In a story she set in Devon, "Mothers," Plath called her alter ego by the same name she used in *The Bell Jar*, Esther, and had her express the same misgivings Plath must have felt as a newcomer in the close community. A new neighbor tells Esther she knows "hardly a soul" in the village, "causing misgivings, like a flock of chilly-toed birds, to clutter at Esther's heart. If Mrs Nolan, an Englishwoman by her looks and accent, and a pub-keeper's wife as well, felt herself a stranger in Devon after six years, what hope had Esther, an American, of infiltrating that rooted society ever at all?" This new country, in Hughes's poem, is a prison, ending under dark cloud and rainy hills: "A thin squandering of blood-water— / Searched for the river and the sea," as she, in her work seemed to search for it, her primal ocean. It was in October that she wrote the snarling, bitter "Daddy," with its "freakish Atlantic," "bean green over blue," and the terrifying, risen father, the "man in black with a Meinkampf look."

It was while living in Devon—county of their willed idyll—that Hughes began an affair with Assia Wevill, new resident of the flat in Chalcot Square. "Error" cannot fail to recall another of Hughes's poems: "The Error," written in the aftermath of Wevill's death.

She, too, committed suicide by gassing herself, along with her daughter by Hughes, Shura, in 1969. In this poem, too, a trail, like the "thin squandering of blood-water," leads to death—the fascination Wevill seems to have felt for Hughes's late wife.

When her grave opened its ugly mouth
Why didn't you just fly,
Wrap yourself in your hair and make yourself scarce,
Why did you kneel down at the grave's edge
To be identified
Accused and convicted
By all who held in their hands
Pieces of the gravestone grey granite
Proof of their innocence?

He paints Wevill, who was a Jewish refugee from Germany, as being fascinated by death as Plath was: the way he depicts her nursing this fascination as if she were feeding a child looks forward to his similar observation of Plath in "Suttee," later in the sequence. Hughes finds himself in a hermetically sealed, death-bounded world: but he bears the blame for choosing it. In "Error," he sets Plath on a path "aimed at a graveyard." It is recalled by the poet in a kind of awful stillness, "in a bubble," "in a closed brilliance," untouchable as his future self could not touch the past in "The Pan." And his wife so alone she lies even in "a foreign grave"—but never resting; the first reference to the controversy that later surrounded her death and life. "The real bones," he writes, "still undergoing everything."

In *Birthday Letters*, the Hugheses' first months in Devon are lit by the grim, bald light of hindsight, but there was hard work and success too. Plath was able to write in the mornings, while Hughes looked after Frieda; after lunch, Hughes worked and she minded the baby. Hughes was doing a fair amount of writing for the BBC, poetry readings and talks for *Woman's Hour*; his poems and stories appeared in British and American magazines; he also took on book reviews. Plath sold poems to *The New Yorker*, the *Observer*, the *New Statesman* and the *London Magazine*, among others; and in November, she won a $2,000 Eugene Saxton Grant to write prose fiction. They must have taken pleasure, too, in their new home, painted white and pink and with new shelving, built by Hughes, for all their books. One of their plans for country life was to grow their own vegetables, as Hughes relates in "The Lodger," whose opening is buoyant with the fertile discovery of their garden. The swift, lolloping rhythm, the exclamation marks, carry an assurance of comfort—Hughes is home at last.

> Potatoes were growing in the yard corner
> That September. They were the welcome wagon!
> First fruits of our own ground. And their flavour
> Was the first legend. Pioneer
> In our own life, those mornings—
> I bought the spades, the forks, the overalls, the boots.
> And the books. The books! I was a student
> Gluttonous to swallow all horticulture,
> The whole cornucopia.

The brisk notice of the countryside around evokes the ease, the sharp eye and warm voice found in 1979's "Moortown."

But soon, in "The Lodger," he can no longer concentrate on the garden, distracted by the pangs and poundings of his heart, which, he is certain, herald imminent death: "Every heartbeat a fresh throw of the dice— / A click of Russian roulette." Early on, there is an inkling that his heart's distress may not be only physical. The poet refers to "whatever hid in my heart": the panicky, soul-felt knowledge of what was to come, felt in the body before understood in the mind. His heart begins to obsess him, becomes like a "dying child" he carries everywhere with him; he is reduced to keeping a diary of its errata—this strong, powerful man whom Plath had thought of as her Adam.

His heart's lurching, his separation from life and its music, is an obvious metaphor for his distress. He made

> Efforts to make my whole
> Body a conduit of Beethoven,
> To reconduct that music through my aorta
> So he could run me clean and unconstrained
> And release me. I could not reach the music.

Plath, at the time, had a passion for Beethoven's music, part-caught from Hughes, who once said of the composer and his connection to poetry, "Blake I connect inwardly to Beethoven, and if I could dig to the bottom of my strata maybe their names and works would be the deepest traces."

His distress is the more affecting for its plainness:

> My new study
> Was all the ways a heart can kill its owner
> And how mine had killed me.

And yet the real heart of this poem only comes at its end, the revelation of the lodger, the secret hiding in the heart.

Hughes leads the reader in with his sidelong "meanwhile," far out to the right of the page.

> Meanwhile
>
> Who was using my heart,
> Who positioned our bee-hive and planted,
> With my unwitting hands, to amuse himself,
> Nine bean rows?

Bean flowers bloom ominously in Plath's poem of October 1962, "The Bee Meeting," in which the speaker becomes a sacrifice to a mysterious god. In Hughes's poem, "this alien joker / Who had come to evict us" is the same spirit whose "blackness and silence" inhabits the Gothic shape of the yew tree in her poem "The Moon and the Yew Tree"; her black, risen, bee-keeping father (in the new year, in "Little Fugue," she would refer to her father's "yew hedge of orders") inhabiting Hughes as much as he did his daughter.

That winter was very cold. They kept the temperature in the house bearable with portable heaters; they had their first Christmas without parents, just the three of them, a family, and Plath was nearly nine months pregnant. "Our Christmas was the happiest and fullest I had ever known," Plath wrote to her mother.

Nicholas Farrar Hughes was born on 17 January 1962, at Court Green. She described the birth in her journal:

> "Here he is!" I heard Ted say. It was over. I felt the great weight gone in a moment. I felt thin, like air, as if I would float away, and perfectly awake. . . . I lifted my head and saw

my first son, Nicholas Farrar Hughes, blue and glistening on the bed a foot from me, in a pool of wet. . . . Dr Webb put his fingers digging into my stomach and told me to cough. The afterbirth flew out into a pyrex bowl, which crimsoned with blood. It was whole. We had a son. . . .

"Such a shocking / Beauty born," Hughes writes in "The Afterbirth." The difficulty and peculiarity of this poem reflect the complex feelings that jolt the poet like electricity: the joy of his son's bloody birth tangled with the blood of death, with the imagery of a hare killed not once but twice. The swift, elfin hare is a mythic animal in many cultures. To the ancient Egyptians, its hieroglyph signified the concept of being; in ancient Greece the lunar goddess, Hecate, was associated with the hare—the Chinese, too, associate it with the moon and augury. It is also a symbol of fecundity and therefore particularly appropriate to this poem, though its image has drawn Hughes before. In "The Hare," he writes:

> Who is it, at midnight on the A30,
> The Druid soul,
> The night-streaker, the sudden lumpy goblin
> That thumps your car under the belly
> Then cries with human pain
> And becomes a human baby on the road
> That you dare hardly pick up?

The hare is "a moony pond of quaking blood / Twitched with spells." His 1959 story "The Harvesting" has a hunter transformed into the hare that he kills. These spells of mystery and transformation carry over into "The Afterbirth"—though the power of this poem, as in the best work of *Birthday Letters*, is in its everyday particularity: the blood-soaked newsprint, the ovenproof glass bowl, are concrete descriptions that strengthen the hints at myth. Hughes's vision of himself is as "A figure with a dog's head / On a tomb wall in Egypt"—Anubis, god of embalming—as he jugs a dead hare crouching in the "claret" of its blood, a sinister echo of the "fallen Eden" of Nicholas's afterbirth.

It is an echo his wife appears to catch:

> You would eat no more hare
> Jugged in the wine of its own blood
> Out of that bowl. The hare nesting in it
> Had opened its eyes.

This image can be linked to the hare that appears in her poem "Totem," written only days before her suicide, and a work whose images are all of death:

> In the bowl the hare is aborted,
> Its baby head out of the way, embalmed in spice,
>
> Flayed of fur and humanity.
> Let us eat it like Plato's afterbirth,
>
> Let us eat it like Christ . . .

In "The Afterbirth," the ripped-up flower of the dead hare, "Disembowelled, a stunned mask," resonates against the afterbirth of the poem's beginning, "the lotus-eater's whole island

/ Dragged out by its roots," its final scream cut off as if the connection is too terrible to follow through.

Memory, even of joy, in these poems, is weighed down by sorrow. The present holds the future in its palm: as the poet writes in the gentle, evocative "Daffodils," the spring of 1962 was "your last April." "Our daffodils are in full bloom," Plath wrote to her mother on 25 April. "We picked about 1,000 this week, and I look out over a literal sea of several thousand more. . . ." They sold them, as Hughes writes, to the local grocer. Once again the reader encounters the issue of memory, its elusiveness, to whom it really belongs. Here Hughes is categorical, possessive of his memory, his alone: "Remember how we picked the daffodils? / Nobody else remembers, but I remember." It is a prize, this recollection, amongst all the forgetting; Frieda, who helped carry the flowers, ". . . has forgotten. / She cannot even remember you."

The daffodils, like this memory, are a miraculous glory, golden (their lightness can be contrasted with the "sunken church," the "mist of rain" that hazes the Devon of the poems earlier in the sequence), standing in their beautiful fragility for the transient happiness of their marriage: "We thought they were a windfall. / Never guessed they were a last blessing." The same nimbus hangs about them in a poem that comes slightly later in the sequence, "Perfect Light," in which Plath is described as she was caught in the camera's eye—perhaps on Easter Sunday, 1962, when in her notes Plath describes Hughes taking her picture and Frieda's, writing to her mother:

These photographs are meant for a late birthday surprise. We took them Easter Sunday, the first day of real spring. I think you can see some of the reason I am so happy. This is just the very smallest corner of our daffodils. Frieda is an expert at picking handsome bouquets—you simply mention the word "daffodil" and she is off.

Hughes writes that "Perfect light in your face lights it up / Like a daffodil." The poet closes in again on how the brightness of the image accents its finality: "It was to be your only April on earth / Among your daffodils." Her voice, however—perhaps standing for her real self—is lost in the still image:

> And beside you, laughing up at you,
> Your daughter, barely two. Like a daffodil
> You turn your face down to her, saying something.
> Your words were lost in the camera.

As "Daffodils" draws to a close, the flowers' darker side is revealed: the poet suddenly seems to see them as Plath might, in language that echoes the black light of her work, when the daffodils become

> Wind-wounds, spasms from the dark earth,
> With their odourless metals,
> A flamy purification of the deep grave's stony cold
> As if ice had a breath—

Selling them then seems a sacrilege, a fatal error: "We sold them, to wither." Furthermore, in cutting them, they lost, significantly, their wedding-present scissors.

Memory, as Hughes indicates at the beginning of this poem, is elusive. And yet at the end of the poem he hints at the possibility of permanence, too, of memorial in life or objects less fallible than mere human beings. The daffodils, rising again each March, "baby-cries from the thaw," rise "on that same groundswell of memory"; although their resurrection "forget[s]" Plath, their simple existence calls her to the poet's mind. Their scissors, lost in the earth, are not gone, but "here somewhere," "an anchor, a cross of rust." It is their loss that, in the face of the breakdown of their marriage, ensures their survival as a memorial. They are tarnished but they survive, each April moving into closer communion with the earth. The image of a cross of rust calls to mind a soldier's grave. "Perfect Light" is even more explicitly military, as, beyond the photograph, Plath's "next moment" was "coming towards you like an infantryman / Returning slowly out of no-man's-land"; it never reaches her. Perhaps because the photograph stops time; perhaps because her own time comes to an end. The poem allows for both.

The blood of the afterbirth and Plath's demanding dark god, the golden yellow of the daffodils and her happy, *Letters Home* self, are woven together in "The Rag Rug." When the Hugheses lived in Boston, Plath's friend Shirley Norton had taught her how to plait rag rugs; she took to this again in Devon. But it is soon much more than the casual occupation that the poem's first line indicates; in Hughes's account, it is hooked out of herself, "issuing like a fugue out of the whorls / Of your fingertips." She wrote in her journal in the spring of 1962: "Braided violently on rug . . . and felt anger flow harmlessly away into the cores of bright soft colored wool. It will be not a prayer rug but an anger rug. . . ." Again Hughes contrasts his lack of understanding at the time—"it calmed you," he writes of her braiding, though the works he apparently chooses to read her as she plaits hint at an understanding of her distress: Conrad's *Heart of Darkness* and *The Secret Sharer*. That the rug was a receptacle for her furies—"As if you had dragged it, like your own entrails, / Out through your navel"—is indicated by this passage from *The Bell Jar* (which, though reflecting her life in the 1950s, was written in 1961):

> Once when I visited Buddy I found Mrs Willard braiding a rug out of strips of wool from Mr Willard's old suits . . . [but] instead of hanging the rug on the wall the way I would have done, she put it down in place of her kitchen mat, and in a few days it was soiled and dull. . . . And I knew that in spite of all the roses and kisses and restaurant dinners a man showered on a woman before he married her, what he secretly wanted when the wedding service ended was for her to flatten out underneath his feet like Mrs Willard's kitchen mat.

The rug is indeed, as the end of the poem indicates, like a serpent in Eden, holding mysteriously within itself the secret of her destruction. Its colors run with her blood, making their evenings "crimson-shadowed," and when the coils of the rug became "a mamba, fatal," her tread upon it "would alter your blood." It is the serpent he dreamed, golden—as the daffodils are golden—and it turns their house upside down "with an earthquake jolt." Only the rug—inert, like the daffodils, the wedding scissors—"survived our Eden."

Hughes has written about the poetic transformation Plath underwent that spring; necessarily a personal transformation, too. In March, she had written a verse play for radio, *Three Women*, a long poem of childbirth, which ends on a note of contentment and reconciliation:

> . . . I am a wife.
> The city waits and aches. The little grasses
> Crack through stone, and they are green with life.

But then, something changed: "After *Three Women*," Hughes writes in an essay on her journals, ". . . quite suddenly the ghost of her father reappears, for the first time in two and a half years, and meets a daunting, point-blank, demythologized assessment." "Such a dark funnel, my father!" she writes in "Little Fugue," in early April ". . . Do you say nothing? / I am lame in the memory." She was finding the voice of her *Ariel* poems, work unlike anything she had done before. Her poem "Elm," written in April, begins:

> I know the bottom, she says. I know it with my
>   great tap root:
> It is what you fear.
> I do not fear it: I have been there.

It is a voice fearless of the worst, a voice that has "suffered the atrocity of sunsets," that is "scorched to the root." She has found her trajectory. The poem closes, ominously: "These are the isolate, slow faults / That kill, that kill, that kill."

The table at which she wrote this was of elm, made by

Hughes for his wife, as he writes in "The Table." It is a poem that, like his notes to her *Journals*, acknowledges the sudden reappearance of her father. The poet's intentions are the best: "I wanted to make you a solid writing-table / That would last a lifetime." A heavy irony, underscored by the use the plank was intended for: "rough-cut for coffin timber." In a poem slightly earlier in the sequence, "Setebos," Hughes hears the "bellow" in Plath's voice when she is, nearly like Ariel (whose tree of imprisonment, in *The Tempest*, was an oak), "freed from the Elm." Here the elm frees her voice but imprisons her:

> With a plane
> I revealed a perfect landing pad
> For your inspiration. I did not
> Know I had made and fitted a door
> Opening downwards into your Daddy's grave.

Hughes seems helpless against the force that flings open this door, that devours Plath.

> Incredulous
> I saw rise through it, in broad daylight,
> Your Daddy resurrected,
> Blue-eyed, that German cuckoo
> Still calling the hour,
> Impersonating your whole memory.

Like the cuckoo, the resurrected Daddy usurps Hughes's place, the impersonation of her memory a reference to her conflation, revealed in her journals, of her husband and her father. " 'Wait!' I said. 'Wait! / What's this?' " He does not know. He is once more the sleepwalker, and now too an actor, unable to alter the lines he's been given. Then even that is taken from him:

> I woke up on the empty stage with the props,
> The paltry painted masks. And the script
> Ripped up and scattered, its code scrambled,
> Like the blades and slivers
> Of a shattered mirror.

The lines are a reminder of how Plath once ripped up and scattered his work, tore the pages from his treasured edition of Shakespeare in a jealous rage when she believed he was having an affair with a BBC producer, Moira Doolan. She saw rivals for Hughes's affection everywhere, anxiously possessive: now her greatest rival seems to be her alter ego, Lady Death, though Hughes's "embrace" of her foreshadows the affair that will mark the real end of their marriage. At the end of the poem, the table, like the rag rug before it, seems to lose its significance; without her presence becoming again simply a thing, "a curio." But its memory holds bitter and recriminatory associations for Hughes, who closes by imagining the desk washed up years later, "far side of the Atlantic,"

> Scoured of the sweat I soaked into
> Finding your father for you and then
> Leaving you to him.

The table, the work it brought, pulled her away from him. There had always been differences between them: "I saw my world again through your eyes," Hughes wrote with wonder in "The Owl" of their different attitudes to the natural world. It is a theme he returns to in "The Rabbit Catcher," written in reflection after a day spent in the country when she had torn up snares set to catch rabbits. Behind this poem is her poem of the same name. "It was a place of force—" she begins. A natural force, but a terrible one, the lives of the dead singing in the wind. In her poem the gorse is malignant, its yellow flowers "extravagant, like torture." There is accusation in his understanding of the snares: she sees not the rhythm of country life—to which he alludes in his poem—but sadism. "How they awaited him, those little deaths! / They waited like sweethearts. They excited him." The snares, set tight, are likened to a relationship—between the poet and the unnamed "him", but perhaps between the poet and Death, too:

> And we, too, had a relationship—
> Tight wires between us,
> Pegs too deep to uproot, and a mind like a ring
> Sliding shut on some quick thing,
> The constriction killing me also.

His poem begins more gently. "It was May." His persona in this poem is ignorant, innocent, uncomprehending, a victim of her "dybbuk fury"—a dybbuk, in Jewish folklore, a disembodied human spirit that wanders the earth until it can find refuge in the body of a living person. And in this poem she seems to be some other creature, with "iron in your face," "your Germanic scowl, edged like a helmet," as if the fero-

cious face of her Daddy was inside her. The gorse, to him, is
homely, not threatening, "A gorse cliff, / Brambly, oak-packed
combes"; he is "baffled," not seeing what she sees, only able to
trail after her like a dog when she tears up the set-out snare.

They look upon the same thing: what they see is entirely
separate.

> You saw baby-eyed
> Strangled innocents, I saw sacred
> Ancient custom.

Her attack on the snares is an attack on his being, just as her
poem was an attack upon him, and nothing to do with rabbits: "You were weeping with a rage / That cared nothing for
rabbits." He is helpless. He cannot reach her. And yet he
acknowledges that her rage might have an object in him
("Had you caught something in me, / Nocturnal and
unknown to me?") even if he was not, at this point, aware of
what it might be. Or her rage might have come from her
catching sight of "your doomed self." In the end, in his view,
it does not matter. The result is the same.

> Whichever,
> Those terrible, hypersensitive
> Fingers of your verse closed round it and
> Felt it alive. The poems, like smoking entrails,
> Came soft into your hands.

Plath's poem "The Rabbit Catcher" was completed on 21
May 1962, along with "Event," in which she writes, "Love

cannot come here." In Hughes's "Rabbit Catcher," he is unaware of the event that prompted the fury that set them off in the car—the poet would, however, now be aware of what prompted her to write "The Rabbit Catcher" and "Event": the visit, on the weekend of 18 May, of David and Assia Wevill, the couple who had taken the lease on their Chalcot Square flat, and with whom, through mutual friends, they had stayed in touch.

Assia had been born in Berlin in 1927; her father—Lonya Gutman, a physician—was a Russian Jew. In the late 1930s, the family fled to Tel Aviv and Assia ended up in Canada. Married twice before, she had met David, ten years her junior, on board ship in 1956; three years later they had married in Burma, where David was teaching, then moved to London in 1960. David Wevill recalls the weekend they spent together as "cordial, exploratory, gracious"; and Plath had written to her mother in happily bland anticipation on 14 May: "We have a nice young Canadian poet and his very attractive, intelligent wife coming down for this weekend— they're the ones who took over our lease for the London flat."

From her poems, however, it seems that Plath felt under threat. If her feelings were at the time unfounded, it cannot be denied that Hughes was drawn to Assia Wevill: they began an affair that summer. On 11 July, Plath wrote the disgusted "Words heard, by accident, over the phone" when she had overheard a conversation between her husband and Assia.

What are these words, these words?
They are plopping like mud.

O god, how shall I ever clean the phone table?
They are pressing out of the many-holed earpiece, they
    are looking for a listener.
Is he here?

Afterwards she had ripped the phone from the wall. That month, too, *The Colossus* was published in New York, but was hardly noticed; there were no reviews in the major papers, not even in her hometown *Boston Herald* or *Globe*. Hughes, in contrast, was already deemed worthy of a *Selected Poems*—published that same month by Faber, along with the work of Thom Gunn.

"Event" is explicitly echoed in "Setebos," which takes its name and theme from *The Tempest*. If Hughes saw that play as the culmination of Shakespeare's work and the reconcilia- tion of the forces that drove him, "Setebos" is a cruel play on that resolution. Hughes's view of *The Tempest* was that it was only Ariel, aiding Prospero's magic, who allowed the Duke to "arrest the mechanism of the Tragic Equation," and hap- pily marry Ferdinand to Miranda. Setebos, a devil, is the father of Caliban, the "savage and deformed slave" made to serve Prospero. Caliban's mother is Sycorax, an incarnation, in Hughes's view, of the goddess whose triple aspect (the Mother, the Sacred Bride, and the Queen of the Under- world) he drew in part from Robert Graves's *The White Goddess*, first published in 1948 and a book that greatly influenced both Plath and Hughes. Miranda is Sycorax's opposite and parallel.

As in Shakespeare's play, Ferdinand and Miranda— Hughes and Plath—are not active agents in their own right but pawns of Prospero, here Aurelia Plath. He equates their wedding, for which Aurelia had donated her own suit, and after which she had paid for their summer in Cape Cod, with the strange, artificial Masque that the lovers of *The Tempest* watch:

> Your mother
> Played Prospero, flying her magic in
> To stage the Masque, and bless the marriage . . .

Of *The Tempest*'s end, Hughes has written that Prospero

marries a Diana-like Miranda to an uncorrupted, idyllic Ferdinand. That is to say, he has solved the never-before-solved tragic problem of the Mythic Equation. But he has done all this through Ariel. Just as Ulysses did, he has brought the island under control, and transformed the evil on it, with Ariel's flower-magic. And it is Ariel who stages the ritual betrothal, and raises the magic ramparts encircling Ferdinand and Miranda, patrolled by the benign powers of Heaven—in the Masque.

In the end, the magic of Prospero is as nothing compared to the powers of Ariel.

In Hughes's own life, the magic cannot be maintained. At the beginning of this poem they are lulled by the "Sounds and sweet airs" that fill the island of *The Tempest*'s air and soothe the savage Caliban; and Caliban seems their happy servant, sharing with them the place's secrets. "I'll show thee every fertile inch o' th' island," he promises his would-be new masters, Stephano and Trinculo. "I'll show thee the best springs; I'll pluck thee berries . . ." Stephano and Trinculo, outwitted in the play by Prospero, do not gain mastery of the island or its native; but Hughes and Plath in this brief, alternative universe, appear to.

Caliban, however, must revert to type, and Plath becomes Ariel, the spirit of her poetry, untameable, while Hughes, a kind of mock Ariel, lies "in the labyrinth of a cowslip / Without a clue." But is he really so unaware?

> I heard the Minotaur
> Coming down its tunnel-groove
> Of old faults deep and bitter.

Here he echoes the bitter division of "Event": "I walk in a ring," Plath writes, "A groove of old faults, deep and bitter." Love cannot cross the "black gap" disclosed. Hughes writes, in another echo of the savaged Orpheus:

> The moon's horns
> Plunged and tossed. I heard your cries
> Bugling through the hot bronze:
> "Who has dismembered us?"

That cry rings first at the end of "Event." The old faults, the black gap, link her father and Hughes: the one who left her, with his death, the other who left her for another woman. In "Setebos," Hughes strengthens that link, her bellow bleeding into that of "King Minos, / Alias Otto." But Hughes cannot lay blame at that door alone. He wonders "which play / Were we in?"; he is "too late to find you / And get to my ship." He could,

it seems, have rescued her, but chose not to, equating himself
with foolish Trinculo, hiding from *The Tempest*'s storm:

> I crawled
> Under a gabardine, hugging tight
> All I could of me, hearing the cry
> Now of hounds.

The theme of the poet's being a part of something over
which he has no control is almost overwhelming now. "Setebos" hints at strange religion, at Plath as sacrifice, trapped in
a burning bronze bull. Hughes's "Apprehensions" and
"Dream Life" make even clearer her service to the fear that
becomes like religion, that turns her into the priestess of her
own cult, tending a bloody shrine. "Apprehensions"—and
apprehension implies foreknowledge of something terrible
to come—focuses on the fear that draws her to her writing
table in an attempt to exorcize it, but also lives in that writing table ("that grain was like its skin, you could stroke it")
and suffuses everything around her. She holds in her hands—
in her Shaeffer pen—the instrument of

> The swelling terror that would any moment
> Suddenly burst out and take from you
> Your husband, your children, your body, your life.
> You could see it, there, in your pen.

The poem implies her understanding that her pen—she
has no control over it—is the agent of her destruction.
Hughes's poem stands as a kind of explanation to her own
poem of the same title. "Is there no way out of the mind?"

she asks, in an abstract work whose colors are flat and stark. In this poem she surrounds herself with walls, colored white, grey, red and black: these are the colors of her desktop.

In Plath's "Apprehensions," the poet is made of "a terror / Of being wheeled off under crosses and a rain of pietàs." Its imagery is one of inchoate fear, which Hughes, in his poem, pins down to concrete objects: a desk, a typewriter, a pen; but the swelling terror is no less terrible for that. It is a fear he had highlighted before, in writing of how she confronted those fears in her journals: "When she came to talk to herself in these pages, that magnetic inner process seemed to engross all her attention, one way or another. And in her poems and stories, throughout this period, she felt her creative dependence on that same process as subjugation to a tyrant. It commandeered every proposal. . . ."

What flows out of her pen is what she draws from her "Dream Life." To Hughes, there was no real poem that did not flow from its author's internal truth. Plath first wrote the bleak "The Moon and the Yew Tree" after Hughes had set the subject for her as an exercise. Of the result, he has written: "It depressed me greatly. It's my suspicion that no poem can be a poem that is not a statement from the powers that control our life, the ultimate suffering and decision in us. . . . And I had no doubt this was a poem, and perhaps a great poem. She insisted it was an exercise on a theme." "Dream Life" attempts to delve—cautiously—into the powers that controlled her life, whose images surfaced in her poems. "Your sleep was a bloody shrine, it seemed," he writes (the last two words significant; the poem hesitates to fathom what it cannot know, to see the images behind her sleeping eyes; Hughes will only venture questions and guesses). He offers her father's gangrenous leg as a possible talisman of her "cult." He recalls, in his reference to her sleep-sea "clogged with corpses, / Death-camp atrocities, mass amputations," the shocking Nazi imagery of "Daddy," the body parts entombed in an icebox in her poem "The Surgeon at 2 a.m.": "Tomorrow they will swim / In vinegar like saints' relics," she wrote.

Her father, too, is transformed into the Ogre of "Fairy Tale." He is totem of both religion and myth; and he is, again, confused with Hughes, as he is her "Ogre lover." He is "the sum, crammed in one voodoo carcase, / Of all your earlier lovers"; but he is also, more significantly, the one who "glowed like a volcano," the one she must die each night to be with—her father. The skeleton key the poet finds to open the door of the Ogre's chamber creates an echo of her death, her last plunge toward her father. The poet only glimpses the Ogre and hears his roar when it's too late, when he has "tripped / Over your corpse."

"Fairy Tale" draws on many mythologies for its primal power. Plath is like the bride of Bluebeard:

> With your smile you listened to me
> Recounting the surprises of one or other
> Of the forty-eight chambers.
> Your happiness made the bed soft.
> A fairy tale? Yes.

As in "The Table," Hughes—Bluebeard—provides access to the Ogre as he helps to release her unconscious. At the same time her father's effigy is "burning in your tears / Like a thing of tar"—the tar baby from West African trickster tales used as a decoy to trap a thief (which Hughes and Plath, who had immersed themselves in Paul Radin's *African Folktales*, would have been acquainted with), who becomes stuck to the tar and trapped. It is a deadly decoy.

Sleep and death are inextricably linked in these poems, the one a foreshadowing of the other; and in "Dream Life," her "God of Sleep" is not a peaceful god but one whose "anatomy" is gathered from her hospital terrors, his stare the blue-eyed stare of her father, the electrodes still in her temples, all these years later.

> Each night you descended again
> Into the temple-crypt,
> That private, primal cave
> Under the public dome of father-worship.
> All night you lolled unconscious
> Over the crevasse
> Inhaling the oracle
> That spoke only conclusions.

It is she, prepared by this god, who is the feast of atonement. This last line leaves a question hanging on air: what was there to atone for?

Plath's character was one of extremes. This can be seen most clearly in the contrast between her *Journals* and *Letters Home*; she could not find a balance between her self-doubt, her suspicion, her fears, and the image of the perfect self, wife, mother, writer she chose to present to the world. The same was true of her marriage. Hughes, when she met him, had been nearly a god to her, perfect: now, as the marriage came up against difficulties, he would be transformed into the opposite, the agent of killing constriction found in "The Rabbit Catcher." The symbiosis between her fragmentation as a person and her growth as a poet is a terrible irony of her life and one that is recognized by Hughes in "Suttee," whose title is taken from the Hindu practice (now outlawed in India) of a wife's throwing herself—or being thrown—onto her husband's funeral pyre. "Suttee" underscores a point first made in "The Table": how, in Hughes's mind, his wish for her success as a writer made him the unwitting midwife to her death.

"Suttee" is, on the surface, a poem of birth, but a birth very different from that of their son. This birth is not a joyous event. It is a birth conceived in the "myth of your first death"—her suicide attempt in 1953:

> begotten
> By that savage act of yours committed
> On your body, battering your face to the concrete,
> Leaving yourself for dead
> (And hoping you were dead) for three days.

Three days: as Christ was in his tomb for three days, so is she resurrected in her own myth, but resurrected into death. What was being born was wanted and feared, like a real birth; and Hughes was "midwife": "I bowed there, as if over a page, / Coaxing it to happen," his image of himself a reflection of Plath bent over her blank page in "Portraits."

The flood of her "new myth," the black tangle of her father, of Hughes, of her impending death, that suffuses the *Ariel* poems "dissolves" him; and he sees what they have made:

> Our newborn
> Was your own self in flames.
> And the tongues of those flames were your tongues.

It is her own work. Yet still, still, despite his being engulfed by them, the poet is uncomprehending:

> "What are these flames?" was all I managed to say,
> Running with my midwife's hands
> Not to wash them, only to extinguish
> The screeching flames that fed on them and dripped from
> them.

It is a fearsome image of blood and fire, echoed by the jacket illustration, painted by Frieda Hughes, for the British hardback edition of *Birthday Letters*, radiant with abstract flames. In his portrait of the end of their marriage and the birth of her new, poetic self, they are trapped in a vacuum, the oxygen sucked out of them.

Happy memories are no salve for torments such as this. Turn back to "A Short Film," which eloquently describes the pain inflicted by something meant to engender only pleasure. "It was not meant to hurt," Hughes writes of the film; but instead, the film—of Plath, aged ten, "skipping and still skipping" (her eternal motion a mockery of life)—is "a dangerous weapon, a time-bomb, / Which is a kind of body-bomb, long-term, too." Here Hughes's free verse seems a kind of tormented explosion of the more formal rhythms of his earlier work: work in which already the notion of the frozen image as agent of damage existed. "Six Young Men", a poem of World War I, appeared in *The Hawk in the Rain*. It is a poem grown from seeing a photograph of six young friends, all dead in the trenches within months of each other.

> To regard this photograph might well dement,
> Such contradictory permanent horrors here
> Smile from the single exposure and shoulder out
> One's own body from its instant and heat.

It is almost as if he has been waiting for that "body-bomb," which, as he writes, maintains its impossibly slow detonation: he is Prometheus chained to the rock. The pain that lies in her grave is still inside the poet and their children, a pain that can be so easily reawakened, even after many years have passed. Present and past, in the final stanza, fuse in a bright flash, as they do in "The Pan." Watching the film, watching her childhood, it seems that her death is "something that has already happened."

9 ◦ "THE CAVE OF THUNDER"

AURELIA PLATH CAME to visit the family in the summer
of 1962, the same time that Plath and Hughes began keeping bees, as "The Bee God" relates. But those bees drew her
ever closer to her father, and Hughes began to pull away
from Plath, drawn into an affair with Assia Wevill, as
"Dreamers" tells. Plath lashed against her Devon confine-
ment: even "The Beach" offered her no solace, its British
bleakness only "the reverse of dazzling Nauset." Hughes and
Plath separated in late summer, and by October 1962, Plath,
now writing her *Ariel* poems, found a flat for herself in Lon-

don. Hughes returned briefly to Court Green in December, "Robbing Myself," as he says, of what little he had left there.

IN JUNE 1962, the Hugheses began keeping bees. Plath wrote to her mother—who was planning to visit them that summer—on the fifteenth of the month about the local "bee meetings" attended by the rector, the midwife and others:

> We all wore masks and it was thrilling. It is expensive to start beekeeping (over $50 outlay) but Mr Pollard let us have an old hive for nothing, which we painted white and green, and today he brought over a swarm of docile Italian hybrid bees we ordered and installed them. We placed the hive in a sheltered out-of-the-way spot in the orchard. . . . The bees were furious from being in a box. Ted had only put a handkerchief over his head where the hat should go in the bee-mask, and the bees crawled into his hair, and he flew off with half-a-dozen stings. I didn't get stung at all, and when I went back to the hive later, I was delighted to see bees entering with pollen sacs full and leaving with them empty—at least I think that's what they were doing.

For Plath, this was more than a country pursuit: her fascination with the bees was a reflection of her obsession with her father and his knowledge of bees (even in his schooldays he had been known to his fellows as *Bienenkönig*, the Bee King). In her private journals, the connection with her father is made explicit; of the same scene she describes to her mother above, she writes:

. . . I was aware of bees buzzing and stalling before my face. The veil seemed hallucinatory. I could not see it for moments at a time. Then I became aware I was in a bone-stiff trance, intolerably tense, and shifted round to where I could see better. "spirit of my dead father, protect me!" I arrogantly prayed. . . .

In October, Plath wrote her remarkable sequence of bee poems—beginning with "The Bee Meeting"—as well as the sinister, angry "Daddy"; its presence shadows "The Bee God."

Hughes explicitly links the bees and her father, making Plath once again into a religious figure, this time not a priestess of a cult but the abbess of a nunnery. He reflects the first of her bee poems, "The Bee Meeting," which is full of images of fear and of herself as a kind of religious adept or sacrifice. "Now I am milkweed silk, the bees will not notice. / They will not smell my fear, my fear, my fear," she writes. In her poem the rector is a "man in black," as her father is in "Daddy." She is led, as if to her death, through bean flowers with "black eyes and leaves like bored hearts." By the end of the poem, when the queen is revealed, Plath the poet is "exhausted," and looks through the trees: "Whose is that long white box in the grove, what have they accomplished, why am I cold."

In "The Bee Meeting," the hive becomes a coffin, and this imagery of doom runs through "The Bee God": "I saw I had given you something / That had carried you off in a cloud of gutturals . . ." Just as when he gave her the table, Hughes is responsible; but only now does he hear how the bees' buzzing echoes the Germanic sound of her father's voice.

Here again, Hughes and Otto Plath are associated: "But when you put on your white regalia, / Your veil, your gloves, I never guessed a wedding."

The bees' home is a "cave of thunder," ominous: and Hughes begins to be stung by a swarm, their stings like bullets, like the electrodes whose volts had once tormented Plath. She attempts to rescue him (flinging off her "ghost-proof" gloves, for they are of little use in protecting her, or him, from the Bee God), but she cannot. The bees are "fanatics for their God, the God of the Bees"—her father. Again, here are the "fixed stars," underwater, that ring at the end of her poem "Words": Hughes seems to wish to bind their beliefs with his language, to allow them, in this way, a kind of shared fate.

The next poem, "Being Christlike," also confronts her father and her fate. "You did not want to be Christlike," it begins—sacrificed for her father, by her father, as Christ could be seen, at a very basic level, to have been sacrificed by his Father for humanity. Christ, too, questioned the sacrifice: in his agony he prayed, saying, "Father, if thou be willing, remove this cup from me: nevertheless not my will, but thine, be done"—though he, too, "walked / In the love of [His] father." Her mother only tries to tempt her away from her father, as Satan tempted Christ:

> When her great hooded eyes lowered
> Their moon so close
> > Promising the earth you saw
> > Your fate and you cried
> > *Get thee behind me.*

His language recalls one of her final poems, "Edge," with the moon "staring from her hood of bone." But while drawing these parallels between Plath and Christ, Hughes rejects them, not once, but three times—as Peter thrice denied Christ.

> You wanted
> To be with your father
> In wherever he was. And your body
> Barred your passage. And your family
> Who were your flesh and blood
> Burdened it. And a god
> That was not your father
> Was a false god. But you did not
> Want to be Christlike.

A series of "and's"—the rhythm of the poem incantatory, as if it is a kind of liturgy—leads to a "but": she is not Christlike, but her father is her god, and she must die to be with him.

For Plath, the time before her father's death had become idealized; in the years before his death, they had lived by the sea: "The center of my whole early life was ocean and boats," she would write in late summer to the poet Richard Murphy. Images of the sea, of her father-god beneath it, suffuse her work.

> Daddy, I have had to kill you.
> You died before I had time—
> Marble-heavy, a bag full of God,
> Ghastly statue with one gray toe
> Big as a Frisco seal

> And a head in the freakish Atlantic
> Where it pours bean green over blue
> In the waters off beautiful Nauset . . .

she wrote in "Daddy." Sometimes (as in the earlier "The Earthenware Head"), it is the poet who seems to be submerged. At
this time—the autumn of 1962—she froze her father there,
and many of her other poems written at this time ("Medusa,"
"Lesbos," "Lyonnesse") are full of images of drowning, of an
enclosing sea, its "clear, green, quite breathable atmosphere."

It is as if she craves and fears the sea, a craving and fear
Hughes confronts in "The Beach." This is a poem that can be
linked to the miry gloom of "Error," in its bald revelation of
her unhappiness with England, its grey raininess "the reverse
of dazzling Nauset." She had expressed her dissatisfaction
with the English sea in "Ocean 1212-W":

> Now and then, when I grow nostalgic about my ocean child-
> hood—the wauling of gulls and the smell of salt, somebody
> solicitous will bundle me into a car and drive me to the near-
> est briny horizon. After all, in England, no place is what?
> more than seventy miles from the sea. "There," I'll be told,
> "there it is." As if the sea were a great oyster on a plate that
> could be served up, tasting just the same, at any restaurant
> the world over. I get out of the car, I stretch my legs, I sniff.
> The sea. But that is not it, that is not it at all.

To her mother, more prosaically, she had written: "There is
something depressingly mucky about English sea resorts. Of
course, the weather is hardly ever sheer fair, so most people
are in woollen suits and coats and tinted plastic raincoats.

The sand is muddy and dirty. . . . My favorite beach in the world is Nauset, and my heart aches for it. . . ."

The poem reveals too, as "The Rabbit Catcher" does, how Hughes and Plath are opposites. "You lashed for release, like a migrant eel in November," he writes. What she yearns for, however, is not available:

> You craved like oxygen
> American earlier summers, yourself burnt dark—
> Some prophecy mislaid, somehow.

What she craves is not just different weather but her idealized past. The dourness of England, where every vehicle is a hearse, "the traffic procession a hushing leftover / Of Victoria's perpetual funeral Sunday," only accentuates the distance from her "flashing thunderclap miles / Of Nauset surf," and her distance from her husband. (The funeral imagery, here, is perhaps an echo of their experiences as mourners at a neighbor's funeral at the end of June, which she sketched in "Johnny Panic" and which she alluded to in "Berck-Plage," written just afterwards. Plath, it should be recalled, did not attend the funeral of her father.)

The poet believes he can provide a replacement, that he could "set inside your head another jewel," just as he imagined he could make her understand his country gods. But his "gentlest electric shock" will do no more good than the electric shocks she suffered at the hands of psychiatrists. His Avalon, a "brilliant original for Hilliard's miniatures" at Woolacombe Sands, proves nothing of the sort: the sea is "stunned after the rain, / Unperforming"; "the flip of an ocean fallen / Dream-face down," and his wife will not leave the car. "You sat behind your mask, inaccessible— / Staring towards the ocean that had failed you."

It is as if this disappointing sea stands for the past ocean she can never recover; and instead of her dream-sea, her dream-father, her dream-self, there is the terror of "the other face, the real, staring upwards." Nothing he could do would reach her desire. The real sea for her is locked away forever. "Ocean 1212-W" ends: "And this is how it stiffens, my vision of that seaside childhood. My father died, we moved inland. Whereupon those nine first years of my life sealed themselves off like a ship in a bottle—beautiful, inaccessible, obsolete, a fine, white flying myth."

Aurelia Plath arrived in late June 1962; and it was around this time that Ted Hughes first made contact with Assia Wevill in London. "Sulferous adulteries grieve in a dream," Plath wrote in "The Other" in July; also that month, while Aurelia Plath was still staying with them but Hughes was in London, Sylvia ransacked his study and burned his letters, finding, in her poem-version of events, "Burning the Letters," "a name with black edges"—Assia's name—confirmation of her fears. In mid-July, she made Hughes leave Court Green.

"Dreamers" charts the beginning of this relationship, which would end in 1969 with Wevill's suicide. Once again the key ingredient is a kind of helplessness, an obedience to Fate. Hughes does not excuse himself: the last line of the poem accepts responsibility for his actions. "That moment the dreamer in me / Fell in love with her, and I knew it." That notwithstanding, all the characters in this story are now part of an irresistible myth:

> The Fable she carried
> Requisitioned you and me and her,
> Puppets for its performance.

In *Bitter Fame*, Anne Stevenson recounts how Plath told Suzette Macedo, a friend both of Plath and Assia Wevill, that she had "conjured up Assia."

In this poem, Assia, for Plath, carries within her the essence of something she felt in herself, or something she desired. In "Lady Lazarus," Plath wrote of her skin "bright as a Nazi lampshade," but it was Assia Wevill who was Jewish, who was a real refugee, whose "many-blooded beauty" was a "dream of your dream-self." It is as if, in this poem, Assia is a figure Plath has drawn from her subconscious, the dark fount of her work. Of Assia, Hughes writes: "Her father / Doctor to the Bolshoi Ballet"—she had all the glamour that Plath, in her college-girl incarnation, had chased; the European sophistication she herself could never achieve.

But of Assia he writes: "she was helpless too," an actor in the play, speaking a script she had not written. Later, he would write that Assia was as drawn to Plath as Plath was to Assia.

> She had too much so with a smile you took some.
> Of everything she had you had
> Absolutely nothing, so you took some.
> At first, just a little,

begins Hughes's poem entitled "The Other," one of the poems about Assia that appears at the end of Hughes's

New Selected Poems, 1957–1994. Too much privilege, too much love, too much poetry—everything. The two women are drawn to each other as if in a dream, and so "Dreamers" continues, "None of us could wake up. / Nightmare looked out at the poppies." (Plath had written "Poppies in July" late in the month, too: "little hell-flames," she called them, longing for "opiates, your nauseous capsules.") At the end of the poem is again a single animal image: Wevill's dream of a fish.

> After a single night under our roof
> She told her dream. A giant fish, a pike
> Had a globed, golden eye, and in that eye
> A throbbing human foetus—
> You were astonished, maybe envious.

Hughes voices no judgment—"I refused to interpret." He seems to wash his hands: but he sees clearly what the dream means. If Assia is Plath's dream-self, then Hughes's dream-self is destined, as he sees it, to fall in love with her.

Plath had lost his heart, it appears; but as Hughes writes in his poem entitled "Totem," she painted hearts, everywhere. Aurelia Plath noted when she arrived: "The welcome I received when I arrived . . . was heartwarming. The threshold to the guest room I was to occupy had an enamelled pink heart and a garland of flowers painted on it. . . ." In her children's bedrooms, Plath had decorated their furniture with enamel paint of flowers and hearts, "an eight-year-old's flowers" (the age she was when her father died); "but mostly hearts." The poem reflects how her own writing, at this time—not just her artwork—was filled with images of blood and beating hearts.

> ... when
> The balled
> Pulp of your heart
> Confronts its small
> Mill of silence
>
> How you jump—
> Trepanned veteran ...

she wrote in "Cut," in October; "Medusa," an embittered poem addressed to her mother, has

> Your stooges
> Plying their wild cells in my keel's shadow,
> Pushing by like hearts,
> Red stigmata at the very center ...

There are also the berries which are "black sweet blood mouthfuls" in "Ariel."

It is almost as if her work, drawn from her very veins, is stained with her blood; *Ariel*, Hughes writes, her "heart-coloured book—the empty mask / Of your Genie." According to Frazer in *The Golden Bough*, totems are "the receptacle in which a man keeps his life." Such totems are generally animals—like the hare in the bowl in Plath's "Totem"—but here the hearts, as the receptacle and symbol of Plath's life, seem equally appropriate. The hearts ward nothing off but are "the track of your panic":

The splashes of a wound.

The spoor
Of the one that caught and devoured you.

On the surface, the heart is an image of vibrant life: Hughes sees it rather as an emblem of life's fragility, as full of death potential as the "glitter of cleavers" in Plath's "Totem," in which

The world is blood-hot and personal

Dawn says, with its blood-flush.
There is no terminus, only suitcases

Out of which the same self unfolds like a suit
Bald and shiny, with pockets of wishes . . .

The strains in their marriage were becoming unbearable: Plath and Hughes agreed to separate. First, however, they would go to Ireland in September, in part with the idea of finding Plath a cottage there. They stayed in Cleggan, in Connemara, with Richard Murphy—a poet Plath had met in judging the 1962 Guinness competition at the Cheltenham Literary Festival. By the time Plath returned to England— she and Hughes had gone their separate ways in Ireland— she was determined to get a divorce, meeting with her solicitor in London on 25 September. Hughes, now in London, stayed with Al Alvarez, or sometimes in a flat owned by Dido Merwin; he sent Plath money. To her friends, she built a picture of herself as a wronged woman, a deserted wife;

this is a notion that Hughes seems cautiously to explore in "The Blackbird."

It is a portrait of his wife as a divided self: "You were the jailer of your murderer." She "played" at feeling safe; yet her "sleepy looks," slid at him, seem duplicitous: she takes the nourishment he offers while underneath she has another agenda. She would tell Richard Murphy that Hughes had "deserted her" in Ireland, and Hughes, for years after her death, would be trapped in her version of events, taken up later by others who saw her as a victim of Hughes's abandonment.

> The lawn lay like the pristine waiting page
>   Of a prison report.
> Who would write what upon it
>   I never gave a thought.

A pen—her pen?—was already writing "wrong is right, right wrong." Her rage is that of a prisoner, and indeed, in "The Jailer," written in October (one of the poems that Hughes kept out of *Ariel* in 1965), she will depict Hughes as the keeper of the keys:

> My night sweats grease his breakfast plate.
> The same placard of blue fog is wheeled into position
> With the same trees and headstones.
> Is that all he can come up with,
> The rattler of keys?

Perhaps "The Blackbird"'s first line turns her accusation back upon herself.

Hughes came to collect his things from Court Green in October and went back to London. Plath was determined to rebuild her life alone. She wrote to her mother: "I haven't the strength to see you for some time. The horror of what you saw and what I saw you see last summer is between us and I cannot face you again until I have a new life."

With Hughes gone from the house, she rose "in the blue hour" to write. This autumn of 1962, through until the end of the year, was miraculously creative for her: the *Ariel* poems arrived, one after another, as can be traced through the *Collected Poems*. She wrote to her mother: "Every morning, when my sleeping pill wears off, I am up about five, in my study with coffee, writing like mad—have managed a poem a day before breakfast. All book poems. Terrific stuff, as if domesticity had choked me." Four days later, 16 October, she wrote: "I am a writer . . . I am a genius of a writer; I have it in me. I am writing the best poems of my life; they will make my name."

Hughes has written of her confidence at this time: "The subject matter [of the *Ariel* poems] didn't alarm her. Why should it, when *Ariel* was doing the very thing it had been created and liberated to do? In each poem, the horror is encountered head on, and the angel is mastered and brought to terms." At the very end of October, she abandoned her plan to winter in Ireland and decided to move to London. She found a flat at 23 Fitzroy Road in Primrose Hill—a house adorned with a blue plaque, for Yeats had lived there. She wrote to her mother, delightedly, that it was "just right . . . with three bedrooms upstairs, lounge, kitchen and bath downstairs and a balcony garden!" "Living apart from Ted is wonderful," she told her mother in early November; "I am no longer in his shadow, and it is heaven to be liked for myself alone, knowing what I want."

She closed Court Green on 12 December and drove to London with the children. "Robbing Myself" recounts a visit that Hughes must have made to their old home after the "cosmic disaster" of their parting. His recollection of the visit is elegiac; uncovering his wintering potatoes, he notes: "They seemed almost warm in their straw. / They exhaled the sweetness / Of the hopes I'd dug into them." It is a "secret family," happy where his own was not. Something of his hope survives in the fruit he has grown: "My summer intact in spite of everything." The house itself, with its jewel colors—the twilight sapphire, the front room a "crimson chamber," the "crimson cataract" of the carpet on the stair—seems a treasure of hope; and yet there is, in all that red, a bloody echo of distress.

There is distress, too, in the closing image of the casket:

> I peered awhile, as through the keyhole,
> Into my darkened, hushed, safe casket
> From which (I did not know)
> I had already lost the treasure.

The casket is a jewel box but also a coffin; and the protection it offers is illusory. But Hughes is all unknowing, his parenthetical ignorance regretful and apologetic.

10 ◇ "The Shock of Her Words from Nowhere"

SYLVIA PLATH COMMITTED suicide in the early morning of Monday, 11 February 1963. From the end of 1962, she had been living on her own in London and writing the poems that, as she said, "would make her name." Separated from his wife, Hughes's poems no longer present images of her life in the way they do in the earlier sections of the book—although "The Inscription," which sees her visiting him in his London flat, is an exception. Rather, works like "Blood and Innocence," "Costly Speech" and "Night-Ride on Ariel" confront her death and its psychic aftermath, envisioning the images evoked by her late work as a kind of "court" in which Hughes, along with Otto and Aurelia Plath, stand helpless, accused of terrible crimes and unable to defend themselves against this powerful voice from beyond the grave.

AT THIS POINT—the very end of 1962—there is a decided shift in the tone of *Birthday Letters*. Hughes and Plath have separated; he is no longer a participant in her daily life, although, of course, he remains involved with her because of Frieda and Nicholas. But the narrative here takes an abstract turn, and it is this change that prompts speculation as to whether these poems might have been composed later than those in the first three-quarters of the book, nearer to the end of the poet's life. There is a more direct engagement on the poet's part with the forces of Fate, with Plath and her parents: as if he now anticipates crossing the border that separates them.

"Blood and Innocence," for instance, is a kind of meditation on the demons that stalked Plath (as they were said to have stalked St. Anthony in the wilderness, a temptation alluded to here). The poet refers to a nameless "they," who demanded "it."

> In the wilderness
> Between the locusts and the honey
> They demanded it. Oh, no problem.
> If that's all you want,
> You said, and you gave it.

Who "they" were, and what "it" was, perhaps was not clear to Plath, either; and that was part of her suffering. "They," in the first stanza, might be said to be the "peanut-crunchers," the gawping spectators she alluded to in "Lady Lazarus," the audience for which her public self always performed, striving for the perfection she might have imagined was "it." Then "they" demand more, until finally

> They wanted
> That—that other. Oh, no problem,
> Why on earth didn't you say.
> Daddy unearthed. And the nine-year-old howl
> Come of age
> Round his good ankle, a cart-rope—
> Hauling him into the light.

Her willingness to give, in the first stanza of this poem, results in her "electrocution," her shock therapy; and in the second stanza, in her first attempt at suicide, when she is "washed and reborn only in your own [blood]." It isn't enough; in the third stanza her father is unearthed, and she is her wounded, childhood self, "hauling him into the light," the "hoof-like thunder on the moor" an echo of *Ariel*—which was the name of the horse she was learning to ride as well as the embodiment of her poetic self. She seeks acknowledgment and approval ("How is that, / Is that OK? you asked"), but at the end of the poem there are only two faces in the crowd that obliterate all the others:

> . . . Mummy Daddy Mummy Daddy—
> Daddy Daddy Daddy Daddy
> Mummy Mummy

—no period, no end, on and on and on.

Even in a poem like "The Inscription," in which there is contact between the poet and his subject, there is the removal first hinted at in "The Pan": this is the only other poem in the book in the third, rather than the second, person. That cold winter—the worst since 1947—she comes to his flat, where he is, it seems, lost without her, a castaway.

> Cold
> His morning flat in bright sun,
> Sooted in Soho. Brick light. New light.
> Cargo-dumped empty lightness.
> Packing-case emptiness, lightness.

She wanted to see "the islet or reef or rock he'd ended up on." The poem is swamped by a joint confusion emanating from both of them: she looks at his life like "a dog in a new home," "like a dog . . . that smelt a rat," but she is also begging for a reassurance that he cannot offer because he does not understand what she wants: "What kind of faith did she mean?" The "red Oxford Shakespeare / That she had ripped to rags" she suddenly sees restored—"resurrected." But what might be a reminder of a time when "happiness / Was invulnerable" strikes her like a "fatal bullet." He returns, at the end of this poem, to the image of wounding that closes "The Shot": the missile that kills her having passed through him first. As for the text of the inscription in the Shakespeare, it is kept hidden from the reader; but its absence—its erasure—calls to mind another inscription, the one on her gravestone. It was also to suffer that fate, although at other hands.

At first, in London, Plath seemed busy and productive. *The New Yorker* accepted "Lyonnesse" for publication; the *Atlantic Monthly* took "The Arrival of the Bee Box" and "Wintering." She wrote "Ocean 1212-W," her lovely evocation of her seaside childhood, for the BBC *Writers on Themselves* series; for *Punch* she wrote "America! America!", a recollection of her schooldays. But as Christmas approached, her spirits became less buoyant; she was anxious about money and the future of her writing. Al Alvarez, who was friendly with her at this time, has written of her then:

> She seemed different. Her hair, which she usually wore in a tight, schoolmistressy bun, was loose. It hung straight to her waist like a tent, giving her pale face and gaunt figure a curiously desolate, rapt air, like a priestess emptied out by the rites of her cult. When she walked in front of me down the hall passage and up the stairs to her apartment . . . her hair gave off a strong smell, sharp as an animal's. The children were already in bed upstairs and the flat was silent. It was newly painted, white and chill . . . rather beautiful in its chaste, stripped-down way, but cold, very cold, and the oddments of flimsy Christmas decoration made it seem doubly forlorn. . . . For the unhappy, Christmas is always a bad time.

The weather was dreadful; Plath and the children caught colds which turned to flu. *The Bell Jar* was turned down by a couple of American publishers; and, when it was published in England (under the pseudonym Victoria Lucas) on 23 January 1963, it received a somewhat lukewarm reception. She was seeing a psychiatrist, Dr. Horder, who had prescribed anti-depressants.

> Dying
> Is an art, like everything else.
> I do it exceptionally well.
>
> I do it so it feels like hell.
> I do it so it feels real.
> I guess you could say I've a call.

She had written these lines, in "Lady Lazarus," at the end of October the previous year; on the morning of Monday, 11 February 1963, a nurse sent by Dr. Horder found her dead in the Fitzroy Road flat, her head in the gas oven. She had protected her children, in their bedroom, from the fumes by pushing wet towels up against the cracks in the doors and leaving their window wide open. She had left milk and bread by their cots.

Birthday Letters does not confront her death explicitly: no single poem relates how Hughes was told of his wife's suicide. He learned of her death from Suzette Macedo, who had heard from Plath's friend Jillian Becker (in the days before her death, Jillian and her husband Gerry had looked after Sylvia, and she had stayed with them; they had been reluctant to allow her to go home alone). But "Telos" is the Greek word for "end," and it is this poem that seems to confront her own end, setting it against all the "Alphas" of her life, "Alpha" the beginning, "Alpha" the success for which she was always striving: her unreachable version of a perfected self. Dorothea Krook, recalling what it was like to teach her, noted:

> She wrote for me, almost every week, an excellent paper: long, full, cogently argued, carefully written—everything that

goes to make an alpha paper. She got her alphas, and I praised the papers as they deserved, yet somewhere in the depths of my mind there was a reservation. . . . I felt in her a certain strain or tension about these essays: arising from an anxiety (I supposed) to "do them well," to excel, to distinguish herself; and not just now and then, but consistently, without lapse.

In "America! America!", collected in *Johnny Panic and the Bible of Dreams*, Plath herself had written—the month before she died—that "The girls' guidance counselor diagnosed my problem straight off. I was just too dangerously brainy. My high, pure string of straight A's might without proper extracurricular tempering, snap me into the void. . . ." No matter what she does, in this poem she is snapped into a void of Alphas. In the poem, she runs from herself but never escapes, the "Furies of Alpha" pursuing her. Hughes accepts the irony that "Alpha" was achieved at the end—after her death, when her poetic work (which she had, during her last months, been sending to magazines with less success than might be imagined) was recognized for what it was:

> And hurling yourself beyond Omega
> fell
> Into a glittering Universe of Alpha.

This "glittering Universe" must have been hard and cold for those she left behind. Plath's poem "Brasilia" imagines a race of "super-people," "with torsos of steel / Winged elbows and eyeholes," "people like light-rays" who appear to embrace, or have within them, "The glory / The power, the glory." Would they be bereft of human feeling, these people? Plath often seemed unaware of how her work, dragged out of not only her own life but the lives of those around her, might have affected those close to her who were depicted in it, a subject already discussed in relation to "The 59th Bear" (and while she published *The Bell Jar* under a pseudonym, this was more because she did not feel the novel was as good as the work she published under her own name than to protect, for instance, her mother—who was deeply hurt by the portrayal of Esther Greenwood's mother).

Hughes's poem "Brasilia" transforms her into one of her "super-people," returning after her death—embodied by her work—"in your steel helm."

> Helpless
> We were dragged into court, your arena,
> Gagged in the hush.

The "three sentences" she passed were those on her father, her mother, her husband, condemned in her verse; and yet her condemnation comes out of her "great love." Her wish was for relationships to be perfect: if they were not that, they were simply the obverse. "The blade of lightning" that was her sentence was also what "snatched you up into Heaven": killed her, but also canonized her as an artist. The "Colosseum flunkeys" who carry out her father's body echo the image of him as a broken statue in "The Colossus"; and her work, like that of a Roman emperor, or the conquistador Cortes, who wrecked the Aztec empire in 1521, builds an "empire"—of images. Images in which there is no resolution, which weep "tearlessly," or cry out "dry-eyed."

The "bronze of immortal poesy," as Hughes writes in the next poem, "The Cast," was her weapon:

> . . . Cupid's bow
> Modified in Peenemünde
> Via Brueghel

—the wounding arrow of love reforged in the deadly rocket factory of Nazi Germany and colored with Brueghel's apocalyptic shades. It was unleashed against her father:

> . . . your cry of deliverance
> Materialized in his
> Sacrificed silence.

Only in her death is he "eased out of your old wound" like shrapnel:

> Healed you vanished
> From the monumental
> Immortal form
> Of your injury: your Daddy's
> Body full of your arrows.

The price of her healing is her vanishing—and her blood. It may be possible, too, to read into this poem an echo of Plath's own confusion of Otto and Hughes: it is hard not to recall Hughes's long silence about his relationship with

Plath—as he was often depicted as the villain of the piece—in the lines

> Helpless
> As weightless, voiceless as lifeless,
> He had to hear it all
> Driven into him up to the feathers,
> Had to stand the stake
> Not through his heart, but upright
> In the town square, him tied to it
> Stark naked full of those arrows . . .

The words ring with a pain that seems more than an imaginative projection of the long-dead Otto's pain. As Otto could never answer his daughter's accusations, so her husband chose for so many years a "voiceless" near silence.

Hughes, in these poems, is forging a mythology that fuses his vision and hers. He takes all the old stories—Greek myth, Aztec sacrifice, astrological prophecy, Christian belief—and uses them in service of his story and Plath's story. He even uses nursery rhyme, as in "The Ventriloquist," whose urgent, primitive, rocking rhythm has the dreadful force and hidden menace of "Rockabye, baby"—or of Plath's "Daddy." The doll doubles for Plath and follows them as Hughes and Plath flee through the woods like Hansel and Gretel. As in "Brasilia" and "The Cast," we end in a court as the doll passes judgment:

> The doll broke in that night
> Killed you and was gone

Screaming at the stars to look
And see Justice done.

The literary legacy of that "doll" was not an easy one. As has already been discussed, even in her lifetime Plath's work, drawing so pointedly and explicitly as it does on her own life and pain, caused hurt and confusion to those around her. The two sides of her personality are strikingly displayed in the contrast between the *Journals*, first published in 1982, and *Letters Home*, published in 1975 by Aurelia Plath as a contrast to the impression of Plath and her relationship to her family given by such work as the *Ariel* poems—collected and published by Hughes in 1965—and *The Bell Jar*, published in Britain the January before she died. Janet Malcolm's significant study of the biographical "industry" that surrounds Plath, *The Silent Woman* (first published in *The New Yorker* in August 1993, and then appearing in book form the following year), details the difficult negotiations that took place not only between Hughes and Plath's putative biographers, but also between Hughes and Aurelia Plath over such matters as the American publication of *The Bell Jar*. In December 1978, Aurelia Plath wrote to Judith Kroll, whose analysis of Plath's poetry, *Chapters in a Mythology*, had appeared in 1976:

[Sylvia] made use of everything and often transmuted gold into lead. . . . These emotions in another person would dissipate with time, but with Sylvia they were written at the moment of intensity to become ineradicable as an epigraph engraved on a tombstone. . . . She has posthumous fame—at what price to her children, to those of us who loved her so dearly and whom she has trapped into her past. The love remains—and the hurt. There is no escape for us.

"Costly Speech" is a reflection of this love and hurt, and the struggles that took place over Plath's memory and legacy. Though she was published in her lifetime, Plath's fame is largely posthumous. The groundswell began only six days after her death, when on 17 February the *Observer*, whose poetry editor was Al Alvarez, ran four of the poems she had written in the last weeks of her life. In April, *London Magazine* ran seven poems and *Atlantic Monthly* two; in August, *The New Yorker* published seven. Many of these poems had been rejected by these magazines before her death.

Hughes assumed the difficult role of her literary executor: difficult both because of his relationship to her and the nature of the material she produced. "Costly Speech" looks specifically over the American publication of *The Bell Jar*, by Harper & Row, in 1971. In a letter written to Janet Malcolm after the initial publication of *The Silent Woman* in *The New Yorker* in 1993, Hughes defends the American publication of the novel. Originally it was not to be published in the States, to spare Aurelia Plath's feelings. She, understandably, had found Plath's portrayal of Esther Greenwood's mother—and the portrayal of other characters in the book, including the writer based on Prouty—extremely distressing. In 1971, she had written to the American publisher, "Practically every character in *The Bell Jar* represents someone—often in caricature—whom Sylvia loved; each person had given freely of time, thought, affection, and, in one case, financial help during those agonizing six months of breakdown in 1953. . . . As this book stands by itself, it represents the basest ingratitude."

As Hughes wrote to Malcolm, it was discovered in 1970 that works published overseas—but not in the United States—by a U.S. citizen who then dies, go out of copyright seven years after the author's death. Unless *The Bell Jar* was published in the United States under the aegis of the Plath estate, it would be pirated anyway. Hughes wrote to Malcolm, "Aurelia accepted the fact: the novel would appear in the U.S. no matter what any of us thought about it. The only question was: who was going to publish it and own the copyright? If not us, then somebody else. Aurelia agreed it had better be us."

Hughes raised this point to counter Malcolm's original assertion that he had wished to publish *The Bell Jar* in the United States in order to finance the purchase of a house. This notion is supported by a letter, written by Hughes to Aurelia Plath in 1970 and mentioning the possibility of the purchase, held in the Plath archive of the Lilly Library in Bloomington, Indiana—missing from the archive is Hughes's letter stating his decision to drop the idea of the purchase when Aurelia objected to publication. When the Harper & Row edition of *The Bell Jar* appeared in the United States in the spring of 1971, it found both critical acclaim and swift sales. Robert Scholes, in the *New York Times Book Review*, said that the book "is literature" and that it "is finding its audience, and will hold it." It remained on the best-seller lists for twenty-four weeks, and the paperback edition brought out the following year went through three editions (the first of 375,000 copies) in a month.

It was this publication of *The Bell Jar* that gave rise to Aurelia Plath publishing *Letters Home*; and so, as Malcolm calls it, Hughes's "corrective to her corrective" of publishing the *Journals*. Once again, Hughes's poetic version of events has an appearance of helplessness and naïveté: it is Plath who seems to act, even from beyond the grave. The "guards" who had charge of her work—her brother, her mother, Hughes—were "simple"

> Ignorant how your left hand wrote in a mirror
> Opposite your right,
> Half of you mortified, half of you smiling.

"Costly Speech" shows Hughes's defensiveness. Hughes's experience with *The Bell Jar* wasn't the only one of its kind. As Plath became the subject of biographers, Hughes became embroiled (or chose to avoid possible embroilment) in lawsuits over use of her material and allegations made—a letter he wrote to the *Independent* in April 1989 is a catalogue of these wrongs. He even entered a dispute over copyright ownership of some of Plath's early poems when the first biography of Plath, by Edward Butscher, appeared in the States. So it seems appropriate that the language of the last stanza of "Costly Speech" is financial, exploitative; publishers are sensitive to the main chance rather than to the true cost of the course they pursue. The guards of her work are

> . . . ignorant of the spooky chemistry
> Of opportunity, of boom and bust
> In the optic nerve of editors.

Ignorant of the tumblers in the lock
Of US Copyright Law
Which your dead fingers so deftly unpicked.

Hughes, despite his role as editor (along with, for the *Journals*, Frances McCullough), is somehow absent even as he is present: "my own airier words, conscripted, reporting for duty, / Forbade it and forbade it." The fact that what exactly was forbidden in this poem—despite the repetition of "forbade it"—is not named, makes the wrong done, the hurt caused, huge and cosmic. Hughes appears to reproach his earlier, airier, heedless self.

Earlier guardians, if so they might be called, are brought to book in "Night-Ride on Ariel," which strongly reflects several of Plath's late poems and identifies the women who influenced her life. The moon was her baleful influence: its pale face appears in so many of her poems, from the "moon-glint" of "Faun" and the "moon's celestial onion" of "Soliloquy of the Solipsist" (both written in 1956) to the moon that stares "from her hood of bone" in "Edge," the last work in the *Collected Poems*. It seemed to pull her to it as it does the tides, and in "Night-Ride," Hughes names the forces that drew her as the moon did. Hughes, in discussing Plath's work, identified the moon as her baleful muse. Of her later poems he wrote: "there is a strange muse, bald, white, and wild, in her 'hood of bone,' floating over a landscape like that of the primitive painters, a burningly luminous vision of a Paradise. A Paradise which is at the same time eerily frightening, an unalterably spot-lit vision of death." Here he links its image with the women Plath looked to for guidance—and also, at some level, resented: "all the old ladies I ever knew wanted to teach me something," she wrote with throwaway irony in *The Bell Jar.*

First there is her mother, "mourning and remaking herself" after her husband's death. "It was always Monday in her mind," he writes. Mondays were black days for Plath, as Hughes himself remarks in his notes to her *Collected Poems,* and his words here echo the shuttered, brittle women's world she conjured in her 1962 poem "An Appearance":

> From her lips ampersands and percent signs
> Exit like kisses.
> It is Monday in her mind: morals
>
> Launder and present themselves.

"The Everlasting Monday" (1957) calls up "the hell of Mondays" "worked" by the moon's man; he is "Fireless, seven chill seas chained to his ankle."

In "An Appearance," love is a "red material," "issuing from the steel needle that flies so blindingly"; in "Night-Ride," her mother's love has the same potential to do damage, as Aurelia Plath makes

> . . . you dance with her magnetic eye
> On your Daddy's coffin
> (There in the family film).

Her mother is the first of four women who will appear in this poem, an echo of Plath's 1957 poem "The Disquieting

Muses" (its own imagery, and title, drawn from the work of the surrealist painter Giorgio de Chirico):

> Mother, whose witches always, always
> Got baked into gingerbread, I wonder
> Whether you saw them, whether you said
> Words to rid me of those three ladies
> Nodding by night around my bed,
> Mouthless, eyeless, with stitched bald head.

"The Disquieting Muses" and "Night-Ride on Ariel" also reflect both Plath's and Hughes's reading of Robert Graves's *The White Goddess*, which argues that the true poetic gift is derived from a matriarchal moon-muse-goddess.

Olive Higgins Prouty, Plath's benefactor, who paid for both her education at Smith and her psychiatric treatment, is given a dainty wand of beams suitable for the romantic novelist she was. The cost of its sparkle was the effort Plath felt obliged to put into being her best self for Prouty, an effort evident in a letter she wrote to her in 1950, her first year at Smith:

> I wonder . . . if I have revealed even a small part of my love for Smith. There are so many little details that are so wonderful—the lights of the houses against the night sky, the chapel bells on Sunday afternoon, the glimpse of Paradise from my window. . . . I just want you to understand that you are responsible, in a sense, for the formation of an individual, and I am fortunate enough to be that person.

Prouty had been so pleased with this letter that she had it copied. "I want others to read it," she wrote to Plath.

Ruth Beuscher, the psychiatrist she met at McLean, put Plath back together while also enabling her to analyze herself in a way that, in Hughes's view, was destructive. As she wrote in her journal in late December 1958, after a session with Beuscher,

> So how do I express my hate for my mother? In my deepest emotions I think of her as an enemy: somebody who "killed" my father, my first male ally in the world. She is a murderess of maleness. I lay in my bed when I thought my mind was going blank forever and thought what a luxury it would be to kill her, to strangle her skinny veined throat which could never be big enough to protect me from the world. But I was too nice for murder. I tried to murder myself: to keep from being an embarrassment to the ones I loved and from living myself in a mindless hell. How thoughtful: Do unto yourself as you would do to others. I'd kill her, so I killed myself.

To Hughes, Beuscher is a

> Moon of dismemberment and resurrection
> Who found enough parts on the floor of her shop
> To fill your old skin and get you walking
> Into Tuesday.

It was working with Beuscher that caused Plath truly to confront the specter of her father and so, in Hughes's eyes, to "jig with your Daddy's bones on a kind of tightrope / Over the gap of your real grave."

Mary Ellen Chase is here, the Smith professor who encouraged her to go to Cambridge and then to return to teach at Smith—where Plath was so unhappy, as recalled in "The Blue Flannel Suit." Hughes is powerless, again, to protect Plath; she is plucked out of his nest with a "chiming claw," Chase attempting to remake Plath in the image of herself, a teacher:

> She propped you
> On her lectern,
> Lecture-timer.

Everything is gathered together in this poem: the imagery of the moon, of blood, of electrocution that fills her work fills this poem. It is both homage and appropriation, as if by using her words and ideas in this way the poet could somehow gather back into himself something that had been lost. Its title can be read in different ways: in a poetic sense it is a kind of ride—riff, even—on *Ariel*, her final, posthumous book of poems; on "Ariel" the individual poem (which Plath wrote on her last birthday), which sees the poet as mythical rider, galloping toward death and rebirth. But Plath did not take her title, *Ariel*, simply from Shakespeare's spirit or the horse she herself rode. Judith Kroll notes that the derivation of the name may be either "lion (lioness) of God" or "altar [hearth] of God"; she quotes the *Catholic Encyclopaedia*: "The altar of holocausts is called the 'ariel of God' . . . on this altar burned the perpetual fire that was used to consume the sacrificial victims (Lev. 6:12)"—and the speaker in Plath's poem calls her horse "God's lioness."

This notion of sacrifice closes "Night-Ride on Ariel." The women she has looked to bring her down, in the end,

> As you flew
> They jammed all your wavelengths
> With their criss-cross instructions . . .

—it is this that causes her flight to fail. They are "crackling and dragging their blacks" just as the moon does in Plath's poem "Edge"; and their hauling of her head "this way and that way" recalls the real ride that inspired "Ariel," reminding the reader of her solid, living self, on horseback, on Ariel. But Plath clings to the fiery altar of the sun, and the shred of the "exploded dawn" that brought news of her death—on a Monday.

11 ◦ "The Jewel
You Lost Was Blue"

AFTER SYLVIA PLATH'S death, Ted Hughes was left with
much more than simply the memory of her and her literary
legacy. There were, of course, Frieda and Nicholas to be
looked after, and in part these last poems of *Birthday Letters*
chart the passage of time as Hughes raises them—as in "Life
after Death"—and looks at the world that is left to them as
they become adults, as in the delicate "Fingers." Poems like
"The Dogs Are Eating Your Mother," warning his children
away from those who would feed on Plath's myths, are like
stones in the wall of "astral fire" he tried to build around his

family in the years following Plath's death. But these final poems also offer a glimpse of reconciliation and peace—extended even toward her father in "A Picture of Otto"—though they acknowledge that the "kindly spirit" that might have been her protector was lost to her in the end.

THE FINAL SECTION of the book cannot, and should not, be placed in any exact chronological sense. These poems, which begin with "Life after Death," are about just that: the stretch of years after Plath's death in which Hughes lived with the day-to-day reality of raising their children, and observed—or fought against, however silently—the myth that started to grow around her. What makes these final poems so powerful is her still-vivid presence in them: "What can I tell you that you do not know / Of the life after death?" he begins in "Life after Death." She is present, the mother of their children, watching as Hughes performs the everyday tasks of fatherhood, while their living selves are both an affirmation of her existence (her son's eyes would become "so perfectly your eyes") and a rejection of her acceptance of death: her son's mouth

> . . . betrayed you—it accepted
> The spoon in my disembodied hand
> That reached through from the life that had survived you.

Hughes's disembodiment, his refusal to speak of his life, only "the life," hint at his suffering, which he elaborates in the fourth stanza, drawing on the imagery of the Tarot again (and reminding the reader again of Plath's "The Hanging Man").

By night I lay awake in my body
The Hanged Man
My neck-nerve uprooted and the tendon
Which fastened the base of my skull
To my left shoulder
Torn from its shoulder-root and cramped into knots—
I fancied the pain could be explained
If I were hanging in the spirit
From a hook under my neck-muscle.

Wolves howl in nearby Regent's Park Zoo; even in the city, the moon is still an overpowering presence. "Wolves consoled us"—though their song is not normally considered consoling. But their sound is one of mourning, as Hughes, Frieda and Nicholas "lay in your death," and Plath's death, her myth, comes to embrace them even as they live. They become orphaned, children in a folktale.

On Friday, 15 February 1963, Ted Hughes attended the inquest into his wife's death, which was held at the St. Pancras County Court, identifying the body of the deceased as that of Sylvia Plath Hughes. Hughes and Plath were newcomers to Devon, and so it was decided that she should be buried near the Hughes family home in Heptonstall, "black village of gravestones," he called it in *Wodwo*. The children did not attend the funeral that took place the following day as the Yorkshire fields lay blanketed in snow: Hughes makes oblique reference to the funeral—"your snowed-on grave, in the Pennines"—at the beginning of "The Prism." The gravestone erected to her memory was carved with an inscription from the *Bhagavadgita*—"Even amidst fierce flames the golden lotus can be planted"—and her name, Sylvia Plath Hughes. This is the stone to which Hughes refers at the end of the poem, the stone that, in the years to come, was frequently defaced by feminists for whom, as Anne Stevenson writes at the end of *Bitter Fame*, "the legacy of Sylvia Plath was no more than a simplified feminist ideology." After her marriage, Plath signed herself "Sylvia Hughes"; the name carved in the stone, Sylvia Plath Hughes, was repeatedly altered, Hughes's name excised or damaged. The arguments about her legacy that ensued disturbed Hughes enough to cause him to break his characteristic silence over his late wife. But "The Prism" slides over this pain, and in it Plath has not departed; her crystal ocean, her "seer's vision-stone," becomes his "lucky stone, my unlucky stone," always with him. The direct memory of her, her sun-browned shoulders, her swimsuit, is a physical, visceral memory. The opening lines of the poem,

> The waters off beautiful Nauset
> Were the ocean sun, the sea-poured crystal
> Behind your efforts . . .

carry a softened echo of "Daddy"'s furious blast.

She has not disappeared. "I still have it. I hold it—" the poet writes of her perfected childhood self. For Plath, too, it was something that could be held in the hand. Hughes echoes the opening of "Ocean 1212-W":

My childhood landscape was not land but the end of the land—the cold, salt, running hills of the Atlantic. I sometimes think my vision of the sea is the clearest thing I own. I pick it up, exile that I am, like the purple "lucky stones" I used to collect with a white ring all the way round, or the shell of a blue mussel with its rainbowy angel's fingernail interior; and in one wash of memory the colors deepen and gleam, the early world draws breath.

Her memory is a prism he can look through, offering him the different colors and sides of herself as the light strikes it:

> That way I see the filmy surf-wind flicker
> Of your ecstasies, your visions in the crystal.
> This way the irreparably-crushed lamp
> In my crypt of dream, totally dark,
> Under your gravestone.

The vision of Plath expressed in these final poems tilts between possessor and possessed. She possesses—and then passes on to Hughes—the prism of her sea-crystal vision: but she is also possessed, both by "The Hands" and "The God." Who is responsible for their separate fates? In "The Hands," the controlling force—the hands—belong and yet do not belong to Plath.

> Sometimes I think
> Finally you yourself were two gloves
> Worn by those two hands.

Was her behavior—her early suicide attempt, her poems, her "last-stand letters" written to friends decrying Hughes's behavior toward her, all "those words you struck me with"—

easier for Hughes to bear if he believed she was moved by some mysterious force outside herself? It would seem so.

A similar theme is explored in "The God," which, in its sixth stanza, also picks up the idea of her hands acting as if of their own accord.

> When you woke
> Your hands moved. You watched them in dismay
> As they made a new sacrifice.
> Two handfuls of blood, your own blood,
> And in that blood gobbets of me . . .

Most significantly, "The God" examines the extreme—and, to Hughes, destructive—self-centeredness of her work. Seamus Heaney, in his lecture on Plath's work, "The Indefatigable Hoof-taps," also saw this as her limitation, and explained it most succinctly:

> There is nothing poetically flawed about Plath's work. What may finally limit it is its dominant theme of self-discovery and self-definition, even though this concern must be understood as a valiantly unremitting campaign against the black hole of depression and suicide. I do not suggest that the self is not the proper arena of poetry. But I believe that the greatest work occurs when a certain self-forgetfulness is attained, or at least a fullness of self-possession denied to Sylvia Plath. . . . In "Lady Lazarus" . . . the cultural resonance of the original story is harnessed to a vehemently self-justifying purpose, so that the supra-personal dimensions of knowledge—to which myth typically gives access—are slighted in favour of the intense personal need of the poet.

As Hughes writes in "The God": "The story that has to be told / Is the writer's God."

What story did Plath have? Nothing, it seems, that was external to herself:

> Your heart, mid-Sahara, raged
> In its emptiness.
> Your dreams were empty.

Bowed at her desk, there was only "a torturing / Vacuum of God," a prayer of sterility. In his introduction to the *Journals*, Hughes wrote:

> Many passages in this present book show the deliberate— almost frantic—effort with which she tried to extend her writing, to turn it toward the world and other people, to stretch it over more of outer reality, to forget herself in some exploration of outer reality—in which she took, after all, such constant, intense delight. But the hidden workshop, the tangle of roots, the crucible, controlled everything. Everything became another image of itself, another lens into itself. And whatever it could not use in this way, to objectify some disclosure of self, did not get on to the page at all.

Wendy Christie, too, recalling her friendship with Plath, noted of her: "Her point of reference was always firmly fixed within herself. She seemed to use her mind as a set of antennae with which she assessed her own experience and felt it over. She wanted 'to know' for her own subjective purposes. Her intellectual traffic was largely with herself and related ultimately to her vision of the world and her experience." Her poetry is made from her distress: she builds an idol from the salt residue of her tears, which Hughes equates with a dead child still nursed—only her blood feeds it, brings it alive, like a revenant, and Hughes is bitterly ironic:

> Its mouth-hole stirred.
> Blood oozed at your nipple,
> A drip-feed of blood. Our happy moment!

In the blood that flows from her—which had in it "gobbets of me"—was, at last, her story.

> An embryo story.
> You could not explain it or who
> Ate at your hands.

Now she must feed the god she has created, and what she gives it is herself: the shells of her Massachusetts childhood, offerings of her mother and father. She offers to Hughes "an effigy—a Salvia / Pressed in a Lutheran Bible"; the flower echoing her name, the Bible her Germanic heritage. She leaves her husband a flattened shadow of herself, and becomes "a trance-dancer / In the smoke in the flames." Now, at last, Hughes recognizes the danger, as he did not, for instance, in "Ouija." "Shall we be famous?" he had asked the little god in that poem—and it was Plath who reacted with horror and dread. Now she is beyond that, and risks to venture that God speaks through her, while Hughes can only stand by,

Watching everything go up
In the flames of your sacrifice
That finally caught you too . . .

But memory of Sylvia Plath, and her legacy, does not belong solely to Hughes. Through her work, Hughes writes in "The God," "suddenly / Everybody knew everything." The phrase is a half-echo of the end of a very striking dream/fantasy that Plath recounts in her journal, as she rails against her mother, and the injustice, too, of her mother's life:

> Something went wrong. How could the fates punish her so if she was so very noble and good? It was her daughter's fault partly. She had a dream: her daughter was all gaudy-dressed about to go out and be a chorus girl, a prostitute too, probably. . . . The husband, brought alive in dream to relive the curse of his old angers, slammed out of the house in a rage that the daughter was going to be a chorus girl. The poor Mother runs along the sand beach, her feet sinking in the sand of life, her money bag open and the money and coins falling into the sand, turning to sand. The father had driven, in a fury, to spite her, off the road bridge and was floating dead, face down and bloated, in the slosh of ocean water by the pillars of the country club. Everybody was looking down from the pier at them. Everyone knew everything.

Her poems expose him to the gaze of the peanut-crunchers, every denizen of the "country club" free to peer at his private tragedy.

In "The Cast," "Costly Speech," and "Brasilia," Hughes has already confronted how her words—those indefatigable hoof-taps—affected those close to her after she died. In "Freedom of Speech" and "The Dogs Are Eating Your Mother," Hughes takes on her more public legacy. Janet Malcolm offers the finest analysis of the wars that began to be waged around the memory of Plath after her death, as friends of Hughes and Plath lined up on opposing sides of a battleground, as critics took their stances. Suffice to say here that in the years after her death, a veritable biographical and critical industry grew up around Sylvia Plath and her work. Hughes nearly always refused to break his silence on the subject—his angry rebuttal of Ronald Hayman's 1989 article in the *Independent* attacking Hughes for not maintaining Plath's grave (following a string of letters on the subject in the *Guardian* earlier that April) is a rare exception. In a letter to Jacqueline Rose, author of *The Haunting of Sylvia Plath*, Ted Hughes wrote:

> Critics established the right to say whatever they pleased about the dead. It is an absolute power, and the corruption that comes with it, very often, is an atrophy of the moral imagination. They move on to the living because they can no longer feel the difference between the living and the dead. They extend over the living that licence to say whatever they please, to ransack their psyche and reinvent them however they please. They stand in front of classes and present this performance as exemplary civilised activity—this utter insensitivity towards other living human beings. Students see the easy power and are enthralled, and begin to outdo their teachers. For a person to be corrupted in that way is to be genuinely corrupted.

Hughes was dismayed, to say the least, by a reading of Plath's poem "The Rabbit Catcher" included in Rose's book, which appeared to raise questions about Plath's sexuality, and asked her to remove it. "When I refused," Rose writes, "I was told by Ted Hughes that my analysis would be damaging for Plath's (now adult) children and that speculation of the kind I was seen as engaging in about Sylvia Plath's sexual identity would in some countries be 'grounds for homicide.' "

Here, in "Freedom of Speech," are the

> famous authors, your court of brilliant minds,
> And publishers and doctors and professors,
> Their eyes creased in delighted laughter

at her sixtieth birthday: an imagined event. But one she had imagined too. In "A Birthday Present," written in the autumn of 1962, the poet waits for a mysterious gift; what it is, exactly, is never revealed, but it bears a relation to Death, with its "deep gravity" and "timeless eyes." The way the gift is transported makes it seem like information, or revelation, and the poet is afraid it will come too late: "Let it not come by word of mouth, I should be sixty / By the time the whole of it was delivered, and too numb to use it." In Hughes's poem the revelation has come, and the audience are "grateful"—grateful for her death, which has allowed their livelihoods? Their laughter is infectious; even those close to her seem to be happy: "Only you and I do not smile," Hughes writes. They know the present's price; it is a truth inaccessible to anyone but the two of them. In "The Dogs Are Eating Your Mother"—its title so stark—the pain of the defaced gravestone is made manifest as he addresses his grown children, Nick in Alaska, Frieda in Australia.

Hughes went to great lengths to protect his privacy and

that of his children. But his silence—his refusal to speak to biographers, to talk about Plath at all—was often interpreted as a continuation of the hostility many perceived had driven his wife to her death. So here the "court of brilliant minds" is transformed into a pack of dogs, savage, like

> the lean hound
> Running up the lane holding high
> The dangling raw windpipe and lungs
> Of a fox . . .

Now Plath is the fox, and Hughes warns his children against speaking about her:

> Protect her
> And they will tear you down
> As if you were more her.

They "jerk their tail-stumps, bristle and vomit / Over their symposia," he writes contemptuously.

Here is a hint of the anger he showed in a letter to Al Alvarez, the second half of whose memoir of Plath (published in full in Alvarez's book on suicide, *The Savage God*) Hughes stopped the *Observer* from publishing in 1971. His children, at that point, still did not know the manner of their mother's death. "You kept saying you would show me what you were writing about her—why didn't you?" Hughes asked. "For you, it was something you wrote, no doubt against great inner resistance, for your readers, it's five interesting minutes, but for us it is permanent dynamite." He contrasts their connection to wife and mother ("You played around the grave. We arranged / Sea-shells and big veined pebbles / Carried from Appledore / As if we were herself") with the "kind / Of hyena" that digs her up: they even "bite the face off her gravestone." She would, in his eyes, be better left for vultures; his children should

> Imagine
> Those bone-crushing mouths the mouths
> That labour for the beetle
> Who will roll her back into the sun.

When *Birthday Letters* was awarded the Forward Prize for poetry in 1998—only weeks before his death—Hughes issued a statement revealing that the work had begun as a way of making a "direct, private, inner contact" with his first wife. The book is that: and it is, too—because of that—a kind of reclamation. "The Dogs Are Eating Your Mother" reveals the poet's contempt for those who would appropriate their story. "Fingers" is a very different kind of poem, its precise, joyous conjuring of her fingers as "they flew / With the light in your look" giving it a redemptive power.

> . . . as you talked, as your eyes signalled
> The strobes of your elation,
> They flared, flicked balletic aerobatics.
> I thought of birds in some tropical sexual
> Play of display, leaping and somersaulting,
> Doing strange things in the air, and dropping to the dust.
> Those dancers of your excess!

These are, unmistakably, her fingers—not fingers belonging to the disembodied hands that pushed her down her tragic course, but emblems of her warm, living self. A self that was not extinguished by her death, but lives on in the fingers of their daughter, Frieda: "Her fingers obey and honour your fingers, / The Lares and Penates of our house."

The warmth of these final poems even extends to Otto Plath. "A Picture of Otto"—with its World War I echoes of Wilfred Owen's "Strange Meeting," the poem Hughes and Seamus Heaney chose to represent Owen in their wide-ranging anthology of poetry, *The School Bag*—imagines meeting him in the Underworld. Where earlier in the book he was "the god with the smoking gun," his psychic presence "the home of anger," here Hughes calls him, at last, "my friend" as they meet "face to face." "You stand there at the blackboard: Lutheran / Minister manqué," he begins. The poem appears to use as its setting-off point a photograph of Otto Plath in his classroom, taken in 1930. Hughes lets go of blame and rage:

> I understand—you never could have released her.
> I was a whole myth too late to replace you.
> This underworld, my friend, is her heart's home.
> Inseparable, here we must remain,
>
> Everything forgiven and in common . . .

Plath is again in her "soldier crypt," a poet killed in battle like Owen, her death haunting Hughes as the deaths of the soldiers killed in World War I haunted him all his life.

The book's final poem, "Red," makes explicit the color theme that can be traced throughout the book. At their first meeting in "St. Botolph's," Hughes is drawn by her crimson mouth; he notes the "blood-raw" light of their honeymoon in "You Hated Spain"; the crimson-shadowed evenings that linger through "The Rag Rug"; the hearts splashed over "Totem." "Red was your colour," the poem begins, reminding the reader of the closing lines of Plath's "Ariel," an intimation of her trajectory toward her end:

> And I
> Am the arrow,
>
> The dew that flies
> Suicidal, at one with the drive
> Into the red
>
> Eye, the cauldron of morning.

For Plath, there was a dangerous vibrancy in the color. In 1958, teaching at Smith, she wrote in her diary after putting on red silk stockings and red shoes, that "the color feels amazing—almost incandescent fire silk sheathing my legs." In November 1961, Plath had written to her mother of decorating Court Green against the "gloominess" that winter invariably brought on in her. "It's incredible to think that carpets can create a state of mind, but I am so suggestible to colors and textures that I'm sure a red carpet would keep me forever optimistic. . . ." In Plath's "Poppies in October," a woman's "red heart blooms through her coat so astoundingly";

in "Nick and the Candlestick," addressed to her son, "the blood blooms clean / In you, ruby."

In *Chapters in a Mythology*, Judith Kroll writes of red's "dominance": "It is a color naturally associated with blood, danger and violence, as well as with vitality." Red, in Kroll's view, is the color that calls to the true, vital self sleeping within the poet, who, in "Poppies in July," is "colorless." Plath observes the red of "Tulips": "Their redness talks to my wound, it corresponds." Its opposite is white: moon-color, the color of bone, the dead children like white serpents in her final poem, "Edge"; the hills stepping off into whiteness in the bleak "Sheep in Fog." "But red / Was what you wrapped around you," Hughes writes. The poem reprises the image of the casket, which first appears in "Robbing Myself"; the savage Aztec sacrifice of "The God"; and links her—even through her name, *Salvia splendens*, a blood-red flower— with blood that beats with life but beats it out, too: "the heart's last gouts, / Catastrophic, arterial, doomed."

Hughes contrasts this flow with the kingfisher blue silk that "Folded your pregnancy / In crucible caresses." Blue is a kindly spirit like "The Prism," which refracts the image of her beloved ocean.

> In the pit of red
> You hid from the bone-clinic whiteness.
>
> But the jewel you lost was blue.

It is the same blue that he alone recalls as the color of the scarf he took from her at their first meeting—although she had written in her journal of how she had lost "the red ban-deau which I loved with all the redness in my heart." He writes as if the jewel, like the prism, was something that could be held in the hand; it slipped from her grasp as Plath, in these poems over and over, slips from Hughes's grasp, eluding him finally even as he creates a vital, vivid portrait of her on the page. It is a final image, too, of his helplessness. It was not for him to keep this jewel of her happiness. It was for her to do so, and she did not, or could not.

The last line of the final poem of *Birthday Letters* is a sim-ple statement of loss—which holds within it the resonance of the greater loss with which the whole book echoes. "But the jewel you lost was blue." Plath, however, had claimed the color too. It seems for her a color of distance, of unattach-ment. In "The Moon and the Yew Tree," written in October 1961, she writes:

> Clouds are flowering
> Blue and mystical over the face of the stars.
> Inside the church, the saints will be all blue,
> Floating on their delicate feet over the cold pews,
> Their hands and faces stiff with holiness.

A little more than a year later she describes the clouds float-ing above a pinned-down "Gulliver":

> Unlike swans,
> Having no reflections;
>
> Unlike you,

With no strings attached.
All cool, all blue.

The world is "blood-hot and personal"; blue allows a little space to breathe.

The blue jewel was her inner sea, lost in her eighth year with the death of her father, her move away from the ocean, never to be reclaimed. Or could it have been? "Blue is my new color, royal, midnight (not aqua!)," she wrote to her mother barely two months before she died. She adds: "Ted never liked blue. . . ."

REFERENCES

Note: Page references are to the first listed edition in the Bibliography.

INTRODUCTION: THE ECSTASY OF INFLUENCE

16 • "a bristling, badger-silence": Andrew Motion, *The Times*, 17 January 1998.

17 • "I think those letters": Letter from Ted Hughes to an unnamed friend, read aloud by Frieda Hughes at Whitbread Award ceremony, 10 January 1999.

21 • "Nothing refreshed her": Hughes, in Plath, *Johnny Panic and the Bible of Dreams*, p. 12.

21 • "I shall perish": Plath, *Journals*, p. 325.

22 • "Living apart from Ted": Plath, *Letters Home*, p. 479.

23 • but it ended with "Wintering": Pollitt, in Alexander, ed., *Ariel Ascending*, p. 95.

24 • "The *Ariel* we know": *Ibid.*

24 • "I wanted the book": Interview published in *Paris Review*, Spring 1995.

25 • Hughes made material available: Stevenson, *Bitter Fame*, Author's note.

25 • "I have never attempted": Hughes, in Malcolm, *The Silent Woman*, p. 141.

26 • "Feminists never had": Greer, in *Close Up*, BBC TV, December 1998.

27 • "Sylvia Plath's journals": Hughes, in Alexander, ed., *op. cit.*, p. 152.

28 • "How can we content": *Washington Post*, 18 April 1982; Alexander, *Rough Magic*, p. 355.

28 • "What I actually destroyed": *Paris Review*, Spring 1995.

29 • "It is important": Kroll, *Chapters in a Mythology*, p. 49.

30 • "An early dramatic death": Hardwick, in Alexander, ed., *op. cit.*, p. 101.

30 • "The Movement": See Drabble, ed., *Oxford Companion to English Literature*, p. 674.

32 • "The point here" "systole-diastole": Hughes, *Shakespeare and the Goddess of Complete Being*, p. 479.

33 • "The poet is in love": Graves, *The White Goddess*, p. 448.

34 • "Goethe called": Hughes, in *Paris Review*, Spring 1995.

34 • "stands in confusion": Hughes, *Gaudete*, pp. 14–15.

35 • "In his vision": Carey, in the *Sunday Times*, 27 January 1998.

35 • "Most readers will perceive": Hughes, in Newman, ed., *The Art of Sylvia Plath*, p. 187.

36 • "All creative work": Hughes, in *Daily Telegraph*, 31 October 1998.

37 • "In this . . . poem": Hughes, in Alexander, ed., *op. cit.*, p. 157.

38 • "It is doubtful": *Ibid.*, pp. 157–58.

38 • "And at once": *Ibid.*, p. 162.

38*n* • "psychological, irreligious": Berryman, in Perkins, et al., eds., *Bënet's Reader's Encyclopedia of American Literature*, p. 921.

39 • "I don't think": Alvarez, *Where Did It All Go Right?*, pp. 204–5.

40 • "There was no rivalry": Hughes, in *Manchester Guardian*, 23 March 1965.

40 • "Our minds soon became": Hughes, in *Paris Review*, Spring 1995.

41 • the "supportive atmosphere": Hughes, in *Daily Telegraph*, 31 October 1998.

41 • "My book *Birthday Letters*": Statement by Ted Hughes on winning the Forward Prize, 9 October 1998.

43 • "Why did you give no hint": T. Hardy, in Armstrong, ed., *Thomas Hardy: Selected Poems*, p. 153.

43 • "The will of man": F. E. Hardy, in *ibid.*, p. 8.

44 • "You have taken": Heaney and Hughes, eds., *The Rattle Bag*, pp. 132–33.

45 • "At the end of the lunch": Conversation with Matthew Evans, 13 April 1999.

45 • "It wasn't just the extraordinary": Conversation with Peter Stothard, 15 April 1999.

46 • "takes the bare bones": Alvarez, in *The New Yorker*, 2 February 1998.

46 • "a book of poems": Heaney, in *Irish Times*, 31 January 1998.

47 • "In the short term": Motion, in *The Times*, 17 January 1998.

47 • "Written over the last": Kakutani, in *New York Times*, 13 February 1998.

48 • "To the hostile ear": Fenton, in *New York Review of Books*, 5 March 1998.

48 • "It means the world": Hughes, in the *Independent on Sunday*, 5 September 1993.

49 • "presenting Plath's suicide": Warn, in *Seattle Weekly*, 5 March 1998.

49 • "my teeth began to grind": Morgan, in *Newsweek*, 2 February 1998.

49 • "In the book's angriest poem": Wood, in *Prospect*, May 1998.

50 • "Now he has issued": Glover, in *New Statesman*, 30 January 1998.

50 • "as if to answer": Pollitt, in *New York Times Book Review*, 1 March 1998.

51 • "Imagine what you are writing": Hughes, *Winter Pollen*, p. 13.

51 • "Some sort of language": Hughes, in Sagar, *The Art of Ted Hughes*, p. 64.

52 • "I grew up in": Hughes, in Sagar, ed., *The Achievement of Ted Hughes*, p. 19.

52 • "its sensuous fetch": Heaney, in *ibid.*, p. 17.

53 • "To bathe in": Blake, "Milton," II, pl. 41, 1.Iff.

CHAPTER 1: "A CRUSH OF DIAMONDS"

58 • "I feel that": Plath, in *Letters Home*, p. 184.

59 • "Everything in West Yorkshire": Hughes, in *The Listener*, 19 September 1963; Sagar, *The Art of Ted Hughes*, p. 6.

60 • "At Cambridge": Merwin, in Sagar, *The Art of Ted Hughes*, p. 8.

60 • "I saw that its body": Hughes, *Winter Pollen*, p. 9.

61 • pseudonym of Daniel Hearing: Sagar, *The Art of Ted Hughes*, p. 9.

61 • J. Arthur Rank: Stevenson, *op. cit.*, p. 77.

61 • "He was an inch": *Ibid.*, p. 308.

62 • "same black sweater": Plath, *Letters Home*, p. 244.

62 • "The seventy-plus": *Ibid.*, p. 12.

63 • that appeared to rule the poet's life: Stevenson, *op. cit.*, p. 8.

64 • had gone undiagnosed and unchecked: *Ibid.*, p. 10.

64 • "I'll never speak": Plath, *Letters Home*, p. 25.

64 • away from the ocean: Stevenson, *op. cit.*, p. 11.

65 • "I was only purely happy": Plath, *The Bell Jar*, pp. 60–61.

65 • "What is my life for": Plath, unpublished journals, 1950, ms p. 81.

65 • sending in forty-five stories: Brown, in Alexander, ed., *op. cit.*, p. 117.

65 • in the same month: Stevenson, *op. cit.*, pp. 18–19.

65 • "After a while": Plath, unpublished journals, 1950, ms pp. 31–32.

66 • "Today was good": Plath, *Journals*, p. 57.

66 • "I love this place so": Plath, *Letters Home*, p. 85.

67 • "Sunday at the Mintons": Stevenson, *op. cit.*, p. 30.

67 • "It is like lifting": Plath, *Journals*, p. 51.

67 • "I would be sitting": Plath, *The Bell Jar*, p. 152.

67 • her novel, *The Bell Jar*: Stevenson, *op. cit.*, p. 39.

68 • "Only I wasn't steering": Plath, *The Bell Jar*, p. 2.

68 • "a great change in her": Plath, *Letters Home*, p. 123.

68 • "Then something bent down": Plath, *The Bell Jar*, p. 117–18.

69 • with her suicide attempt: Stevenson, *op. cit.*, p. 45.

69 • "I waited until my mother": Plath, *Letters Home*, p. 131.

69 • "Cobwebs touched": Plath, *The Bell Jar*, p. 149.

70 • "She was incapable": Hughes, in Alexander, ed., *op. cit.*, p. 158.

71 • "Being dead": Plath, *Journals*, p. 100.

72 • "Sylvia's psychotherapy": Stevenson, *op. cit.*, p. 47.

72 • "I rail and rage": Plath, *Journals*, p. 129.

72 • "I identify him": *Ibid.*, p. 279.

73 • "Guess what": Plath, *Letters Home*, p. 100.

74 • "The marriage to": Kroll, *Chapters in a Mythology*, p. 124.

75 • *Harper's* published her poem "Doomsday": Stevenson, *op. cit.*, p. 51.

75 • "contrasting and comparing": Plath, *Letters Home*, p. 145.

75 • "My main bother": *Ibid.*, p. 141.

76 • News of her success: *Ibid.*, p. 175.

76 • "the importance of personal responsibility": *Ibid.*, p. 153.

76 • worth $100: *Ibid.*, p. 173, in Alexander, *Rough Magic*, p. 156.

76 • "The roof slants": *Ibid.*, p. 183.

77 • an "almost professional sense": Baltzell, in Butscher, ed., *Sylvia Plath*, p. 62.

77 • "the concentrated intensity": *Ibid.*, p. 49.

79 • "We disapproved of": Myers, in Stevenson, *op. cit.*, p. 312.

80 • "is really a brilliant": Plath, *Letters Home*, p. 219.

80 • the magazine contained: Sagar, *The Art of Ted Hughes*, p. 10.

80 • "that big, dark, hunky boy": Plath, *Journals*, p. 110.

80 • "to blast over Richard": Plath, *Journals*, p. 110.

81 • "I was stamping": *Ibid.*, p. 113, and unpublished, from ms.

81 • "Teeth gouged": Plath, *Johnny Panic and the Bible of Dreams*, p. 309.

81 • "What to do?": Plath, unpublished journals, ms p. 409.

83 • "Met, by the way": Plath, *Letters Home*, p. 221.

84 • "the biggest seducer": Plath, unpublished journals, 26 February 1956.

84 • "He is on the prowl": Plath, *Journals*, p. 133.

85 • "let me have him": *Ibid.*, p. 131.

88 • "It is, of course": *Ibid.*, p. 222.

CHAPTER 2: "BEAUTIFUL, BEAUTIFUL AMERICA!"

92 • "a small early Georgian": Huws, in Stevenson, *op. cit.*, p. 179.

92 • "you know I am": Plath, *Letters Home*, p. 228.

92 • "I had been ready": Plath, *Journals*, p. 135.

93 • "I have the loveliest": Plath, *Letters Home*, pp. 231–32.

93 • "which gave her the gay side": Plath, unpublished journals, 26 March–5 April, ms p. 11.

95 • "Arrived in Paris early": *Ibid.*

95 • "practical satisfaction" "technical virginity": *Ibid.*, Summer 1952, ms p. 325.

96 • "I took a plane": Plath, *Journals*, p. 214.

96 • "It is this man": Plath, *Letters Home*, p. 234.

96 • "I need Ted": Plath, *Journals*, p. 200.

96 • Alexandra House: *Cambridge News*, 22 October 1964; Payne, *Down Your Street*, p. 168.

98 • "a large, hulking, healthy Adam": Stevenson, *op. cit.*, pp. 85–86; Plath, *Letters Home*, p. 233.

99 • "the fatal bellman": Shakespeare, *Macbeth*, Act II, scene ii, ll. 3–4.

99 • "as if a great muscular owl": Plath, *Journals*, p. 239.

99 • and final oblivion: Heaney, *Critical Writings*, p. 153.

100 • "Don't blab too much": Stevenson, *op. cit.*, p. 84; Plath, *Journals*, pp. 137–38.

100 • "You have accepted": Plath, unpublished journals.

101 • "a source of great depression": *Ibid.*, 15 September 1958.

103 • "prevented . . . from absorbing": Plath, *Letters Home*, p. 316.

104 • "I was furious": Plath, *Journals*, p. 127.

CHAPTER 3: "SPAIN WAS THE LAND OF YOUR DREAMS"

108 • "a huge and miraculous secret": Plath, *Letters Home*, p. 258.

108 • "When Ted and I see": Plath, *Letters Home*, p. 258.

108 • "We rushed about": *Ibid.*

109 • "Act of faith": Plath, *Journals*, p. 153.

110 • to London from Heptonstall: Plath, *Letters Home*, p. 277; Stevenson, *op. cit.*, p. 97.

110 • "I was really frantic": Plath, *Letters Home*, p. 278.

111 • "They left to honeymoon: Stevenson, *op. cit.*, p. 91.

113 • "Anyway, I have never felt": Plath, *Letters Home*, p. 261.

114 • "The continuous poise": Plath, *Johnny Panic and the Bible of Dreams*, p. 218.

115 • "Alone, deepening": Plath, *Journals*, pp. 146–47.

117 • particularly that of de Chirico: Stevenson, *op. cit.*, p. 123.

119 • "We wake about seven": *Ibid.*, p. 94; Plath, *Letters Home*, p. 265, and unpublished, from Lilly Library, Indiana University.

119 • "went about with Ted": Plath, *Letters Home*, p. 267.

CHAPTER 4: "THAT HOME WAS OUR FIRST CAMP"

122 • met Plath's brother Warren: Stevenson, *op. cit.*, p. 95.

122 • "an incredible, wild": Plath, *Letters Home*, p. 268.

122 • "We had a picnic": *Ibid.*, p. 269.

125 • "We share a bathroom": *Ibid.*, p. 283.

125 • poems by Yeats for the BBC: *Ibid.*, p. 276; Stevenson, *op. cit.*, p. 96.

125 • a local boys school: Plath, *Letters Home*, p. 247.

125 • *Nimbus*: *Ibid.*, p. 289.

126 • Plath moved in with Hughes: Stevenson, *op. cit.*, p. 98.

126 • "We have such lovely": Plath, *Letters Home*, p. 289.

126 • "About this time": Campbell, in Newman, ed., *The Art of Sylvia Plath*, pp. 183–84.

127 • "the passionate rage": Stevenson, *op. cit.*, p. 97; Krook, in Butscher, ed., *Sylvia Plath*, p. 55.

128 • "my man": Plath, *Journals*, p. 153.

128 • One of the poems she composed: Stevenson, *op. cit.*, p. 105.

129 • "too fancy": Quoted in Plath, *Collected Poems*, p. 13.

130 • "I returned there": Plath, *Letters Home*, p. 294.

130 • won the New York Poetry Center competition: *Ibid.*, p. 296.

131 • a teaching post at Smith: *Ibid.*, p. 300.

131 • "frightens me a little" ". . . Sometime write me": *Ibid.*, p. 306.

131 • "SP occasionally amused herself": Hughes, in Plath, *Collected Poems*, p. 276, n. 62.

132 • "I do wish": Plath, *Letters Home*, p. 294.

133 • "Her father's name": Hughes, in Alexander, ed., *Ariel Ascending*, p. 155.

133 • "Pan claims": Plath, *Letters Home*, p. 346.

135 • literary criticism and Chaucer: Stevenson, *op. cit.*, p. 106.

136 • "We began mooing": Plath, *Letters Home*, p. 307.

136 • "Her immediate 'face' ": Hughes, in Stevenson, *op. cit.*, p. 110.

137 • chosen as a finalist for the prize: Plath, *Letters Home*, p. 315.

137 • "FABER & FABER": *Ibid.*, p. 312.

CHAPTER 5: "WHAT HAPPENS IN THE HEART SIMPLY HAPPENS"

141 • the teeth of near disaster: Stevenson, *op cit.*, p. 111.

141 • "Yesterday was the first": Plath, *Journals*, p. 164.

142 • "No children": *Ibid.*, p. 165.

142 • rejected a year earlier: Plath, *Letters Home*, p. 324.

142 • "Last night I felt": Plath, *Journals*, p. 176.

143 • "Woke up after": Plath, unpublished journals.

143 • "I keep feeling": Plath, *Letters Home*, p. 328.

144 • "Girls with bear-skin caps": Plath, unpublished letter to Dorothea Krook, 25 September 1958, courtesy Anita Jackson.

144 • "I am thinking of": Plath, *Letters Home*, p. 301.

145 • "which in American usually means": Plath, unpublished letter to Krook.

145 • "overflowing with ideas": Plath, *Letters Home*, p. 336.

146 • "These girls were": Plath, *Journals*, p. 236.

147 • the Winthrop Cemetery: In Plath, *Collected Poems*, p. 289, n. 103.

147 • the "celestial occasion": Alexander, *Rough Magic*, p. 44.

147 • "It relates more richly": Plath, *Journals*, p. 222.

148 • Her father's death she had viewed: Plath, *Johnny Panic and the Bible of Dreams*, p. 266.

148 • "I cry so": *Ibid.*, p. 205.

148 • "was lovely at her home": Plath, *Letters Home*, p. 340.

149 • "a queerly ambiguous": Plath, *Journals*, p. 250.

149 • "wade / through black jade": Moore, in Williams and Honig, eds., *The Mentor Book of Major American Poets*, p. 372.

151 • The literary life beckoned: Stevenson, *op cit.*, p. 141.

151 • "We have a little": Plath, unpublished letter to Krook.

151 • won the Guinness Prize back in England: Stevenson, *op. cit.*, p. 140.

152 • "But although it makes": Plath, *Journals*, p. 226.

152 • reappearing "conquered": *Ibid.*, p. 305.

155 • "In the third yard": *Ibid.*, p. 298.

156 • in a "glass caul": *Ibid.*, p. 297.

156 • "great, stark, bloody play": *Ibid.*, pp. 286–87.

157 • Panic was much in her mind: Stevenson, *op. cit.*, p. 144.

158 • "The crown of wire": Plath, *Johnny Panic and the Bible of Dreams*, p. 166.

160 • "I hate her for that": Plath, *Journals*, p. 267, in Stevenson, *op. cit.*, p. 146.

160 • "felt a fear also": Plath, *Journals*, ms p. 349.

160 • invited to Yaddo: Stevenson, *op. cit.*, pp. 155–56.

160 • "I feel that this month": *Ibid.*, p. 157; Plath, *Journals*, p. 307.

CHAPTER 6: "RIGHT ACROSS AMERICA WE WENT LOOKING FOR YOU"

166 • "There in the blue": Plath, *Letters Home*, p. 349.

167 • "a stiff artificial piece": Plath, *Journals*, p. 312.

167 • Sadie does not attempt: Plath, *Johnny Panic and the Bible of Dreams*, p. 104.

168 • she was temporarily infertile: Plath, *Journals*, p. 310.

168 • "I would bear children": *Ibid.*, p. 312.

169 • "one of the main regeneration dramas": Hughes, *Winter Pollen*, p. 58.

169 • "a descent into destruction": Hughes, in Faas, *Ted Hughes*, p. 205.

171 • "low-ceilinged, painted white": Plath, *Letters Home*, p. 353.

171 • "I particularly love": Plath, cited by Schulman, "Sylvia Plath at Yaddo," in Alexander, ed., *Ariel Ascending*, p. 166.

172 • "Sylvia seemed egotistical": Stevenson, *op. cit.*, pp. 164–65.

173 • "It is unlike anything": Hughes, *Winter Pollen*, p. 183.

CHAPTER 7: "I LET THAT FOX CUB GO"

178 • Douglas Cleverdon, a radio producer: Stevenson, *op cit.*, p. 182.

178 • *The House of Aries*: Plath, *Letters Home*, p. 389.

178 • *Meet My Folks!*: *Ibid.*, p. 386.

178 • contract with Heinemann: Stevenson, *op. cit.*, p. 184.

178 • "They do very few": Plath, *Letters Home*, p. 366.

178 • the Somerset Maugham Award: Stevenson, *op. cit.*, p. 189.

179 • "I think being mountainous-pregnant": *Ibid.*, p. 190; Plath, letter to Lynne Lawner, 30 September 1960, published in *Antaeus*, no. 28, p. 50.

179 • The Hugheses had a print of Isis: Stevenson, *op. cit.*, p. 183.

180 • "The Hugheses' flat": Alvarez, in Alexander, ed., *Ariel Ascending*, p. 187.

181 • "He was marvelous": Plath, *Letters Home*, pp. 380–81, in Stevenson, *op. cit.*, p. 195.

181 • "the inescapable blast": Merwin, in Stevenson, *op. cit.*, p. 193.

182 • Hughes . . . compared the guarding: Stevenson, *Between the Iceberg and the Ship*, p. 30.

183 • Hughes's work, however: Stevenson, *Bitter Fame*, p. 201.

183 • broadcast in November: *Ibid.*, p. 202.

183 • the prestigious Hawthornden Prize: Plath, *Letters Home*, p. 415.

183 • Peter Hall commissioned him: Stevenson, *Bitter Fame*, p. 213.

183 • their parting was not a happy one: *Ibid.*, p. 205.

184 • "GOOD NEWS": Plath, *Letters Home*, p. 417.

185 • "It was Ted who": Merwin, in Stevenson, *Bitter Fame*, p. 341.

186 • no sign of distress: *Ibid.*, p. 215.

186 • "the *Ariel* poems": Hughes, *Winter Pollen*, p. 165.

188 • "The poetry of the *Ariel* poems": *Ibid.*

CHAPTER 8: "THEN THE SCRIPT OVERTOOK US"

190 • "It is . . . very, very ancient": Plath to Helga Huws, in Stevenson, *Bitter Fame*, p. 222.

191 • *The Colossus* would be published: *Ibid.*, p. 220.

193 • "what I held in focus": Hughes, in Bentley, *The Poetry of Ted Hughes*, p. 63, from unpublished letter to Terry Gifford and Neil Roberts.

194 • "When I set out": in Armstrong, ed., *Thomas Hardy*, p. 141.

195 • "hardly a soul": Plath, *Johnny Panic and the Bible of Dreams*, p. 108.

197 • Eugene Saxton Grant: Stevenson, *Bitter Fame*, pp. 225–26.

198 • a passion for Beethoven's music: *Ibid.*, p. 238.

198 • "Blake I connect": Hughes, in Faas, *Ted Hughes*, p. 202.

199 • "Our Christmas": Plath, *Letters Home*, p. 440.

199 • "Here he is!": Plath, unpublished journals, 17 January 1962.

200 • His 1959 story "The Harvesting": Hughes, *Difficulties of a Bridegroom*, p. 79.

202 • "Our daffodils": Plath, *Letters Home*, p. 453.

202 • her picture and Frieda's: Plath, *Johnny Panic and the Bible of Dreams*, p. 232.

202 • "These photographs are meant": Plath, *Letters Home*, p. 454.

204 • how to plait rag rugs: Stevenson, *Bitter Fame*, p. 140.

204 • "Braided violently": Plath, unpublished journals, 20 May 1962.

205 • "Once when I visited": Plath, *The Bell Jar*, p. 69.

206 • "After *Three Women*": Hughes, "Sylvia Plath and Her *Journals*," in Alexander, ed., *Ariel Ascending*.

208 • a BBC producer, Moira Doolan: Stevenson, *Bitter Fame*, p. 206.

211 • they had stayed in touch: *Ibid.*, p. 245.

211 • "cordial, exploratory, gracious": Wevill, p. 242.

211 • "We have a nice young": Plath, *Letters Home*, p. 454.

212 • Hughes, in contrast, was already: Alexander, *Rough Magic*, p. 279.

213 • marries a Diana-like Miranda: Hughes, *Shakespeare and the Goddess of Complete Being*, p. 436.

213 • "I'll show thee": Shakespeare, *The Tempest*, Act II, scene ii, 152.

216 • "When she came to talk": Hughes, in Alexander, ed., *Ariel Ascending*, p. 156.

216 • "It depressed me greatly": Hughes, "Notes on the Chronological Order of Sylvia Plath's Poems," in Newman, ed., *The Art of Sylvia Plath*.

CHAPTER 9: "THE CAVE OF THUNDER"

224 • "We all wore masks": Plath, *Letters Home*, p. 457.

224 • *Bienenkönig*, the Bee King: *Ibid.*, p. 9.

225 • ". . . I was aware of bees": Plath, *Journals*, ms p. 518.

226 • "Father, if thou be willing": Luke 22:42.

227 • "The center of my whole": Stevenson, *Bitter Fame*, p. 253.

228 • "Now and then": Plath, *Johnny Panic and the Bible of Dreams*, p. 253.

228 • "There is something": Plath, *Letters Home*, p. 391.

229 • The funeral imagery: Plath, *Johnny Panic and the Bible of Dreams*, pp. 74–75.

230 • "And this is how": *Ibid.*, p. 124.

230 • contact with Assia Wevill: Stevenson, *Bitter Fame*, p. 248.

230 • confirmation of her fears: *Ibid.*, p. 250.

231 • "conjured up Assia": *Ibid.*, p. 273.

232 • "The welcome I received": Plath, *Letters Home*, p. 458.

233 • "the receptacle in which a man": Frazer, *The Golden Bough*, p. 800.

234 • Richard Murphy: Stevenson, *Bitter Fame*, p. 253.

234 • meeting with her solicitor: *Ibid.*, p. 258.

235 • Hughes had "deserted her": *Ibid.*, p. 257.

236 • "I haven't the strength": Plath, *Letters Home*, p. 465.

236 • "Every morning": *Ibid.*, p. 466.

236 • "I am a writer": *Ibid.*, p. 468.

236 • "The subject matter": Hughes, *Winter Pollen*, p. 188.

236 • "just right": Plath, *Letters Home*, p. 477.

237 • "I am no longer": *Ibid.*, p. 479.

CHAPTER 10: "THE SHOCK OF HER WORDS FROM NOWHERE"

243 • At first, in London: Stevenson, *Bitter Fame*, pp. 279–80.

243 • "she seemed different": Alvarez, in Alexander, ed., *Ariel Ascending*, p. 205.

244 • "she wrote for me": Krook, in Butscher, ed., *Sylvia Plath*, p. 52.

245 • "The girls' guidance counselor": Plath, *Johnny Panic and the Bible of Dreams*, p. 36.

249 • "[Sylvia] made use": Stevenson, *Bitter Fame*, p. 302; Aurelia Plath to Judith Kroll, 1 December 1978, Neilson Library, Smith College.

250 • Many of these poems: Alexander, ed., *op. cit.*, p. x.

250 • "Practically every character": Aurelia Plath, in Malcolm, *The Silent Woman*, p. 33.

251 • "Aurelia accepted the fact": Hughes in *ibid.*, p. 210.

251 • when Aurelia objected to publication: *Ibid.*, p. 209.

251 • went through three editions: Alexander, *Rough Magic*, p. 348.

253 • "there is a strange muse": Hughes, in *Poetry Book Society Bulletin* (London), no. 44 (February 1965), p. 1; quoted in Newman, ed., *The Art of Sylvia Plath*, p. 73.

254 • "all the old ladies": Plath, *The Bell Jar*, p. 5.

255 • "I wonder . . . if I have revealed": Plath, *Letters Home*, p. 62.

256 • "I want others": Plath, *Letters Home*, p. 62.

256 • "So how do I express": Plath, unpublished journals, 12 December 1958.

257 • But Plath did not take her title: Kroll, *Chapters in a Mythology*, p. 181.

CHAPTER 11: "THE JEWEL YOU LOST WAS BLUE"

262 • "the legacy of Sylvia Plath": Stevenson, *Bitter Fame*, p. 302–4.

262 • "My childhood landscape": Plath, *Johnny Panic and the Bible of Dreams*, p. 117.

264 • "There is nothing": Heaney, *The Government of the Tongue*, p. 168.

265 • "Many passages": Hughes, *Winter Pollen*, p. 181.

265 • "Her point of reference": Christie, in Newman, ed., *The Art of Sylvia Plath*, p. 183.

267 • "Something went wrong": Plath, *Journals*, pp. 267–68.

268 • his angry rebuttal: *Independent*, 19/20 April 1989.

268 • "Critics established": Hughes, in Malcolm, *The Silent Woman*, pp. 46–47.

269 • "When I refused": Rose, *The Haunting of Sylvia Plath*, p. xv.

270 • "You kept saying": Hughes, in Malcolm, *The Silent Woman*, p. 124.

272 • Otto Plath in his classroom: Plath, *Letters Home*, p. 17.

273 • "the color feels amazing": Plath, *Journals*, p. 221.

273 • "It's incredible to think": Plath, *Letters Home*, p. 435.

274 • "It is a color": Kroll, *Chapters in a Mythology*, p. 17.

275 • "the red bandeau": Plath, *Journals*, p. 114.

276 • "Ted never liked blue": Plath, *Letters Home*, p. 492.

BIBLIOGRAPHY

WORKS BY TED HUGHES

For the ease of the reader, I have tried for the most part to take quotations from Hughes's work from the *New Selected Poems* of 1995; a good bibliography of Hughes's work may be found in Nick Gammage, ed., *The Epic Poise*.

The Hawk in the Rain. London: Faber & Faber, 1957. New York: Harper, 1957.
Lupercal. London: Faber & Faber, 1960. New York: Harper, 1960.
Wodwo. London: Faber & Faber, 1967. New York: Harper & Row, 1967.
Crow: From the Life and Songs of Crow. London: Faber & Faber, 1970, 1972.
    New York: Harper & Row, 1971.
Gaudete. London: Faber & Faber, 1977. New York: Harper & Row, 1977.

Cave Birds. London: Faber & Faber, 1978. New York: Viking Press, 1978.

Moortown. London: Faber & Faber, 1979. New York: Harper & Row, 1979.

Rain Charm for the Duchy and Other Laureate Poems. London: Faber & Faber, 1992.

Shakespeare and the Goddess of Complete Being. London: Faber & Faber, 1992. New York: Farrar, Straus & Giroux, 1992.

New Selected Poems, 1957–1994. London: Faber & Faber, 1995. New York: Harper & Row, 1982.

Winter Pollen: Occasional Prose, edited by William Scammell. London: Faber & Faber, 1995. New York: Picador USA, 1995.

Difficulties of a Bridegroom: Collected Short Stories. London: Faber & Faber, 1995. New York: Picador USA, 1995. Picardy Press, 1997.

Tales from Ovid: Twenty-four Passages from the Metamorphoses. London: Faber & Faber, 1997. New York: Farrar, Straus & Giroux, 1997; 1999.

Birthday Letters. London: Faber & Faber, 1998. New York: Farrar, Straus & Giroux, 1998; 1999.

Phèdre by Jean Racine: A New Version by Ted Hughes. London: Faber & Faber, 1998. New York: Farrar, Straus & Giroux, 1999; 2000.

Alcestis by Euripides: A New Version by Ted Hughes. London: Faber & Faber, 1999. New York: Farrar, Straus & Giroux, 1999; 2000.

WORKS BY SYLVIA PLATH

Letters Home: Correspondence 1950–1963, edited by Aurelia Plath. London: Faber & Faber, 1975. New York: Harper & Row, 1975.

Johnny Panic and the Bible of Dreams and Other Prose Writings. London: Faber & Faber, 1979. New York: Harper & Row, 1979. New York: Harperperennial Library, 2000.

The Bell Jar. New York: Bantam Books, 1981. New York: Alfred A. Knopf, 1998. New York: Harperperennial Library, 2000.

Collected Poems, edited with an introduction by Ted Hughes. London: Faber & Faber, 1981. Buccaneer Books, 1998. New York: HarperCollins, 1986.

The Journals of Sylvia Plath, edited by Ted Hughes and Frances McCullough. New York: Ballantine Books, 1991. New York: Anchor Books, 1998. Plath's unpublished journals, later published in Britain as *The Journals of Sylvia Plath, 1950–1962*, ed. Karen V. Kukil (London: Faber & Faber, 2000) were also consulted; however, citations in the notes refer to the earlier American edition.

OTHER WORKS

Alexander, Paul. *Rough Magic: A Biography of Sylvia Plath*. New York: Penguin, 1992. New York: Da Capo Press, 1999.

———, ed. *Ariel Ascending: Writings About Sylvia Plath*. New York: Harper & Row, 1985.

Alvarez, A. *The Savage God*. London: Weidenfeld & Nicolson, 1971. New York: W. W. Norton, 1990.

———. *Where Did It All Go Right? An Autiobiography*. London: Richard Cohen Books, 1999. New York: HarperCollins, 2000.

Armstrong, Tim, ed. *Thomas Hardy: Selected Poems*. Harlow, Essex: Longman, 1993.

BBC Television. *Close Up: Ted Hughes, Force of Nature*. December 1998, produced and directed by David Kerr.

Bentley, Paul. *The Poetry of Ted Hughes: Language, Illusion and Beyond*. Harlow, Essex: Addison Wesley Longman, 1998.

Butscher, Edward, ed. *Sylvia Plath: The Woman and the Work*. London: Peter Owen, 1979. New York: Dodd, Mead, 1985, 1977.

Cirlot, J. E. *A Dictionary of Symbols*. New York: Dorset Press, 1971.

Drabble, Margaret, ed. *The Oxford Companion to English Literature*. Oxford and New York: Oxford University Press, 1985; 6th ed., 2000.

Faas, Ekbert. *Ted Hughes: The Unaccommodated Universe, with selected critical writings by Ted Hughes and two interviews*. Santa Barbara: Black Sparrow Press, 1980.

Frazer, Sir James George. *The Golden Bough: A Study in Magic and Religion*, 1 vol. abridged ed. New York: Macmillan, 1963. New York: Simon & Schuster, 1996.

Gammage, Nick, ed. *The Epic Poise: A Celebration of Ted Hughes*. London: Faber & Faber, 1999.

Hamilton, Ian. *Keepers of the Flame: Literary Estates and the Rise of Biography*. London: Hutchinson, 1992. Boston: Faber & Faber, 1994.

Heaney, Seamus. *The Government of the Tongue: The 1986 T. S. Eliot Memorial Lectures and Other Critical Writings*. London: Faber & Faber, 1988. Noonday Press, 1990.

Heaney, Seamus, and Ted Hughes, eds. *The Rattle Bag*. London: Faber & Faber, 1982.

———. *The School Bag*. London: Faber & Faber, 1997.

Jung, C. J. *Psychology and Alchemy*, rev. edn. London: Routledge, 1968. Princeton, N.J.: Princeton University Press, 1968.

Kroll, Judith. *Chapters in a Mythology: The Poetry of Sylvia Plath*. New York: Harper & Row, 1976.

Malcolm, Janet. *The Silent Woman: Sylvia Plath and Ted Hughes*. New York: Vintage Books, 1995.

Newman, Charles, ed. *The Art of Sylvia Plath: A Symposium*. London: Faber & Faber, 1970. Bloomington: Indiana University Press, 1970.

Payne, S. *Down Your Street, Cambridge Past and Present*, Vol. 1. Cambridge, UK: The Pevensey Press, 1983.

Perkins, George, Barbara Perkins, and Phillip Leininger, eds. *Bënet's Reader's Encyclopedia of American Literature*. London and New York: HarperCollins, 1992.

Rose, Jacqueline. *The Haunting of Sylvia Plath*. London: Virago, 1997. Cambridge, Mass.: Harvard Unviersity Press, 1992; 1993.

Sagar, Keith. *The Art of Ted Hughes*. Cambridge, UK: Cambridge University Press, 1978.

———, ed. *The Achievement of Ted Hughes*. Manchester: Manchester University Press, 1983. Athens: University of Georgia Press, 1983.

Stevenson, Anne. *Between the Iceberg and the Ship: Selected Essays*. Ann Arbor: University of Michigan Press, 1998.

———. *Bitter Fame: A Life of Sylvia Plath*. London: Penguin, 1998. Boston: Houghton Mifflin, 1989; 1998.

Wagner-Martin, Linda. *Sylvia Plath, A Biography*. London: Chatto & Windus, 1988. New York: Simon & Schuster, 1987.

Williams, O., and E. Honig, eds. *The Mentor Book of Major American Poets*. New York: New American Library, 1972.

ACKNOWLEDGMENTS

FIRST, PETER STOTHARD, in whose office at *The Times* I first saw the manuscript of *Birthday Letters*. I am grateful beyond measure for the opportunity he gave me to work with Hughes's book, and for the freedom he gave me to write my own. Immeasurable thanks too to Joanna Mackle, publishing director at Faber & Faber, with whom I worked on the serialization (and who was my liaison with Ted Hughes) and later, this book. I gained a friend as well as a colleague in the course of our collaboration. Matthew Evans, chairman of Faber & Faber, provided insight into how

Birthday Letters came to be; I am grateful too to Melvyn Bragg, who first put the idea for this book in Evans's head. Before Paul Keegan took over as my astute editor, Christopher Reid gave me some fine advice, which informed this manuscript too. Everyone at Faber has been helpful and kind; Queen Square has been a fine place to fit myself into. Thanks also to Charles Boyle, Matthew de Ville and Ron Costley. At W. W. Norton, thanks to Jill Bialosky for taking on *Ariel's Gift*; also to Drake Bennett and Ann Adelman. Special thanks to Thomas Lynch for pointing me in the right direction.

At *The Times*, this book would not have been written without the sterling support of my assistant, James Eve. Alex O'Connell was working with me when this project began, and has been there all the way through. At the Lilly Library in Indiana, thanks to Julia Simic and Catherine Johnson; at Emory University, thanks to Steve Enniss of the Special Collections Department, and to Kathy Shoemaker.

Andrew Motion spoke to me at length about Hughes and his work, and read the manuscript when I would have thought he had more pressing commitments. His wise scribbles in the margin were invaluable to me. Elaine Showalter (who kindly donated to me the title of a phantom lecture series, "The Ecstasy of Influence," for my introduction), Diane Wood Middlebrook, Lisa Jardine and Al Alvarez all provided incisive comments. Ruth Scurr wandered the streets of Cambridge on my behalf; Ben Haggarty pointed me to footnotes and led me through myth; the staff of the London Library fed my endless hunger for books. I am particularly indebted to the work of Anne Stevenson, Jacqueline

Rose and Janet Malcolm. My agent, Antony Harwood, is my champion. Grateful thanks, too, to Frieda Hughes and Olwyn Hughes.

A book like this is not the product of scholarly support alone. Des Jenson, Tara McNicholas, Brian MacArthur and Jeanette Winterson have been there when the seas became heavy. My amazing parents, Arthur and Ellen Wagner, have searched for out-of-print books on my behalf, clipped acres of newsprint and sent it to me, and have been and continue to be the world's best cheerleaders.

Speaking in 1996, Ted Hughes described the nature of his early partnership with Sylvia Plath:

> When you are the only creative writer it can give rise to jealousy and opposition in a family that does not understand why you shut yourself away in a room alone with your thoughts, trying to woo the muse. By contrast, when there are two of you, the atmosphere is supportive. It's easier to concentrate on what you are doing, because both of you do the same thing. It's like singing together in the dark.

For seven years I have found my song with my husband, Francis Gilbert. His comments on *Ariel's Gift* made it by far a better book than it would have been without his keen eye; but more than that—without him beside me it would simply never have been written. To my love, my companion, my good right arm: my thanks, my admiration, eternally.

General Index

Guardian, 268
Guinness competition (1962), 234
Gunn, Thom, 212
Gutman, Lonya, 211

Hall, Sir Peter, 183
Hardwick, Elizabeth, 30, 151
Hardy, Thomas, 194
  compared with TH, 42–43, 44
  "Family Portraits," 43
  "The Going," 43
  "The Pedigree," 43
  Poems of 1912–13, 14, 42–43
  Some Recollections, 42
  "When I set out for Lyonnesse," 194
Harper & Row, 250, 251
Harper Brothers Publishers, 128
Harper's, 75
Harrison, Tony: School of Eloquence, 14
Harvard University, 62, 63
Haworth, West Yorkshire, 122
Hayman, Ronald, 268
Heaney, Seamus, 46–47, 53, 99, 272
  "The Indefatigable Hoof-taps," 264
  "On a New Work in the English Tongue," 7
"Hearing, Daniel" (Ted Hughes), 61
Hecate, 200
Heinemann, 178
Hemingway, Ernest, 111
Heptonstall, West Yorkshire, 110, 120, 122, 261
Hilliard, Nicholas, 229
Hiroshima, 162
Homer: Odyssey, 183
Hopkins, Gerard Manley, 52

Horder, Dr., 243
Hughes, Carol, 45
Hughes, Edith (TH's mother), 59, 60
Hughes, Frieda Rebecca (TH's daughter), 17, 19, 188, 196, 240, 244, 259, 261, 269
  Aurelia looks after, 184, 190
  in Australia, 269
  birth (1 April 1960), 175, 179, 180
  and Birthday Letters, 220
  and Letters Home, 27, 28
  TH protects, 15
Hughes, Nicholas Farrar (TH's son), 19, 93, 184, 240, 243, 259, 261, 269
  in Alaska, 269
  birth (17 January 1962), 189, 199–200, 201, 219
  and Letters Home, 27, 28
  TH protects, 15
Hughes, Olwyn (TH's sister), 25, 136, 183
Hughes, Shura (TH's daughter), death of, 15, 32, 195
Hughes, Ted:
  birth (17 August 1930), 59
  appearance, 58, 61, 80, 98, 100
  background, 19, 59
  bee-keeping, 223–25
  and Beethoven, 198
  begins an affair with Assia Wevill, 195, 211–12, 223, 230–31
  and Blake, 53, 98
  cancer, 15
  collaboration with SP, 40–41
  compared with Hardy, 42–43, 44
  demonization, 23, 26

education, 19, 57, 60, 61
fatalism, 35
first published, 61
first voyage to America, 138
and the First World War, 32, 60, 61, 221
Forward Prize for Poetry, 41, 271
the Great Will, 43
Guggenheim grant, 160
Guinness Prize, 151
Hawthornden Prize, 183
holistic approach, 32, 53
lawsuits over SP, 252–53
and *Letters Home*, 27–28
marriage to SP, 14–15, 20, 22, 40, 47, 58, 73, 126–27, 188, 208, 220, 234
meets SP, 80–81, 83
and myth, 33, 35, 61, 157
National Service, 60
New York Poetry Center prize, 130–31
ouija board, 131–34
protects Frieda and Nicholas, 15
the publication of *Ariel*, 23–25
publication of *Birthday Letters*, 44–50
separation from SP, 16, 20, 22, 223, 234, 236–37, 239
and shamanism, 170
Somerset Maugham Award, 178
SP's "abandonment" story, 235
on SP's later poems, 253
SP's literary executor, 20
on SP's method, 21
SP's spirit survived in, 44

and SP's suicide, 15, 18, 20–21, 32, 49, 244
success, 183
and the supernatural, 121
teaching, 125, 128, 145
voice, 61, 98, 100
wedding and honeymoon, 107–20, 122
Whitbread Book of the Year awards, 16–17, 33
The White Goddess influences, 212
works for J. Arthur Rank, 61, 83
Yaddo residency, 160, 161–62, 171–72
death, 15
–, PERSONALITY
ambition, 58
an intensely private man, 14–15, 269–70
lack of self–consciousness, 126
vehemence, 126
–, STYLE
form, 51–52, 74
fox totem, 61, 182
free verse, 221
hare image, 200–201
language, 52, 74–75
memory, 202, 204
work connected to the natural world, 30–31, 98
Hughes, William (TH's father), 59
Hughes family, 138, 175, 183, 261
Huws, Daniel, 61, 77, 92, 178
Huws, Helga, 178

Ibsen, Henrik: *The Master Builder*, 143

"Insect Societies" (in *A Handbook of Social Psychology*), 62

Plath, Sylvia:

"abandonment" story, 234–35

in analysis, 71–72, 139–40, 152, 159–60, 256

appearance, 63–64, 77, 140, 144, 243

archive, 251

background, 265, 266

bee-keeping, 223–25

and Beethoven, 198

begins work on *The Bell Jar*, 184

birth (27 October 1932), 62

birth of Frieda, 175, 178–79, 181

birth of Nicholas, 189, 199–200

collaboration with TH, 40–41

compared with Dickinson, 42

compared with Emily Brontë, 123–24

completes *The Bell Jar*, 191

drawing, 119–20

ECT, 68–69, 94, 226, 229, 241

education, 19, 57–58, 66, 75–77, 102–3, 125–26, 135, 137, 255

on England, 228–29

estate, 25, 27, 250

Eugene Saxton grant, 149

her father's death, 39–40, 64, 72, 73, 148, 160, 227, 229, 230, 256, 276

feminist icon, 23

filmed aged ten, 220–21

first published, 65

Fulbright Scholarship, 58, 75, 108, 125

grave headstone defaced, 26, 262, 269

haunted by her father's ghost, 189–90, 206, 207–8, 256

influenced by primitivist art, 117

inquest and funeral, 261

instructions to herself, 100

and Isis, 179–80

"last-stand letters," 263

her literary executor, 20

marriage to TH, 15, 19–20, 22–23, 40, 46, 58, 73, 126–27, 188, 208, 220, 234

meets Ruth Beuscher, 71

meets TH, 80–81, 83

method, 21

miscarriage (1961), 183

"new voice," 37–38, 173

The New Yorker publishes, 150

ouija board, 131–33

the Panic Bird, 152, 156, 160

poetic stature, 20, 22–23

pregnancies, 161, 168–71, 176, 178–79, 184, 199

"psychic gifts," 36, 39

Pulitzer Prize, 24

and red, 273–75

relationship with her mother, 36, 160, 256

rhythmic tension in her work, 50–51

scarred face, 71, 95, 135, 144

separation from TH, 16, 20, 22, 223, 234, 236–37

spirit survived in TH, 44

struggles with short stories, 141–42

successful, 103

suicide, 15, 16, 18, 20–21, 23, 32,
38, 49, 157, 158, 188, 239,
244
suicide attempt/breakdown, 21,
68–75, 162, 219, 241, 263
and the supernatural, 121
teaches at Smith, 117, 131, 138,
139, 142–43, 257, 273
TH on her later poems, 253
TH honours in *Birthday Letters*, 54
in TH's artistic shadow, 22
wars waged around her memory,
268
wedding and honeymoon, 107–20,
122
The White Goddess influences, 212
works for *Mademoiselle* magazine, 67
Yaddo residency, 160, 161–62, 167,
171–72, 173
–, PERSONALITY
aggression, 179
ambition, 58, 63, 65, 72, 79
anger, 104, 113, 127, 147, 181,
204–5, 208
bitterness, 115, 137, 172, 195
distant, 184–86
dual nature, 130, 163, 172, 249
possessiveness of TH, 179
presents image of perfection, 218
self-doubt, 218
violence, 187, 208, 212
world of slights and damage, 103
–, STYLE
drowning images, 228
head image, 130
work springs from her inner self,
98, 264, 265

Plath, Warren (SP's brother), 62, 71,
108
Poetry (Chicago), 125
The Poet's Voice series (BBC radio),
183
Pollard, Mr (beekeeper), 224
Pollitt, Katha, 24, 50
Prouty, Olive Higgins, 58, 71, 131,
255
Punch, 243

Queen Elizabeth (ship), 76, 138
quipu (ancient Peruvian device),
184–85

Racine, Jean: *Phèdre*, 7
Radin, Paul: *African Folktales*, 31, 218
Rank, J. Arthur, 61, 83
Redpath, Professor, 72
Rheims, 184, 186
Rich, Adrienne, 151
Rock Lake, Ontario, 164
Roethke, Theodore, 37, 38n, 172
Romanticism, 14, 30
Rose, Jacqueline: *The Haunting of
Sylvia Plath*, 268–69
Rosenberg, Ethel, 162
Rosenberg, Julius, 162
Rousseau, Jean Jacques, 145
Confessions, 13
Royal Air Force (RAF), 60
Royal Shakespeare Company, 183
rue Duvivier, Paris, 92
Rugby Street, Bloomsbury (No. 18), 92

St. Botolph's Rectory, Cambridge, 79
St. Botolph's Review, 79–80, 83

St. George the Martyr church,
Bloomsbury, 108
St. Juliot, Cornwall, 194
St. Pancras County court, 261
San Francisco, 162
Sartre, Jean-Paul, 144
Sassoon, Richard, 75, 77, 80, 85, 87,
92, 96, 112
Sassoon, Siegfried, 75
Saturday Evening Post, 141
Scholes, Robert, 251
Scott, J. D., 30
The Secret Sharer, 205
Seventeen magazine, 65, 151
Sexton, Anne, 14, 151
Shakespeare, William, 32, 34, 44, 82,
208
Macbeth, 99
The Tempest, 82, 109, 147, 207,
212–15
shamanism, 170
Shirley (a girlfriend of TH's), 81, 85
Smith College, Northampton, Massa-
chusetts, 19, 40, 57, 58, 63*n*,
66, 75, 76, 102, 117, 129, 131,
138, 139, 142–43, 255, 257,
273
Smith Review, 66
Sophocles:
Antigone, 143
Oedipus Rex, 143
South Yorkshire, 60
Spain, 46, 113–19
Spectator magazine, 30
Spender, Stephen, 128
Starbuck, George, 151
Stevenson, Anne, 72, 130, 182

Bitter Fame, 25, 172, 181, 231, 262
Stothard, Peter, 45
Swinburne, Algernon, 194

Tenison Road, Cambridge, 96
Tennessee, 162
Tennyson, Alfred, Lord, 194
Thomas, Dylan: *Under Milk Wood*, 178
Thoreau, Henry, 145
The Times, 16, 45, 47
Toulouse-Lautrec, Henri de, 112

United States of America, 46, 98,
118, 138, 139–41, 157,
161–62, 163, 176
University of Massachusetts, Amherst,
145

Voltaire, 117

Wain, John, 30
Walter, Uncle (TH's uncle), 122
Warn, Emily, 49
Washington, DC, 162
Washington Post, 28
Webb, Dr, 200
Webster, John: *The Duchess of Malfi*,
143
Wellesley, Massachusetts, 64
Wertz, Dick, 89
West Yorkshire:
dialect, 52
TH on, 59–60
Wevill, Assia:
background, 211
and the Chalcot Square flat, 191,
211

and death of Shura, 15, 32, 195
glamour, 231
suicide, 15, 32, 195
TH begins an affair with, 195,
211–12, 223, 230–31
TH depicts, 196
Wevill, David, 191, 211
Whitstead House, Barton Road, Cambridge, 76, 95
Willard, Mr and Mrs, 205
Willow Street, Boston (No. 9), 139,
151
Winthrop, Massachusetts, 62, 84
Winthrop Cemetery, Massachusetts,
147, 155
Wisconsin, 162, 164
Withins, West Yorkshire, 122
Woman's Hour (BBC radio programme), 197

Women's Volunteer Service, 96
Wood, James, 49
Woolacombe Sands, 229
Wordsworth, William, 31
The Prelude, 13, 99
Writers on Themselves series (BBC),
243

Yaddo artists' colony, Saratoga
Springs, 160, 161–62, 167,
171–72, 173, 176
Yale Series of Younger Poets, 137
Yale University, 73, 75, 142
Yeats, W. B., 125, 143, 236
Yellowstone, 162, 165
Yorkshire, 122, 138, 175, 177, 183,
261

INDEX OF WORKS BY TED
HUGHES AND SYLVIA PLATH